World-
Famous
Rebels

World-Famous Rebels

Charles Connell

Odhams Books

First published: 1970

Published for Odhams Books by
The Hamlyn Publishing Group Limited,
Hamlyn House, 42 The Centre,
Feltham, Middlesex.

SBN 600 72653 3

Printed in Great Britain by C. Tinling & Co. Ltd.
London & Prescot

Contents

Illustrations

Introduction

The Oxford Dictionary defines a rebel as "a person who rises in arms against, resists, or refuses allegiance to, the established government; a person or thing that resists authority or control". It will be found that all the rebels who appear in this volume fall into one or other of these two categories. Julian the Apostate, Wat Tyler, John Hampden, Alexander Hamilton, Danton, Lenin and Michael Collins certainly resisted the established government, whereas rebels such as Buddha, Socrates, Martin Luther, Galileo, Toussaint L'Ouverture, Shelley and the rest resisted authority or control. What they all have in common is expressed metaphorically in the proverb: "Who draws his sword against his prince must throw away the scabbard."

In a sense everybody is a rebel at one time or another, for it is impossible to go through life without occasionally resisting authority or control. Even infants in arms are sometimes wilful and refuse to do as they are told. There comes a stage in the career of every schoolboy when he clashes with the disciplinary system. Young people nowadays seem to be in a constant state of rebellion, some taking issue with the authorities on genuinely serious matters, such as their education, their financial situation, political questions and social problems; others refusing to accept apparently unimportant restrictions with regard to their clothing, the length of their hair or their skirts, their recreational activities, their use of cosmetics, the books they may read or the films they may attend. Lastly, in the grown-up years between adolescence and old age, all of us feel rebellious whenever our personal liberties are threatened. In a greater or lesser degree we object to such impositions as the foreign travel allowance, prescription charges, licensing laws, toll bridges, speed limits and breathalyser tests.

We are all rebels, and if we are honest we will readily admit that we have often drawn and flourished our swords, but very few of us can claim that we have thrown away the scabbards. We have been circumstantial rebels, our outbursts of rebellion having been provoked by prevailing conditions, responding to excesses of anger or resentment usually of temporary duration. It is here, in our momentary flashes of rebellion against minor irritations, that we differ from the 21 rebels in this book. Matters of supreme importance set alight the fires of *their* rebelliousness, and in many cases even their own deaths could not extinguish the flames. To return to the original metaphor, once their swords were out, they were never sheathed again.

For that is the way of the truly great rebel. He sees something wrong – in religion, in politics, in established opinions, in art, in the social structure, in the moral code – and he dedicates his whole life to putting it right. Argument, criticism, ostracism, threats, oppression, persecution, imprisonment, even death cannot divert him from the path he has chosen. This means that as long as men like Socrates and Bertrand Russell are conscious of humbug and self-deception, they will rebel against them right up to the end. Mary Wollstonecraft and Mrs. Pankhurst raised their voices defiantly against social and political conditions that put women at extreme disadvantage and deprived them of basic rights. As long as white people oppress coloured people, men of the calibre of Toussaint L'Ouverture and John Brown will fight racial prejudice. Let tyranny raise its ugly head in Ireland, and patriots such as Michael Collins and his fellow rebels will do battle for freedom until they are silenced for ever. And if literature, sculpture or music lapses into conventionality, then along will come a Lawrence, an Epstein or a Wagner to revolutionize his own particular area of creative expression.

Since nothing is perfect, there will always be rebels, for it is nothing less than perfection that the rebel is seeking – perfection according to his own lights. To men like Wat Tyler, John Hampden, Danton and Lenin, certain modifications of the political system were essential preliminaries to the coming of Utopia. Socrates's only quarrel with the world was that mankind was ignorant, so he tackled the problem with his two devastating weapons, logic and ratiocination. The only flaw Galileo could find in the whole universe was that the earth was not its centre, so he preached heliocentrism. Aneurin Bevan's drastic cure for social and political evils was the elimination of capitalism, so he set out to reform the social system.

The rebel, then, is invariably a crusader for a cause in which he believes implicitly. If his rebellion is to succeed, then he must have certain qualities such as courage, patience, persistence, vision and a rare single-mindedness. He must also be blessed with an aggressiveness that is sometimes indistinguishable from pugnacity. Furthermore, he needs moral strength and physical resilience, since at no time will his individual campaign be free from attack and he must always be ready to fight back. Like Socrates, Wat Tyler, John Brown and Michael Collins, he must even be prepared to die for his beliefs, for rebellion all too frequently demands its martyrs.

All 21 of them, then, are rebels and every one has earned his place in the story. Their various exploits bear out Daniel Webster's shrewd observation that repression is the seed of revolution, words that have a special significance today.

One salutary lesson to be learned is that once the rebel has committed himself to a certain line of action, opposition inevitably tends to increase his rebelliousness. All those in authority, whether they are parents or heads of states, if called upon to suppress a rebellion, should first examine its causes, bearing in mind that an insurrection does not start by spontaneous combustion. It is no use blaming the rebels when the guilt lies with those who created the conditions that made rebellion necessary.

Finally, those who attempt to crush a revolt would do well to remember that it is when a rebel has been forced to conform that he becomes doubly dangerous. His physical resistance may be checked for a time, but he can never be effectively restrained either mentally or spiritually. In his own subtle way he will continue the struggle, for every rebel firmly believes in his heart that rebellion against tyranny means obedience to God.

Charles Connell

Chapter 1 Buddha c. 560–480 BC

It seems difficult to believe that a man known as the Blessed One, the Holy One, the Perfect in Enlightenment, the Exalted One, the World-Honoured and the Awakened One should also have distinguished himself as a rebel. Yet a proper understanding of the life and doctrines of the Buddha, one of the world's great spiritual leaders, leads inevitably to the conclusion that this essentially non-violent teacher was breaking the chains of caste and giving the common people hope, courage and a universal faith. In short, Buddha rebelled against the social system and against the Brahmin priesthood that fostered it.

Philosophically speaking, there is not a great deal of difference between Buddhism and the more advanced levels of Brahmanical thought. The Brahmans were equally aware of the hopeless and irremediable state of the world; they believed that because salvation could not be attained on earth, it had to be searched for in a rebirth in heaven. Any distinction between them is largely temperamental. If he had been called upon to argue with a really competent exponent of the more abstruse vedantic idealism, Buddha would have been forced to acknowledge that he shared many of his opponent's views. After all, it was not Buddha who first propounded the twin laws of Reincarnation and Karma. Both doctrines had been fundamental tenets of Hinduism for centuries. What Buddha reacted against, however, was the popular side of Brahmanism.

To understand the extent to which Buddha rebelled against the established religion of India, it is necessary to examine briefly the story, first of the living and then of the legendary Buddha. In the one case the facts are regrettably all too few; in the other there is obviously much that is pure invention. Sometimes the truth about Buddha contrasts sharply with the extravagantly imaginative accounts of his youth and early manhood. Sometimes significant parallels can be drawn. Frequently the discrepancies are as revealing as the similarities.

Siddhartha Gautama, subsequently known as the Buddha, was born (perhaps in the year 560 B.C.) at Lumbini, in the little Himalayan kingdom of Sakya, north-east of the province of Oudh. His father Suddhodana was ruler of the Sakya tribe. When Siddhartha's mother died, seven days after his birth, the child was brought up by his aunt in the busy provincial capital of Kapilavatthu.

As heir to the kingdom, Siddhartha lacked for nothing. During his boyhood he received the usual training given to a princeling, practising martial exercises, learning to ride, pursuing a healthy outdoor life and acquiring the customary knightly skills and accomplishments. He was strikingly handsome and reputed to be anatomically perfect. He excelled at all sports and had a remarkable intelligence. There is no evidence that at that time he displayed any special interest in Brahmanical lore.

Following the normal pattern of aristocratic families, he changed his house to suit the season, spending part of the year in a summer residence, part in winter quarters and the rest in a locality where the heavy rains caused least inconvenience. Later his outlook was broadened by extensive travel. He visited a number of educational centres where he met and conversed with some of the most important Hindu teachers of his day. At the end of his wanderings he came home, married his beautiful cousin Yasodhara and tried to settle down to the life of pleasure and luxury that was his rightful heritage.

Siddhartha, however, was unable to reconcile himself to the easy-going leisurely atmosphere of the court with its rigid social code and its intolerable attitude towards the less fortunate. Even when his wife presented him with a son, Rahula, he still hankered after something more than a routine domesticity. Intellectually and spiritually he was far from satisfied with the world as he saw it. Material possessions and comforts meant little or nothing in an existence where man himself was so transient, where there was no certainty, where everybody was subject to the countless ills of mortality. The more he thought about mankind's miserable lot, the more he was determined to seek out a way by which his fellow men could make the most of their brief appearances in bodily shape. During the whole of his swift passage from birth to death, man was virtually in thrall to his own flesh and blood. Siddhartha resolved to liberate him.

Precisely as his father had feared, Siddhartha's first revolutionary move was to become a hermit. Like many a young Hindu looking for an answer to the eternal problem of evil and evil-doers, he chose to adopt the homeless life of the ascetic, forsaking his wife, his child and all earthly ambitions, and wandering from place to place entirely dependent on such scraps as were put into his begging bowl. His hope was that through self-denial and mortification of the flesh he would attain to a visionary state in which the secret of the universe would be revealed to him. When he took this momentous step, Siddhartha was not yet in his thirtieth year.

For six long years he eked out a wretched existence, subsisting on the bare minimum of food and drink. In the company of other ascetics he endured extreme forms of bodily austerity. He also seized the opportunity of delving into the philosophical systems of the Brahman teachers, always aspiring towards the Enlightenment that would give him a proper understanding of the mystery of life.

Then he noticed corruptions in the teaching of the Brahman priests; in their perverseness they were causing schisms and internal conflicts. Siddhartha made his second revolutionary gesture. Reduced by his voluntary privations to a walking skeleton, he experienced what can only be described as a religious trance. He suffered excruciating pains and fell to the ground senseless. Nobody knows what visions were vouchsafed him during this seizure, but when he recovered he knew beyond all doubt that he had been following the wrong path. Not by rigorous asceticism would he be finally awakened to the truth concerning ultimate wisdom. Salvation lay in steering a "middle way" between the physical torture of strict self-denial and the sensuality of unbridled licence.

In so far as Siddhartha was unsympathetic towards the caste system and because his mission was to free people from the despotic Brahman priests, he was certainly a rebel against the whole religious culture of India. Even his tiny group of fellow ascetics were shocked by his unorthodox aims. They disassociated themselves from their former leader; they also denounced him as a renegade. Was he not challenging the Brahman priesthood's claim to a monopoly in religion? Had he not bypassed the traditional source of Hindu thought as set down in the ancient Vedas?

One day he made up his mind to sit under a sacred fig tree and remain there until he attained the spiritual enlightenment he had sought for so long. Throughout the night he waited for a sign, and then at last, in the hush that precedes the dawn, he sank into a trance. In this mystical state he saw as in a vision the complicated pattern of cause and effect that rules life here on earth. At the same time the true path to happiness was revealed to him.

Thereafter he knew that he was the Buddha, the Enlightened One, the Perfect One. Under the pipal-tree at Gaya in what is today the Indian State of Bihar, he had achieved a full understanding of the meaning of life. He had experienced Nirvana.

For the rest of his life he devoted himself to sharing his new religion with others. The handful of disciples who had branded him a renegade were among the first to acknowledge him as Buddha and soon his doctrine, or *dharma,* was bringing peace and joy to thousands of converts throughout India. Expressed in simple terms, this doctrine comprises four truths: suffering exists; it has a cause; it can be suppressed; the suppression is accomplished by following the "Path". The nature of the Path which leads to blessedness is eightfold. It can be trod only by those who practise "right vision, right thoughts, right speech, right action, right livelihood, right efforts, right mindfulness and right concentration". In other words, the goal can be won only by those who possess a mental and moral discipline.

Buddha's purpose was to liberate man from all those evil passions that interfere with the development of the soul. He taught that such vices as hatred, lust and envy are obstacles that lie between the aspiring soul and that unspeakable happiness which is Nirvana. The old Hindu belief was that life on earth implied an endless series of rebirths and that nobody could escape from this recurring pattern. Buddha believed that it was possible – through love, self-control, willpower and compassion – for man's spiritual essence to free itself from the narrow confines of its earthly prison-house and rejoin the mysterious Whole from whence it came.

Such was the comforting gospel that Buddha preached until his eightieth year when he died peacefully on a couch spread beneath two trees at Kusinagara in Oudh. He was cremated and his ashes were housed in eight urns so that they could be divided among his devotees.

It is significant that for a long time after his death Buddha's bodily form was deemed too sacred for reproduction in painting or sculpture. For decades he was represented by the wild fig-tree under which he became enlightened, by his empty preaching throne, by his footprints and by other relevant symbols. The statues that appeared later (which seem to suggest that he was too well-fed and self-satisfied to have been a Holy Man), tend to emphasize the physical characteristics of the countries in which they were fashioned. Any resemblance between many of them and the real Buddha may well be coincidental. The facts are clear. In the first place, after his six years in the "wilderness", fasting and other deprivations reduced him to little more than skin and bones. Furthermore, even when he abandoned the ascetic life and pursued his "middle way", he relied on one fairly substantial meal of curry and rice, with maybe a few spoonfuls of gruel for supper. Perhaps the image-makers decided that a plump, healthy-looking Buddha would be considered more worthy of veneration.

According to Buddhist tradition, there were also at least 24 legendary Buddhas as distinct from Siddhartha Gautama. The simple term "Buddha" could refer to any one of those fabulous teachers who belong to prehistoric times, whereas "the Buddha" specifically means the man from Lumbini who founded a new religion in the sixth century B.C. No study of the real Buddha, however, would be complete without a glance at the story that begins with the Brahman Sumedha's decision to become a Buddha in some future birth so that he might lead suffering humanity into the way of salvation.

Sumedha, too, sought for the path leading to release from the recurring pattern of existence here on earth; he too freed himself from material things and become a forest hermit. Moreover, after his last birth, he knew that his destiny was to become a Buddha. Other incidents where fact and fiction are practically identical include the legendary Buddha's realization that mortification of the flesh was not calculated to liberate the soul and flood it with enlightenment, his period of meditation leading to a state of enlightenment, his experience of Nibbana (Nirvana) and his discovery of the Eightfold Path. The detailed description of miraculous events following the death of Sumedha, such as his ceremonial cremation and the celestial and terrestrial waters that extinguished the flames of the funeral pyre, seems to stretch credulity too far, but on the other hand the remains were stored in eight vessels and kept in different territories, exactly as had happened to the real Buddha.

From a careful comparison of the two accounts certain conclusions may be drawn. The virtual inseparability of legend and reality partly explains why the Buddhist creed has but one distinct flavour, is always consistent and was clearly hammered out by one highly individual rationalist. It was largely due to Buddha's singleness of purpose that his activities as a missionary enjoyed such widespread success.

Everybody will agree that the Buddha round whom so many legends were woven was a far more colourful figure than the historical Buddha. He also strikes one as being altogether gentler, more tolerant, less complicated. Viewed with understanding, however, he has all the qualities of a disarming rebel whose tactful handling of potentially explosive situations seems to rob rebellion of its customary aggressiveness. His revolt against his father's possessiveness, presented allegorically, does not shock the reader who, on the other hand, is deeply moved when the authentic Siddhartha ruthlessly breaks away from his father, his wife and his only child.

The same argument applies to the legendary Buddha's major rebellion against the existing religious system. The significant passage in the Buddha legend occurs shortly after the Bodhisatta rode away from riches to rags. The actual reference is to the "Supreme Brahman, constant, eternal, and without distinctive signs, which the wise who know reality declare to be liberation". The Bodhisatta was not prepared to accept the important phrase "without distinctive signs". Moreover, he did not see eye to eye with the dualistic terminology of soul and body. He believed that the soul freed from its fleshy tenement is still a soul and no matter what changes it has undergone as a result of its earthly sojourn, it remains essentially a soul and will inevitably be born again. Only in complete abandonment of things physical can it attain Nirvana. This is the fundamental issue on which Buddhist and Brahman thought part company.

To measure the full extent of Buddha's "rebellion" it is necessary to remember first of all that when he was born, Hinduism was already a very ancient religion, and secondly that in so far as it did not originate from a single founder like Christ or Mohammed, it is a faith that cannot easily be defined. Its character is essentially ethnic, whereas Buddhism has all the elements of a missionary growth.

The Hindus whose religion was eventually challenged by Buddha based their way of life on a number of beliefs that had developed organically in India over many centuries. They believed in the inspired teachings of the Brahman, in caste, in transmigration, in successive rebirths of the individual soul, in an endless cycle of spiritual comings and goings. They considered certain animals and trees to be sacred. Extravagant ceremonies and sacrifices also figured in their religious rituals. As for their gods, although Hinduism was and still is fundamentally monotheistic, Vishnu has always been supreme, while Siva and Durga or Parvati have played secondary roles. Lesser deities include Siva's son Ganesh, elephant-headed and a bringer of good fortune; the six-headed war-god Skanda; the sun-god Surya; Sarasvati, the beautiful patroness of art and learning; Hanuman, Sitala, Brahma, Indra and many others. Finally, lower down the Hindu scale of divinity come the sacred animals and trees already referred to, and then all mountains and rivers and rocks. In short, the Hindu sees everything in nature as possessing, in various stages, the divine essence.

Not only did Buddha have to decide where he stood in relation to current theological beliefs; he also had to make up his mind on an issue of vital concern to the Hindu. Could he accept and follow the traditional way of life as practised by his fellow-countrymen, sometimes in the temple but principally in the home? Was he prepared, for instance, to subscribe to the numerous rites and sacraments which hedged in the Hindu from conception to a stage well beyond the grave?

The answer is that although Buddha had no quarrel with many of the basic tenements of Hinduism, he could not agree that one man could be better than another and therefore he could not go along with the classical Hindu idea that Aryan society comprised four distinct class groups. Convinced that all men were equal, Buddha could not reconcile his egalitarianism with the rigid class divisions of the Hindu who believed that the Brahman studied and taught at the head of the social hierarchy; that on a lower level the nobleman maintained law and order and was responsible for his country's defence; that below him came the merchants and peasants; that the lowest class of all consisted of menials and labourers whose duty it was to serve their social superiors.

In Buddha's opinion, *dharma* (that "which was right and as it ought to be") was a message sent to all who desired it. It was not something that was reserved for a special clique, nor was it intended to be monopolized by a privileged band of Brahman teachers. Expounded by one who could explain its meaning to people of varying intellectual levels, it offered wisdom and comfort to everybody. *Dharma* benefited every man according to his capacity.

By subordinating all natural activity to ceremonial and ritualistic laws, the Brahmans had restricted the unfettered development of national power. Their efforts to subjugate ordinary people to priestly domination had spread a mantle of gloom over the lives of the common folk. Buddha's reformed doctrine pointed out a way of escape from the terrible consequences of the Brahmanical system. Beginning with the suppression of desire for the material things of this world, passing through the rejection even of self-denial, it ended in the very negation of existence – Nirvana.

Although Buddha's influence gradually made itself felt over the whole of India and subsequently spread to Tibet, Ceylon, Siam, Burma, China and Japan, Buddha never set himself up to be worshipped as a god. All he asked of his followers was that they should listen to his teaching and be guided along the road to spiritual happiness. Because of his all-embracing wisdom and unfathomable knowledge, all those who came into contact with him learned to revere and obey him.

A general survey of his life and times serves to emphasize the fact that Buddha's chief contribution to civilization was his restatement of the philosophy that ignorance is death while knowledge is life. It is through ignorance that man craves satisfaction for a self that has no separate existence. It is through knowledge and understanding that he will so nurture his soul that it will ultimately attain the perfection of the universal soul of which it is an infinitesimal but vital part. In so far as his teaching clashed with the Hindu doctrines of his era, it was undeniably revolutionary.

Buddha himself said: "I do not say to you, Believe this, for so it is told you, but DO this. And, little by little, as when a man climbs a mountain, the earth unfolds beneath him, for yourselves you shall see and know, needing no testimony from another – no, not even from the ancient Scriptures, the Vedas, the Vedanta or any Brahmin, nor another. For the kingdom of heaven is within you. Look inward, and see it, and be glad."

These are surely the words of a rebel, but a rebel whose cause was no less than spiritual liberation.

Chapter 2
Socrates
c. 470–399 BC

Before examining any account of the life of the famous Athenian philosopher, Socrates, the reader must take into consideration certain significant circumstances. In the first place, Socrates himself left behind no written records of what he thought and did during the seventy years that passed before he drank that fatal cup of hemlock in an Athenian prison. In fact, despite his outstanding intellect and skill with words, he clung to the convention of all Athenians belonging to the great age of Pericles. He wrote no books at all. Consequently, for any information concerning the man we must rely entirely on the observations, memories and indeed imaginations of his contemporaries.

A further difficulty arises in that no one thought of writing about him until Socrates was almost fifty years old. The greater part of his life, therefore, can be known only through the memories of others. Thereafter the would-be biographer is compelled to draw upon three very diverse sources. The Athenian playwright Aristophanes, although he was a personal friend of Socrates, chose to ridicule him in his comedy *The Clouds*. The brilliant philosopher Plato, who studied under Socrates and was also his close friend, reproduced in his dialogues the Socratic method of question and answer, dealt with Socrates's trial in his *Apology*, and in his *Phaedo* set down Socrates's last conversation in which he described the immortality of the soul. And finally, the Greek historian Xenophon, who also came under Socrates's influence, illustrated the life and character of his hero in his *Memorials of Socrates* and other works.

All three sources, however, should be approached with caution. Because he was a satirist, Aristophanes by the very nature of his profession was bound to present an exaggerated and distorted picture. Because at times he may have used Socrates as a mere mouthpiece for his own opinions, Plato possibly fell a victim to his own inventiveness in some of the dialogues. And because Xenophon lacked humour and a proper understanding of ethics, he was unable to penetrate to the true meaning of the more abstruse Socratic pronouncements. Each one had his shortcomings, but in the absence of any other relevant material, none of the three can be ignored. Of them all, Plato commands the most respect. In any event, he was present throughout Socrates's trial, and in much that he has written about the occasion he is obviously trying to capture familiar aspects of the accused, his attitude towards both judges and witnesses, and the prisoner's philosophic acceptance of his fate. Then again, some of Plato's descriptions and comments are corroborated in Xenophon's writings. None of them is contradicted by the historian.

From the writings of his contemporaries, then, we learn that Socrates was born in Athens in the fifth century B.C. His father, Sophroniscus, last of a long line of stone-cutters, had once worked under the direction of the master sculptor Phidias. His mother, Phaenerete, was a woman of good family and reputedly a highly competent amateur midwife. They were comfortably off, occupying a pleasantly situated old house in the suburb of Alopeke, and were able to keep their son in comparative luxury until the sudden death of Sophroniscus. Young Socrates then inherited the business, tried to make a success of it, but soon found that he had no talent as a sculptor. He had no reason to worry, however, for his inheritance also included the ancient dwelling-house and enough money to live on. His mother married again, so he had only his own modest requirements to think about.

If the small statue of Socrates in the British Museum in any way resembles the original, Socrates must have been something of a physical oddity. He had wide nostrils, blubbery lips, a snub nose, a suspicion of a squint and the pot-bellied figure of a faun. According to Aristophanes, he walked with a characteristic strut and had a habit of rolling his eyes. Although his body was big and awkward, he possessed great physical strength and remarkable powers of endurance. Later on, as a hoplite or citizen soldier (the equivalent of a fully-armed infantryman), he was often called upon to march long distances carrying about seventy pounds of equipment. He was to fight valiantly at the siege of Potidaea, and years afterwards when the Boeotians drove the Athenian army ignominiously from Delium, Socrates figured among those who were last to leave the battlefield. If his fellow soldiers had displayed the same courage and presence of mind, disaster at Delium would have been averted.

Socrates's physical peculiarities were matched only by his extraordinary mental processes. In a city that was already famous for its intellectual atmosphere, he towered head and shoulders above all the brilliant thinkers of his day. It is not surprising that just before the outbreak of the Peloponnesian War, the Delphic oracle announced that Socrates was the wisest man alive.

While still a young man Socrates was widely read in both the sciences and the arts. He had begun by trying to solve the twin mysteries of life and death. From this starting-point his acute mind had ranged over the whole field of knowledge. He had pondered over the shape of the earth, a subject about which even the experts failed to agree. He had studied the workings of the human brain and to what extent it was responsible for controlling not only man's everyday actions but also the vast scheme of things men called the universe. Dissatisfied with existing theories and conjectures, Socrates decided to pursue a different line of investigation. His original approach to scientific, social and religious problems caused many eminent Athenians to regard him as an intellectual rebel. His ideas on a number of topics were certainly revolutionary.

By the time he was forty Socrates's fame was no longer confined to the little world of Athens. He was already building up an international reputation. Apollo's startling pronouncement at Delphi probably marked the turning-point in his career. Before the oracular bombshell Socrates had been content to meander unhurriedly through life, culling the flowers of wisdom, inhaling their delicate perfumes and constantly moving on to fresh pastures. After the priests had consulted the oracle and had written on the wax tablet the challenging statement *Socrates is the wisest man in the world,* he became a man with a mission. He knew now that he had to make people aware of their ignorance and persuade them to cultivate their souls. His most difficult task, he decided, would be to teach men to think logically.

He began by analysing to his own satisfaction the oracular hyperbole. He had scant respect for the Olympians; but for Apollo, the god of the Muses, he had always felt a certain affection. Yet here was his favourite deity making a solemn declaration that could not possibly be true. There must be many men in the world, he reasoned to himself, who were wiser than Socrates. What then did Apollo mean? Was he perhaps implying paradoxically that Socrates was the wisest of men because he was the only one who knew that he knew nothing?

At any rate he could prove that Apollo was wrong. All he had to do was to find somebody wiser than himself.

Socrates started his search among politicians and drew an immediate blank. Then he turned to the poets and was equally unsuccessful. His investigations forced him to the reluctant conclusion that neither statesmen nor "the unacknowledged legislators of mankind" had any real knowledge. Descending the social scale, he questioned ordinary workmen and shopkeepers. He discovered that at least they had some understanding of their various jobs, but unfortunately most of them were convinced that they also understood more important matters.

It was true, then, that the oracle had been indulging in paradox. Apollo had been pointing out subtly that people were misusing the precious gift of life simply because they were ignorant without being aware of it. Socrates had been named as the wisest man alive because none but he appreciated the inestimable value of life and at the same time his own ignorance about it. Clearly his bounden duty was to pursue knowledge, and having found it, to make it available to others. The Delphic oracle did not want him to change his ways as a result of its cryptic utterance. He was not expected to become either a model citizen or a successful politician. Apollo did not want him to shave off his beard, to dress more elegantly and to abandon his habit of going about bare-footed. On the contrary, Socrates had to imbue his fellow Athenians with some of his own independence, his own freedom from external pressures, his own indifference to material possessions. The god of the Muses had called upon him to liberate mankind from humbug and self-deception.

Then and there Socrates proposed to devote his life to pondering over problems of behaviour, politics and religion. He became a moral philosopher.

Accompanied by young men who were eager to learn, he used to wander through the city, lingering in public places to express his views on moral and social principles. Using a revolutionary technique that came to be known as the "Socratic method", he would draw out the thoughts and opinions of his followers. By a series of persistent questions he induced men to pour out their ideas on such abstractions as happiness, justice and knowledge. Gently guiding them from one conclusion to another, Socrates kept up his purposeful interrogation until the principle under discussion stood out in crystal clarity. The whole cross-examination was conducted with such an inexorable logic that all who listened were held spellbound. In a book written shortly after Socrates's death, Xenophon said that "nothing could be more beneficial than to be in the company of Socrates and to talk with him at any time".

Those who doubt or disbelieve the story of the oracle may feel more inclined to accept the report about Socrates's mysterious "voice" that had been speaking to him at intervals ever since childhood. It was neither an over-developed conscience pointing out right and wrong nor yet a guide to moral conduct, but rather a sort of personal demon that came to warn him whenever bad luck was impending. If Socrates chose to disregard these inner promptings, then unpleasant consequences usually followed. Like Joan of Arc later, he was a visionary, liable at times to fall into a trance and become as it were inspired. The difference seems to be that Joan's guardian angel told her what to do; Socrates's tutelary spirit told him what to avoid.

Socrates's popularity as a preacher and teacher steadily increased and many youths of good family came to join his circle of admirers and devotees. They all wanted to hear the truth, the whole truth and nothing but the truth. Attracted by his magnetic personality, his original approach and his eccentricity, young people neglected their duties to their parents and to the State. The son of Anytus the tanner, for instance, refused to learn his father's trade. Socrates had taught him that a good character was more valuable than good leather. Henceforth, said Anytus's son, he intended to learn about life from the great free-thinker and paradox-monger.

It was this sort of rebellion, son turning against father to pursue knowledge, that led to foolish accusations being levelled against Socrates. Angry parents charged the philosopher with leading their offsprings astray. They called him a corrupter of youth and unfortunately the name stuck.

The Athenian authorities had also noted that Socrates showed little respect for the gods. Because of his reputation as a sage, they had tended to tolerate the philosopher's unequivocal attitude towards the State religion, but in the year 430 B.C. the situation changed almost overnight. Starting in Abyssinia, spreading to Libya and sweeping rapidly into the countries that fringed the Mediterranean, the plague found its way into Hellas and devastated the countryside. If Athens was to survive, then there was only one course of action to be taken. Every citizen would have to pray and do sacrifice to the god of medicine, Aesculapius. Deliverance from the evil that was striking down men, women and children indiscriminately depended on each conscientious Athenian bringing a propitiatory cock, Aesculapius's favourite titbit, slitting its throat and flinging the bloody offering on the god's own altar. Everybody responded to the appeal – everybody except one man.

Socrates, the rebel philosopher, deliberately abstained from the religious rites. Worse still, it was rumoured he had said that Pericles would have been better advised to have concentrated on the waterworks at Piraeus instead of wasting his time trying to bribe Aesculapius. If Socrates *had* made such a remark, it would not have been intended as blasphemy. It would surely have been prompted by the fact that one of the symptoms of the plague was an inordinate thirst. True or false, however, the story was subsequently used to discredit the philosopher during his trial.

After the plague had spent its fury came the battle of Delium, already mentioned. Socrates marched as a hoplite with the second regiment and was one of the few in that undisciplined mob who ever looked like soldiers. Although it was late autumn and the way over the mountains was cold and rough, he wore no sandals, trudging along over icy rocks and jagged stones without complaining, showing no signs of fatigue.

Then came the catastrophe. The Athenians could not withstand the Boeotians' fierce onslaught and were compelled to retire. Many were the cowards who fled in panic that day, but Socrates was not one of them. Alcibiades described him in these words: "Strutting, his eyes turned searchingly in all directions – that is how he came home, the only hero in the defeat."

Some time after the battle of Delium, Socrates married a young lady of independent means named Xanthippe. He was informed that he would find his bride-to-be "rather difficult". His philosophic reply was: "The best rider will pick the wildest horse." He had already voiced his opinions on marriage, boldly declaring his belief in equal rights for women, an incomprehensible and revolutionary notion in those days, but once he had a wife of his own, he promptly abandoned it. According to Plato and Xenophon, Xanthippe appears to have been an affectionate partner and not at all the shrew she is made out to be by her Alexandrian biographers. She was to bear him three children: Lamprocles, Sophroniscus, and in his sixty-ninth year Menexenus.

Socrates was with Xanthippe at the theatre in 423 B.C. when Aristophanes's comedy *The Clouds* was first presented. It was a memorable occasion. Before an audience of about thirty-five thousand, Socrates was openly branded as a dangerous revolutionary. Ugly, bare-footed and badly dressed, the actor impersonating the philosopher in the scene showing the idea factory spoke a line that was to make history: "Gods are not current coin with us!" Hardly had the audience recovered from this assault on their religious susceptibilities than they were again shocked by the stage Socrates's bold declaration: "There is no Zeus!" Quotations such as these were remembered long afterwards and used against the philosopher to prove him an atheist.

Nor was this all. After the interval Aristophanes burlesqued the manner in which Socrates had been stirring up sons against their fathers. In reply to the argument that there was no law in Athens allowing a son to strike his father, the stage Socrates said:

"The law? Who makes it, Men like you and me.

Why should we not be law-givers for coming generations?

Just take a look at the young barnyard cocks, how they attack their fathers!

Where is the difference, pray, between ourselves and them?

They make no laws, and that's the whole of it."

Such observations could have only one interpretation. The whole speech was clearly an incitement to rebellion.

The Clouds, intended to be an *exposé* of the literary and philosophical humbug of the period, had been entered in the annual festival competition. It failed to win the first prize for Aristophanes, but by its vicious gibes and wild exaggerations it established an image of Socrates that the philosopher could never live down. This was the image that persisted in men's minds when Alcibiades fell from grace and practised treachery against the State. Many a worthy citizen recalled that Alcibiades had been a pupil of Socrates. They agreed that he must have picked up his disloyalty from the peripatetic philosopher.

Then, in the autumn of 406 B.C., the Athenians inflicted a crushing defeat on the Spartans in a sea engagement that took place between Lesbos and the Asiatic mainland. Unfortunately for the eight commanding admirals, their victory had been dearly bought at the expense of twenty-five warships and four thousand men. On their return to Athens they immediately faced charges of negligence. One admiral who had denounced the rest was not proceeded against. Two of the others had the good sense to withdraw into voluntary exile. The fate of the remaining five who were chained together like slaves was to be decided by a single vote, but Socrates, who was chairman of the court, refused to accept such unconstitutional procedure. He insisted that each commander should be treated as an individual, stipulating that "each one of the accused . . . be judged upon his personal behaviour or guilt". By popular acclaim, however, Socrates's plea was ignored, a verdict was passed on all five simultaneously, and next day they were given hemlock to drink. Naturally, all who attended the trial saw Socrates's advocacy of the admirals' constitutional rights as yet another example of his general rebelliousness.

A few years later Socrates found himself in even deeper waters. After Lysander and his Spartans had overrun Greece and Athens had been occupied by the enemy, a Council of Thirty was elected to organize the city's future government. The creation of this corrupt body was the signal for a veritable reign of terror. The Long Walls were torn down, arsenals were destroyed, harbour buildings were razed to the ground and the secret police executed hundreds of malcontents. Many fled to avoid the persecution.

Because he believed that his rightful place was in Athens, Socrates refused to leave. When an army of exiles and emigrés swept back into power, Socrates was suspected of hobnobbing with traitors. Furthermore, when the liberators set out *en masse* for the Acropolis to give thanks to the tutelary goddess, Socrates did not join the marchers. His absence did not pass unnoticed.

In the old easy-going days the Athenians had been well aware of his unorthodoxy, his originality, his revolutionary tendencies, and had been prepared to tolerate them. But times had changed and under the new regime a citizen was expected to conform. There was no room now for a man who would not honour Pallas Athene, for a man who taught young people to be cleverer than their parents, for a man who encouraged his pupils to forsake business and pursue philosophy instead. Socrates had become a kind of public enemy.

The blow fell at the turn of the century. Prompted by Anytus, one of the leaders of the restored democrats, an obscure poet called Meletus accused Socrates on two main counts. To begin with, he had committed a crime in not worshipping the gods whom the city worshipped; and he had introduced religious novelties. Secondly, the philosopher was charged with "corruption of the young". The prosecutor concluded by demanding the death penalty.

The first part of the indictment presented few problems. The Athenians had never yet put a man to death for a crime against religion. The heaviest penalties hitherto incurred by such offenders had been expulsion or voluntary exile. As for the other charge, that was a clear case of misrepresentation. Far from corrupting Athenian youths, Socrates had led them along the path of wisdom. Plato's older relatives and certain young companions could testify that the philosopher had always considered it to be his mission to combat ignorance and conduct men towards enlightenment.

At the actual trial Socrates treated Meletus and his absurd accusations with the contempt they deserved. In his own defence he did his best to destroy the false image the people had so carefully built up during the last quarter of a century. Then he went on to say: "I know you would prefer to turn me loose – but on condition that from now on I hold my tongue and do not annoy my fellow citizens. But I may as well tell you now that I cannot do it. . . ."

Of the 500 judges responsible for the verdict, 280 voted for a conviction while the rest favoured an acquittal. Hardly a big enough majority to warrant the death penalty. After the count it seemed highly probable that the death sentence would be reduced to exile, confiscation of property or a considerable fine. According to the Athenian law, the accused was entitled to propose a suitable alternative punishment, and if he had chosen banishment, the authorities would have been eminently satisfied.

Tired but resolute, Socrates addressed the court. After denying the charges, he said he was not prepared to plead for his life, either personally or through the medium of his family and friends. He then turned to the question of a fitting counterproposal. "What do I deserve," he demanded, "for not having spent my life peaceably, caring neither for household nor wealth, greedy for no offices or honours, but concerned only to make you ever better and more reasonable?" As he had always acted for the good of Athens, they ought to *reward* him with the privilege usually accorded to winners at the Olympic Games – a daily meal at the public table in the Prytaneum.

When the uproar caused by Socrates's arrogant suggestion had subsided, the irrepressible old rebel maintained that his proposal had been a serious one. He certainly had no intention either of going to prison to be treated as a slave or of trying to start a new life at his age in an alien land where, because he could not keep his mouth shut, his troubles would surely begin all over again. If he had been a wealthy man, he would have proposed a heavy fine on himself. As he had no money, all he could offer was what he could raise at that moment – one mina. As an alternative to death, then, his punishment should be a fine of precisely that amount.

Before the angry judges could explode, his friends hastily increased Socrates's over-modest bid to 30 minae. They would stand surety for that amount.

Exasperated by Socrates's uncompromising attitude, the jury voted again. This time there was an overwhelming majority in favour of the death penalty. The "criminal" was handed over to the "Eleven", the prison bailiffs, who chained him hand and foot and dragged him away to a dark airless cell. There, manacled but otherwise not badly treated, Socrates remained for the space of one month. His friends made plans for his escape, bribing the guards and arranging for him to live peacefully in Thessaly, but the philosopher refused to take a way out that would be an act of treachery against the State. After all, even if the verdict had been wrong, it had been legally arrived at by a properly constituted court. Socrates would do nothing to outrage the laws of his fatherland.

Xanthippe and the three children came to say goodbye on the final day. At sunset Socrates was handed a goblet containing the usual draught of poison (most likely hemlock), prayed calmly for a "fortunate journey", raised the fatal cup to his lips and drained it. He then paced to and fro until walking became too difficult. He lay down on the wooden plank that was his bed, and as he thought fitting at the approach of death, drew his gown over his head. Before all feeling had left him, he suddenly wrenched away the covering to say to his old friend Crito who was present, "We owe Aesculapius a cock. Don't forget to pay the debt."

Chapter 3
Julian the Apostate
AD 331–363

The youngest son of Julius Constantius, Flavius Claudius Julianus (later to be known as Julian the Apostate) was born in Constantinople in A.D. 331. After the Roman Emperor Constantine's death six years later, there was a general massacre of males belonging to the (imperial) Flavian race, and when the promiscuous slaughter ended Julian and his half-brother Gallus were the only two of the line left alive. There can be no doubt that this family tragedy left the boy Julian deeply embittered. It was impossible for him thereafter to reconcile such happenings with the Christian belief as it was then established.

The Empire had been divided among Constantine's three sons – Constantine, Constantius and Constans; but after the eldest, Constantine, had been killed in an ambush and Constans had been murdered ten years afterwards, Constantius became sole ruler over the Roman world. He had ordered the massacre of the Flavians but spared Gallus and Julian because they were too young to upset his plans.

First he had sent them to be educated in different cities,

Statue at Ellora of Buddha (*left*), who forsook the luxuries of the court, his beautiful wife and all earthly ambitions for the life of an ascetic. Six years later he discovered the perfect way in the contemplative life. The keynote of his system, a revolutionary reformation of Brahmanism, was that "Nirvana", or – blissful detachment brought release from rebirth and suffering. Nineteenth-century engraving of Socrates in prison, with his friends gathered round him (*below*). As was the Greek custom, the cup of hemlock was given to him to drink. He took the poison as if it were a goblet of wine at a banquet and awaited his death with complete tranquillity. Socrates outraged his fellow citizens by his revolutionary

views on moral and social questions, and by his uncompromising quest to find the truth about everything. – The Emperor Flavius Claudius Julianus, "the Apostate" (*left*), in full armour at the time of his long-meditated expedition against the Persians (from an eighteenth-century engraving). After crossing the Tigris and advancing to Ctesiphon, he was enticed farther by a Persian traitor and forced to retreat across barren country, harassed by Persian cavalry. Repeatedly he beat back the enemy, but at last he was mortally wounded by a spear-thrust.

(*Above*) Nineteenth-century painting of Martin Luther, burning the Pope's order of excommunication in the presence of a multitude of doctors, students and citizens in Wittenberg.

Wat Tyler, the strong leader of the Peasants' Revolt of 1381, was struck down and killed in the presence of the young King Richard II (*below*). (From the Froissart Chronicles.)

in Ionia and Bithynia. As they grew older and consequently more dangerous, he had them moved to virtual imprisonment in the ancient castle of Macellum near Caesarea, formerly the palace of the kings of Cappadocia.

Thus for the next six years Julian and his half-brother were taught by the best possible tutors, growing steadily in wisdom and in strength. Their surroundings were pleasant enough, but they yearned for freedom and for their rightful positions in society. Their opportunity came when Gallus reached the age of twenty-five. For reasons of state Constantius invested the young man with the title of Caesar, married him off to a vicious fury of a princess called Constantina, and allowed him to settle in Antioch. Naturally, brother Julian was not forgotten. He was given status, wealth and the semblance of liberty.

Eventually Gallus fell into disgrace, was stripped of his rank, imprisoned and speedily executed. This left only Julian.

Strongly guarded, the youth was transferred to Milan where for seven harrowing months he lived in daily apprehension of death. In the end, however, he triumphed over adversity, thanks to the good offices of the Empress Eusebia who pleaded his cause successfully with her husband. She wielded such powerful influence over Constantius that he sent for Julian, listened to him with tolerance and understanding, and for their mutual benefit sent him into honourable exile in Athens.

This unexpected change in his fortunes was enthusiastically welcomed by Julian. As far as he was concerned, the Emperor could not have chosen a more delightful location than the capital of Greece. He was at least able to study the Greek language, religion, learning and way of life, all of which he admired. For six enchanting months he strolled through the groves of the Academy, discussing his problems with famous philosophers. Every day he gained in intellectual stature and achieved a certain popularity among Athenian scholars and students. Never again was he to know the happiness and contentment that he experienced during his stay in Athens.

Meanwhile the Empress Eusebia continued to sing Julian's praises whenever her husband was in a receptive mood. She skilfully drew Constantius's attention to the

B

contrasting characters of Julian and the over-ambitious Gallus. She argued that the Emperor's best policy would be to earn the everlasting gratitude and loyalty of such a virtuous, modest and impressionable young man. All Constantius had to do, she urged, was to find the exile a suitable wife, to grant him the title of Caesar, and to make him ruler of the countries beyond the Alps. His generous gesture would undoubtedly bind Julian to him for all time.

Convinced by his wife's appreciation of the situation, the Emperor carried out her wishes to the letter. His own sister Helena, he decided, would make a perfect bride for Julian. Consequently he proposed to recall the 25-year-old prince from his beloved Athens, and leading him by the hand, conduct him to his towering tribunal to present him to the people as the new Caesar of the West.

When he had to quit Athens Julian wept bitterly. For one thing, he had totally succumbed to the charm and beauty of the city. For another, he had little confidence in the kind of reception that was waiting for him. He could not trust the crafty Constantius.

A brief consultation with the goddess Minerva dispelled all Julian's doubts and suspicions. He returned to the Emperor's court, celebrated his nuptials with Helena, and was duly appointed Caesar and given the task of administering the West. He had shaved off his beard and had put on the military garment of a Roman prince in honour of the solemn occasion. After the ceremonial investiture Constantius exhorted him to perform heroic deeds and gave him every assurance of sincere friendship. The rank and file banged their shields on their knees, while their officers signified their approval less ostentatiously.

Then, riding together in the same chariot, Constantius and Julian went back to the palace. The new Caesar immediately made for Mediolanum (Milan) where he spent rather more than three weeks of laughter and merry-making. The only drawback was that at all times Julian was well aware that he was under surveillance. His letters were carefully censored and none of his friends had access to him. His servants and household staff were screened and he was allowed to retain only four – his doctor, his librarian and a couple of pages. There were plenty of slaves to carry out his orders, but he dared not trust a single one of them. His marriage, from which he might have derived some measure of relief from all these minor irritations, was wrecked at the outset through Eusebia's unbridled jealousy.

While Constantius was away defending his frontiers, Julian was given a chance to show his true worth. Escorted by no more than four hundred soldiers he went to the Roman province of Gaul which was being systematically pillaged by swarms of marauding Germanic barbarians. At least forty-five wealthy cities and hundreds of towns and villages had been overrun and plundered by the time the small contingent of Romans began their march across the Gallic countryside.

On the face of it, Julian's sheltered upbringing hardly seemed to have fitted him for a military career, but surprisingly he soon proved himself to be a natural leader. Abstemious and unacquainted with luxuries, he easily adapted himself to camp life, eating the same simple fare as was provided for the common soldiers and sleeping rough like a seasoned campaigner. At the head of his resolute little force, he made his way to the ancient city of Autun and thence to the Roman camp just outside Rheims. He must have had that indefinable aura that emanates from a good general and inspires his men to inexplicable feats of valour, for on his arrival the legionaries in the camp, who until that moment had been feeling depressed and demoralized, were filled with new confidence and courage. Led by Julian, they sallied forth in search of the enemy.

In this, his first action, Julian's inexperience proved costly. His failure to post proper sentries resulted in an attack upon his unprepared rearguard. Two legions were wiped out before the situation was restored.

It was in his second action that Julian earned his military reputation. Although he was unable to destroy the enemy, he drove the Germans back as far as the banks of the Rhine. Across the broad river he could see the ruins of Cologne, but with winter fast approaching, he decided to abandon the pursuit and pull back his army into Gaul. He withdrew to Sens, and shortly after he had established his headquarters there the Germans appeared in strength, surrounded the place and pinned down the Romans for about a month. Thanks to Julian's tactical skill and fearlessness, the siege was at last broken and the barbarians compelled to retire.

Encouraged no doubt by this success, Julian began to take a more independent line. He knew that Marcellus, master-general of the Roman cavalry in Gaul, could have effected an earlier relief at Sens if he had acted with the promptitude the circumstances had warranted. In the final analysis, Constantius was probably responsible for Marcellus's unco-operative attitude, but that thought did not deter Julian from disciplining the treacherous general. He sent for Marcellus and dismissed him, appointing in his stead a loyal, courageous and faithful officer named Severus. Strongly supported by Eusebia, Julian himself was officially put in supreme command of all Roman troops in Gaul.

But Marcellus was not the only officer to work secretly against Julian. When the campaign was resumed in the spring, the young Caesar and his army boldly attacked the German cantonments. Simultaneously the Roman infantry general Barbatio, with a force of some thirty thousand legionaries, swept northwards from Milan, crossed the mountains and penetrated as far as the Rhine. Logically the Germans could do nothing but evacuate Gaul and hurry to the defence of their own country. At the critical moment, however, Barbatio deliberately failed to press home the advantage he had gained, thus leaving Julian without the support on which he had counted.

Quick to profit from Barbatio's curious reluctance to fight, the Germans poured reinforcements across the Rhine to help their comrades in Gaul until they outnumbered the Romans by about three to one. Nevertheless Julian resolved to attack, with himself at the head of the Roman army's right flank. Then was fought the memorable battle of Strasbourg, a bloody and determined conflict. Roman losses included four tribunes and nearly two hundred and fifty soldiers; German casualties ran to six thousand killed in action, plus many more drowned or pierced with darts while trying to swim across the Rhine. The outcome of the affair was that the Germans were driven from the Upper Rhine provinces.

The victorious Julian then transferred his attention to the Franks, probably the most warlike of the barbarians. He had to contend with a strong body of these fierce fighters who had occupied two castles on the river Meuse. After a siege lasting 44 days, they surrendered, thus breaking away for the first time from their ancient traditions that they must conquer or die. Prisoners – and there were many – were sent as a gift to Constantius.

Before the rest of the Franks could get their second wind, Julian kept up the pressure, his battle-line stretching from Cologne to the coast. Surprised by the swiftness of his advance, the barbarians could not withstand the onslaught and it was not long before they were expelled from every Gallic province.

During the interval of peace that followed the successful campaigns, the indefatigable Caesar concentrated his energies on furthering the welfare of his subjects, rebuilding their devastated cities, strengthening the Rhine outposts, and providing adequate food stocks from places as far afield as Britain. He even found time to deal with administrative matters and improve the fiscal system. He expressed his views on tax collectors in a letter to a friend: "Was it possible for the disciple of Plato and Aristotle to act otherwise than I have done? Could I abandon the unhappy subjects intrusted to my care? Was I not called upon to defend them from the repeated injuries of these unfeeling robbers?"

Julian moved his headquarters to the city he loved, Paris. and Gaul enjoyed a period of comparative tranquillity. Praised and admired throughout the Empire, except of course by Constantius who was jealous of the youthful Caesar's growing popularity, he still had a few detractors.

It was when Julian's star seemed to be in the ascendant that Constantius struck. With a view to weakening his rival, he decided to recall soldiers from Gaul to fight in the eastern provinces against the Persian monarch. Consequently a tribune and a lawyer were sent to Paris to arrange the transfer of troops. Julian was horrified to learn that he would lose four legions, together with 300 brave youths from each of the remaining formations. He admitted that the Gallic provinces were at peace while there was always trouble on the eastern frontier, but to rob him of his best men would solve nothing. The Persians would continue to threaten and a few more Roman legions pitched into the battle-line would have no appreciable effect. To leave Julian unguarded and the Gallic provinces unprotected would be an open invitation to the barbarians to swarm back into Gaul. The good work already done would thus be wasted.

There was also another matter to consider. Julian had

promised most of the auxiliaries that they would never be called upon to cross the Alps. He had pledged his own and his country's honour on that score. How could he ask soldiers who had just started to relax after an arduous campaign to undertake the agonizingly laborious march to the eastern front, to risk their lives against crack Persian archers and to suffer the intolerable heat of the burning Asian deserts? And without them, how could he cope with the Germans and Franks who would come seeking revenge?

Constantius obviously had Julian at his mercy. If he obeyed the Emperor's commands, he would be inviting his own destruction. If he disobeyed, he would be branded as a rebel. Faced with these equally unpleasant alternatives, Julian was on the point of withdrawing from public life.

He thought about the situation, however, and reluctantly decided to carry out Constantius's orders. Soon long columns of unhappy legionaries were trudging towards the Alps. Elsewhere detachments from various formations were converging on the appointed assembly area where wagons awaited to transport wives and families. Even the most casual observer would have seen that these warriors were dissatisfied, resentful and not far removed from mutiny.

When all the troops had arrived, Julian spoke to them from a tribunal in front of the gates of Paris. He commended their past deeds, emphasized that he dared not ignore the Emperor's commands, and after urging them to serve Constantius loyally bade them dismiss. There were no cheers, no demonstrations. The auxiliaries simply broke ranks and strode away wrapped in a dismal silence. Only the officers over a farewell drink expressed their grief at leaving their esteemed general and their homes in Gaul.

At midnight, unable to contain their emotions any longer, the people of Paris, brandishing weapons and torches, surrounded Julian's palace and began calling out, "Julian Augustus" over and over again. Then, as dawn broke, the military burst into the building, insisted on taking Julian to the tribunal, and there they named him their emperor.

Embarrassed by such adulation, Julian begged them to give their allegiance to the only man who was entitled to it, Constantius. But by that time the soldiers were too incensed to listen to reason. They presented their commander-in-chief with an ultimatum. Either he was to become their emperor or, despite their deep affection for him, they would have to finish him off. Julian put up a token resistance and then yielded to popular pressure. From the moment he accepted their terms he automatically labelled himself a rebel.

Although there is evidence to show that Julian was not wholly aware of what was going on and that he had submitted unwillingly to the troops' demands, there are also in the records dark hints that he was guilty of shaping events. He certainly did not want a civil war and still less did he seek a confrontation with Constantius. He undoubtedly had ambition and may well have hankered after ultimate power, but it must also be remembered that to a large extent Constantius himself had pushed him into action. As soon as Julian found his life in jeopardy, he had nothing to lose by choosing rebellion.

Once he was set on his revolutionary course, Julian knew exactly what he had to do. Decked out in all the panoply of war, he assembled his supporters in the field of Mars and delivered the customary harangue. He was careful to point out that all they wanted were the Gallic provinces. As long as Constantius agreed to a treaty, they had no quarrel with him. He then wrote to Constantius explaining what had happened. He admitted the illegality of his election, but stressed the fact that the troops had been subjected to considerable pressure. He was not challenging the Emperor's supremacy. He would in fact be sending him rich gifts annually, together with a number of young barbarians for his army, and would be delighted to accommodate a Praetorian prefect who could keep an eye on Constantius's interests. For himself he claimed no more than he already held. He signed his message "Caesar" and requested the title "Augustus".

While Julian was coping with a tribe of recalcitrant Franks, his ambassadors travelled slowly across country to hand Julian's report to Constantius. They were frigidly received and contemptuously dismissed. The Emperor was clearly in no mood to grant concessions. The title "Augustus" would *not* be conferred on Julian; political and military power in the Gallic provinces would be wielded by men appointed by the Imperial Court; a suitable treaty would be hammered out at a place somewhere between Paris and Antioch.

Julian summoned his supporters again, and when he read

out the Emperor's haughty reply and said he was prepared to give up the title "Augustus", their response was unequivocal. "Julian Augustus," they shouted, "continue to reign, by the authority of the army, of the people, of the republic which you have saved!"

Thereafter Julian's only recourse was war. Thoroughly disillusioned, he renounced Christianity and declared that any friendship that had existed between him and Constantius was now at an end. His soldiers, admiring him as the man who had liberated Gaul and trounced the Germans, vowed that they would never let him down. No matter what happened, he could depend on their loyalty at all times. With Julian as their leader, they were ready to march anywhere.

Following a plan devised by Julian, two fighting columns converged on Sirmium where they were met by Julian's own contingent of 3,000 volunteers who had approached by way of the Black Forest. Welcomed by soldiers and civilians alike, the rebels entered the town in triumph. Sweeping on relentlessly through the provinces of Illyricum, Julian soon established himself as master of Italy.

A civil war would have been inevitable, for Constantius had every intention of crushing the rebellion, but he contracted a fever and died at Mopsucrene, not far from Tarsus. It is believed that on his death-bed he nominated Julian as his successor.

So the rebel Caesar, who had made his way victoriously across Europe from the Atlantic to the Bosphorus, returned to the city of his birth and the new capital of the Empire, and ringing in his ears were the acclamations of the whole population of Constantinople. He was only thirty-two, but he was the undisputed master of the Roman Empire. The man who despised honours, pomp and royalty, had attained to the highest honour of all.

He began his reign by reforming the Imperial Court, eliminating its extravagance and corruption. He also removed from office the numerous informers and spies who had been employed by Constantius. Criminals who had flourished during the reign of his predecessor were promptly punished, and under Julian's dispensation every effort was made to make the punishment fit the crime. One of the corner-stones of his legal policy was justice, especially for his poorer subjects whose distresses he did his best to relieve. He was, in short, a good and wise ruler.

No description of Julian's character would be complete without some reference being made to his religious beliefs and his apostasy. For one who was so well informed in most matters, he seemed to have entertained strangely prejudiced views on religion. Perhaps his hostility towards Christianity stemmed from the early part of his life when most of his relatives were butchered and he was left an orphan in the hands of their murderers. As a boy he must have associated the Christian religion with cruelty, persecution and slavery. Educated as a young saint by the Bishop of Nicomedia, Julian probably developed a smouldering resentment against the puffed-up, supercilious ministers appointed by the Bishop. Moreover, these very pillars of the Church did nothing but wrangle among themselves, amending their creeds to suit particular circumstances, and frequently giving the impression that they did not really understand much of what they professed.

It is hardly surprising that at the first opportunity an intelligent young man like Julian rebelled against all the sham and hypocrisy that had surrounded his upbringing. As a disciple of Plato, he turned towards the Eternal Cause of the universe, believing in a supreme god and a number of inferior gods who were responsible for maintaining harmony in the animal, vegetable and mineral kingdoms. Then, when he was twenty, Julian was secretly initiated at Ephesus into the sacred and solemn mysteries of Eleusis. From that moment on he was an ardent worshipper of the gods and goddesses of Olympus.

What is remarkable about Julian's apostasy is that he managed to hide it from the world for rather more than a decade. Only when Constantius's hatred and envy drove him into rebellion did he announce his earlier rebellion against Christ.

Still more remarkable in that intolerant era was Julian's humane attitude towards his subjects after he became all-powerful. Christians feared and pagans expected he would launch a terrifying programme of persecution. He surprised believers and unbelievers alike by observing a strict neutrality. Although he personally dedicated his life to the deities of Olympus, he made it abundantly clear that the citizens of the Roman world were free to choose their own gods.

No sooner had he assumed the Imperial purple than he decided to deal with the Persian threat once and for all. In an incredible march that started at Constantinople and finished up outside the heavily fortified city of Ctesiphon, Julian met with success all along the route. Advised that a siege was out of the question, he swung inland towards the Tigris. The enemy attacked in strength and a stray javelin pierced Julian's ribs and penetrated his liver. He tried to pull it out but the effort was too much for him and he fainted. He was carried into his tent, and realizing that the wound was fatal, he delivered his own funeral oration. "I die without remorse as I have lived without guilt. I am pleased to reflect on the innocence of my private life; and I can affirm with confidence that the supreme authority, that emanation of the Divine Power, has been preserved in my hands pure and immaculate. Detesting the corrupt and destructive maxims of despotism, I have considered the happiness of the people as the end of government . . . I now offer my tribute to the Eternal Being, who has not suffered me to perish by the cruelty of a tyrant, by the secret dagger of conspiracy, or by the slow tortures of lingering disease."

After these moving words, Julian implored those who were in attendance not to mourn and then launched a metaphysical argument concerning the nature of the soul. But blood poured afresh from his wound and he found it difficult to breathe. At about midnight Julian the Apostate, who had rebelled against his Emperor and against Christianity, reached the end of his brief reign. According to some of the early Christian writers, his last words were, "Thou hast conquered, O Galilean", but in view of Julian's devotion to the old religion, such an acknowledgement would have been completely out of character. His revolt against Constantius had been born of expediency; his revolt against that same Galilean had stemmed from an unshakeable conviction.

Chapter 4
Wat Tyler
d. 1381

Some time before the Great Revolt of 1381, the English poet Gower, in his *Mirour de l'Omme,* wrote these significant words: "Three things, all of the same sort, are merciless when they get the upper hand: a water-flood, a wasting fire, and the common multitude of small folk. For these will never be checked by reason or discipline."

The Peasants' Revolt towards the end of the fourteenth century is the story of just such a "common multitude of small folk". It was brilliantly organized, intelligently handled and immediately effective. Although the historical records of the period provide but little information about its captain and leader, we know that he was a man of courage and integrity, was highly esteemed by his fellow rebels, and according to his contemporaries, he was blessed with an "excellent wit". We know neither his age nor what he looked like, and yet the cause for which he fought and died will forever remain a part of our national heritage. This unsung hero who became ruler over the greater part of south-east England for the space of eight days was named Wat Tyler.

For a proper understanding of the nature of his rebellion, it is necessary first to examine briefly the circumstances that goaded him into action.

To begin with, for centuries before the peasants' rising, the common people of England had been squeezed dry by an iniquitous social system. They were exploited, oppressed, cheated and robbed at every turn. For a long time they had either accepted their miserable lot with sullen resignation, or they had merely grumbled among themselves and prayed secretly for better days. They hoped that conditions would improve, but they made no effort to bring about a change themselves.

In the latter half of the fourteenth century, however, a new spirit of unrest was abroad. The peasants and the ordinary workers were everywhere forming pockets of resistance. Realizing that individual protests were of no value whatsoever, they started to band together for mutual aid and support. From 1377 onwards the authorities were uncomfortably aware of certain confederacies in which the members of some particular work group were learning to co-operate for the benefit of all. On the one hand, the oppressors believed in the principle "Divide and rule". On the other, their victims were discovering that union meant strength. The time had now come for the rebels to declare themselves and try to build a new England.

Each separate faction had its own leader who served as a rallying-point and acted as spokesman for the others. A priest named John Ball, whom the biased chronicler Froissart called "the mad priest of Kent", went about expounding the doctrines of the religious reformer Wycliffe, with special reference to social equality, and was largely responsible for launching the revolt. On the eve of the popular uprising, however, he was flung into Maidstone gaol and excommunicated. By that time one of the local leaders, Wat Tyler, had established himself as the outstanding personality of the movement. He it was who gave the rebellion its shape and direction, planned its overall strategy and made all major decisions. Without his presiding genius there would have been riots and disturbances at a number of isolated points. Tyler transformed what would have been a rabble into a formidable fighting machine.

The people reached breaking-point in November, 1380.

Parliament had demanded the sum of £160,000. The Church agreed to provide a third of this amount; the rest had to be obtained by taxation. Poll-taxes had already been introduced, but during that fatal winter the poor were called upon to pay an average sum of a shilling per head, a crippling levy in those hard times. Even the Treasurer must have disapproved of the tax, for he resigned. His successor, Robert Hales, generally referred to as "Hob the Robber", was less sensitive. Determined to have the money at all costs, in January and February 1381, he sent out teams of collectors who were ordered to enforce payment or to send defaulters to prison.

At first there was no serious trouble. Villagers simply submitted inaccurate lists, and in many cases their falsifications were not challenged either by their own officials or by the collectors themselves. Their tax evasions eventually came to light when their final figures were added together. Compared with the returns for 1377, the population of England had fallen by as much as thirty per cent.

After Parliament had rejected the collectors' findings as unsatisfactory, new commissions were appointed, with instructions to travel from county to county and carry out a thorough investigation. It did not take them long to confirm the authorities' worst suspicions. Their inquiries revealed that citizens everywhere had been dodging the poll-tax.

The people's immediate reactions to the king's commissioners were understandably hostile. Filled with resentment, they staged public demonstrations and indignant protests. Then they revolted against their rulers and flatly refused to pay. The first two counties to carry rebellion to its furthest limits were Kent and Essex. Wat Tyler, who was living in Chelmsford at the time and who had no doubt listened to some of John Ball's fiery speeches, played a prominent part in organizing the rebel army.

The authorities realized that the people meant business when they sent Thomas Bampton and two serjeants-at-arms to collect outstanding taxes at Brentwood. Men from at least three neighbouring villages stubbornly ignored the tax-gatherers' demands. When Bampton threatened the ringleaders with imprisonment, the irate citizens banded together and drove him out of town. News of this successful action quickly spread to laouring communities north and south of the Thames. Arming themselves with whatever was handy – axes, knives, bill-hooks, sticks, scythes and a quantity of rusty weapons and armour brought home by veterans from the French wars – they were more than ready to do battle with their oppressors. On Whit Sunday, also in Brentwood, they laid violent hands on the chief justice of common pleas, Sir Robert Belknap, and gave him the same treatment as they had meted out to the luckless Bampton.

With Wat Tyler whipping up enthusiasm wherever he went, the citizens of Rochester, Dartford, Gravesend and Canterbury swung into action. Rebel columns converged on Maidstone, where they executed a prosperous burgess who had tried to sabotage the revolt in its initial stages. For good measure they also set fire to a number of country mansions belonging to wealthy merchants and land-owners.

In Maidstone there was a meeting of captains to decide on the next move, and it was at this important conference that Wat Tyler was officially elected commander-in-chief. By common consent he was asked "to maintain them and act as counsellor". Then the assembly nominated other leaders, divided the rank and file into companies, chose their concentration areas and added the final touches to their campaign. Church bells would be rung and beacons fired to let the people know that the day of reckoning was at hand.

Henceforth Maidstone became the pivot of the whole operation. Wat Tyler sent out his messengers to the remotest corners of the county; before long every Kentishman's mission was to free himself from the triple tyranny of Church, Law and Government. Serfs and peasants, spurred on by Wat Tyler and others like him, set out to destroy the feudal system.

Tyler's absolute control of the rebels was revealed on the morning of 10 June when he formed up his followers into an orderly procession and led them into Canterbury. At noon, during high mass, the great cathedral was rudely invaded by those who were convinced that the Archbishop had let them down and ought to be "decapitated for his iniquity". Elsewhere in the city, while one lot had a field day breaking into the castle, a second party flung open the prison gates and turned loose the inmates, many of whom were still in their chains and manacles. Archbishop

Sudbury's palace was plundered and more valuable papers destroyed, while the county sheriff himself was apprehended and his personal documents publicly burnt. As soon as Tyler was satisfied that all resistance had been crushed the city officials were herded together and compelled to declare their loyalty to "King Richard and the True Commoners of England".

The uprising was meeting with the same success in other areas of south-east England. In towns such as Colchester, Chelmsford and Brentwood the people acted with the same ruthless audacity, manhandling anyone connected with the government, indulging in an orgy of pillage and vandalism. Wat Tyler and his lieutenants were beginning to think that complete victory could not be long delayed.

On 11 June the insurrectionaries of Essex and Kent started their historic trek towards London. Meeting with little opposition *en route,* the two well-disciplined armies converged relentlessly on the capital. In the words of John Froissart, they "went on their way like a tempest, sweeping and casting down all houses of lawyers and proctors of the King's or Archbishop's courts, on whom they had no mercy". Among the hosts of prisoners they released from gaol was the firebrand John Ball.

All credit must go to Wat Tyler for the speed and smoothness with which the twin prongs of the revolutionary movement made their simultaneous probe in the direction of the capital. Both columns left their respective assembly areas on 11 June, and by the following evening the Kentish contingent were bedding down for the night in the fields near Mile End. It is estimated that a force of thirty thousand was encamped south of the river. Roughly the same number of rebels had leaguered beyond the city walls to the east. To reinforce this double threat, between forty and fifty thousand labourers and artisans were waiting inside the capital, all ready and willing to fight under Wat Tyler's redoubtable leadership.

As night fell, rebel patrols advanced into Southwark. There Wat Tyler and his henchmen were welcomed by an alderman who in secret session guaranteed that the Londoners would assuredly rally round the standard of revolt as soon as it was raised within the city. All Tyler had to do, the alderman insisted, was to head for London Bridge and to initiate a rumour to the effect that the rebels were about to batter their way in. During the resultant confusion, he added, he would be personally responsible for opening the gates and admitting the rebel army.

Wat Tyler gave the alderman's plan his blessing, but took the precaution of sending three of his captains with their ally when he entered the city by stealth that same night. These three were briefed to establish contact with the leaders of the London rebels and to make detailed arrangements with them for what Tyler now had in mind – the complete take-over of the capital of England!

This encounter, so vital to the successful outcome of the whole enterprise, took place in the alderman's house. Discussions continued far into the night and from them emerged a clear picture of the obstacles still to be surmounted. When the representatives of Kent and Essex rejoined their comrades outside the city walls, they had much useful information to pass on to their chief. The wily Wat certainly profited by it.

The situation inside the city was highly encouraging. In so far as England's military machine consisted of a number of private armies commanded by the barons, the authorities in London could not call upon the services of either soldiers or police to help suppress the rebellion. The king's only recourse in a national crisis was to rely on the support of the barons, but he knew that if the barons joined forces, then they would be stronger than the king and the monarchy itself might be in danger. In any event, Richard II was only a boy, so what it all boiled down to was that the privileged few who wished to retain the feudal order were without a competent leader.

Wat Tyler understood that under normal circumstances his people's army had no hope whatsoever of capturing London, protected as it was by its forbidding walls and battlements and outer ditch. He appreciated the fact that the king and his councillors considered themselves perfectly safe inside the impregnable Tower of London. But he was also well aware that the security of the city and its rulers depended entirely on the loyalty of its inhabitants, that whoever controlled the gates controlled London. In the year of grace 1381, Tyler could count on circumstances being very far from normal. For one thing, the capital was swarming with men who wanted to overthrow the régime. For another, at one strategic point his aldermanic friend was in charge of the guardians of the gate.

It so happened that 13 June was a feast day – Corpus Christi. The Kentish men on Blackheath, assembled under the banners of their patron Saint George, listened to an impassioned address delivered by John Ball. They had something other than the Eucharist to celebrate, for Wat Tyler had demanded on their behalf that the young king should come and discuss terms. Word had been sent to Richard that his people were still loyal to him. Their only desire was to rid the kingdom of traitors.

Showing great courage the boy king, accompanied by a few nobles and councillors, left his stronghold in the Tower, stepped into the royal barge and was rowed down river towards Rotherhithe. When the vessel reached the rebel encampment, the oarsmen manoeuvred it to within twenty yards of the shore. After angry exchanges between lords and commoners, Richard asked the men on the bank what exactly they wanted. They shouted back an invitation to him to land so that their leader could confer with him as man to man. Left to himself the youth would doubtless have acceded to their request, but his nobles, fearful for their lives, refused to take the risk. They hurled further abuse at the rebels, ordered the oarsmen to pull away from the danger area and were soon on their way back to the Tower. For the lords the expedition had been a humiliating experience. Richard had privately enjoyed it. Moreover, he felt confident that Wat Tyler and his men would never use physical violence against their king.

Wat Tyler was now more determined than ever to win control of London. It seemed to him that although the Bridge was strongly fortified, it would have to be seized as a preliminary to storming the city. To persuade the guards to lower the drawbridge, he told them he would first destroy the bridge by fire and then have his men ferried across the river in boats. The terrified guards promptly unfastened the chain, wound down the huge drawbridge, and even unbarred the stone gate to let in the rebels. Tyler led his 30,000 Kentishmen over the bridge and into the capital.

As the men of Kent marched into the city from the south, their fellow rebels from Essex and other counties entered from the north by way of Aldgate. It was there that the alderman who was in command of the gate guards helped the rebel cause by betraying his trust.

London citizens from all walks of life cheered their "liberators" and offered them food and drink. Obedient to Wat Tyler's instructions, the rebels, their numbers swollen by mobs of journeymen, artisans and apprentices, behaved at first in a reasonable manner, neither rioting nor looting. They tried to live up to their leader's proud claim: "We are zealots for truth and justice, not thieves and robbers."

When part of Tyler's army reached the Tower, King Richard and one of his heralds appeared on a turret looking down on St. Katherine's wharf where the rebels were massed. After a few trumpet notes had reduced the crowd to a respectful silence, the herald called upon the people to disperse and return to their homes. He promised that there would be no reprisals and that His Majesty would make it his business to redress their wrongs. But the rebels were far from satisfied. They were even less satisfied later that evening when an official read to them a royal bill in which the king thanked them for their allegiance and declared his readiness to forgive and forget their attempt to overthrow their rightful masters. Their simple answer to such empty words was that all their grievances had to be met without delay.

At last the authorities realized that the rebels were in deadly earnest. It was therefore decided that on the following day Richard would go to Mile End to listen to Wat Tyler's demands. Only the king was likely to gain anything in the way of concessions at that stage of the revolt.

Early in the morning on 14 June, King Richard II and a small escort of knights left the Tower and rode to the appointed rendezvous. Wat Tyler, sitting astride a pony, surrounded by a milling throng of serfs, peasants, farmers and workers of all descriptions, was waiting to greet the youthful monarch. When the royal party arrived, Tyler dismounted, went down on one knee and kissed his king's hand. Then, rising to his feet, he outlined the people's demands which included the total abolition of feudalism, lower rents, hunting and fishing rights, permission to buy and sell in the open market, the repeal of a number of unjust laws, a drastic pruning of the powers of the lords, and an unqualified pardon for all who had taken part in the rebellion.

Richard listened sympathetically and informed Tyler that everything he had asked for would be dealt with. The rebel leader then added one further request, telling the king, "the Commons will that you suffer them to take and deal with all the traitors who have sinned against you and the law."

For the first time Richard started to hedge. All those whose disloyalty could be proved, he assured Tyler, would be apprehended and would receive their just deserts. Then, when he saw that this vague answer was unacceptable, he reluctantly agreed that the rebels could decide the fates of those unpopular ministers who had taken refuge in the Tower.

Delighted with the concessions he had obtained, Wat Tyler next mustered his forces in two long lines. While the king moved slowly along the ranks, a herald formally delivered a verbatim account of the negotiations. To confirm all that had been said, a team of clerks prepared the necessary charters of enfranchisement.

In the meantime a large contingent of armed commoners occupied the Tower and in an outburst of fury beheaded the two men whom they considered their chief oppressors – Archbishop Sudbury and Treasurer Hales. These executions were followed by many other brutal reprisals, although in view of the circumstances the majority of the rebels behaved with remarkable restraint. In fact, hundreds of them, under the impression that the struggle was over, went back to their homes, leaving Tyler and about thirty thousand Kentishmen to establish the new order in London and to ensure that the promised political reforms were carried out.

The king and his councillors, however, supported by the wealthy city merchants and traders, had by this time reviewed the situation and had come to a momentous decision. Since their attempts to appease Tyler and his men had produced nothing but savagery of the worst kind, they agreed that there was only one course to pursue if the constitution was to be preserved. Wat Tyler had to be eliminated.

On 16 June, therefore, Richard's advisers invited Tyler to another conference with the king. On this occasion the meeting place was Smithfield.

Foolishly putting his trust in the people who were out to destroy him, the rebel leader accepted the invitation and with a small band of supporters set out to keep the appointment.

Tyler halted his escort on the western side of St. Bartholomew's. There, with their banners proudly unfurled, the men paraded in good order, little suspecting the treachery that had been planned by the king's officers. They watched Richard and his entourage ride up, all smiles and affability, as though they were seeking to establish friendly relations with Wat Tyler and the commoners.

Astride his favourite pony and with only one man in attendance, Tyler approached the king. He dismounted, seized Richard's hand and shook it enthusiastically. "Brother," he said, "be of good cheer. Thee shall have within a fortnight more thanks from the commons than thee ever had before: we twain shall be right good fellows."

Richard merely repeated the previous requests he had made through his herald that Tyler's army should be disbanded and sent to their homes.

Tyler pointed out that they were still waiting for charters unequivocally setting out the royal concessions. For the king's information he again listed the people's requirements and hinted darkly that the lords would pay dearly if they were not immediately met. He particularly stressed the necessity for repealing many of the existing laws and for passing new legislation that would guarantee freedom, equality, justice and the abolition of privileges.

After Richard had promised him full satisfaction, Wat Tyler asked for a drink. He was handed a flagon of ale which he quaffed at a draught. He then started to ride across the vast open space that lay between his men and the king's.

It was the moment the lords had been waiting for. One of their servants stepped forward and called out provocatively, "Wat Tyler is the greatest thief and robber in Kent!" Naturally Tyler reigned in his pony and summoned the man to him. When the fellow deliberately hung back, the rebel leader whipped out his dagger and went to avenge the insult. Before he had covered half the distance, Major Walworth, an officer in the king's bodyguard, intervened and announced that he was arresting Tyler for violent behaviour in the royal presence. Obviously acting under orders, knights and men-at-arms swiftly closed in, surrounding pony and rider and cutting them off from their only source of help. Wat Tyler was caught in a trap from which there was no escape.

In desperation Tyler stabbed at the major, but to no effect. Drawing his sword, Walworth struck at Tyler's neck and head, while another of the conspirators thrust his sword twice into the rebel captain's body.

Badly wounded, Tyler collapsed across his pony's neck. Somehow he conjured up sufficient strength to break through the hostile ring and began to gallop towards his supporters. He managed to stay in his saddle for a few seconds, but then he lost consciousness and crashed to the ground. Some of his horrified followers discharged a few arrows towards the king's men, causing them to break up and disperse, but Richard himself courageously rode towards them. This manoeuvre certainly threw the rebels into confusion, giving them the impression that the king was on their side. When he begged them to have confidence in him, they drifted away without further incident.

Four or five commoners picked up their dying leader's body and removed it to St. Bartholomew's hospital. It was not allowed to remain there long. Major Walworth, who had ridden to the city to find out what troops were available there, came back to complete his day's work by having Wat Tyler's body transferred to Smithfield and beheaded. With the blood-stained head displayed on a spear, the Major and his soldiers, together with some knights and men-at-arms, encircled the demoralized remnants of the rebel army and drove them out of London. A number of Tyler's lieutenants and other ringleaders, including the notorious John Ball, were rounded up and put to death. These wanton executions marked the collapse of the revolt.

The concessions granted to Wat Tyler by the king were promptly cancelled, the charters of emancipation were not issued, and the betrayed peasants seemed to have gained nothing. But Wat Tyler's work had not been entirely in vain. By his vigorous leadership and uncompromising attitude towards authority, he had taught the common people never to bow down before injustice and oppression.

Chapter 5
Martin Luther
1483–1546

The reformation was undoubtedly precipitated by Martin Luther's spirited attack on abuses in the Catholic Church, notably the Church's practice of selling Indulgences or promises of forgiveness of sin, but ever since the late Middle Ages Roman Catholicism had been slowly drifting towards a major upheaval. Early in the sixteenth century when corruption in the Church was at its worst, the first stirrings of revolt came from Germany where there was widespread disillusionment with religion as observed by many of its priests, especially those in high office. As monks became lazy, vicious and predatory, as bishops forgot their spiritual responsibilities and hankered after worldly gain, as popes themselves concentrated more and more on the pursuit of temporal power, the prestige that Rome had formerly enjoyed began to fade.

Men were ready for a change. Even if Martin Luther had not registered his forceful protest against the sale of indulgences, depravity and degeneracy within the Church had reached such shameful proportions that rebellion was bound to break out. To Martin Luther was given the honour of striking the first blow. His insistence that salvation by faith should replace salvation by good works was the pivot of the whole movement.

Son of a Saxon peasant miner, Martin Luther, who was to become the leader of the Protestant Reformation in Germany, was born in Thuringia in 1483. Even as a boy he had about him some indefinable quality that convinced his parents he was destined for great things. Both his father and his mother hoped that he would concentrate on law, develop into a brilliant jurist, marry advantageously and furnish them with whatever was necessary for a comfortable and prosperous old age.

Although Martin's father had been a miner until he branched out as an iron founder, he had descended from solid peasant stock and consequently the boy was brought up in a simple uncomplicated atmosphere. His parents were deeply religious but they still clung to most of the old country superstitions and had no doubt that fairies and witches really existed. Their son assuredly inherited some of their quaint beliefs and primitive notions.

On the whole Martin's childhood was a happy one. He enjoyed the unsophisticated country life, revelling in the woods and vineyards round about Erfurt. He had a special liking for sacred song and often attended services in the town's many churches. He joined religious processions, rubbed shoulders with monks, and not surprisingly evinced an early interest in the church and in the monastic life.

At school he excelled in Latin, a subject that was then the gateway to so many professions. Discipline was strict and canings were frequent. If a scholar collected an excessive number of demerit marks, he earned for himself a severe birching at the end of the week. A dozen or more strokes of the cane as a punishment was not unusual. Under such circumstances Martin had a healthy respect for his teachers. Because of his enthusiastic approach to his studies, he managed to avoid the more drastic forms of correction. It seems, however, that he fared less fortunately at home for, as he himself tells us, his mother once birched him until she drew blood. His crime – stealing a nut!

Nevertheless Martin was able to look back on his schooldays with a certain amount of affection. It was not until he began studying for his Master's degree at the University of Erfurt that the rebellious streak in him first manifested itself. Despite all the pressure exerted by his parents, the young man abandoned law and turned towards the religious life.

For some time Luther had been troubled by a deep consciousness of sin. His parents themselves, his teachers and the learned professors at Erfurt University had all contributed to what could only be described as an abnormal fear of his Maker. Linked with this unnatural terror was the feeling instilled in him by the scarifying pictures of Christ the Judge in the handbooks of the period. Sometimes, when he considered his spiritual inadequacies, he was inclined to try to save his immortal soul by entering a monastery. Then, in a sudden access of exaltation, he would decide that in so far as God's mercy was all-embracing, such a course was unnecessary.

This state of indecision persisted until a certain hot day in July, 1505. Luther, then a student of twenty-one, was returning to the University after visiting his parents' house. Caught by a sudden summer storm, he was mortally afraid to be struck by lightning and cowered on the ground. "St. Anne, help me!" he exclaimed. "I will become a monk!"

The celestial warning helped resolve all his doubts and perplexities. Clearly God wanted him to take the cowl.

Luther spent the next fortnight putting his affairs straight and wondering which monastic order was the most suitable. Finally he selected the reformed congregation of the Augustinians, a very strict community where he could practise asceticism, scourging and fasting, and follow the rigorous pattern of existence imposed by the prior. It was his desperate struggle to obey the rules of the mediaeval church that subsequently led him into rebellion.

His novitiate, however, passed off peacefully enough. Nearly all his waking hours were taken up with spiritual exercises. There were regular prayers seven times a day. The monk's day started betwen one and two in the morning. Bedtime was correspondingly early so that the novitiate could fit in eight hours' sleep. After twelve months as a novice, Luther made his solemn profession and so became a monk. If the Church was right, he could now assume that he was as innocent as a newly baptized child. All he had to do henceforth was to devote the rest of his life to prayer, sacred song and meditation. His spiritual future was assured.

At least that was what Luther thought until he was saying his first mass. His father, who had felt disappointed when Martin had forsaken the law, accepted his son's invitation to attend and brought a party of twenty with him for the occasion. He saw his son move into position in front of the altar and heard him begin: "We offer unto thee, the living, the true, the eternal God——" Then, there was a long embarrassing silence.

At last Martin continued with the service and struggled on to the end. He explained afterwards that all his old uncertainties had suddenly flooded back and had momentarily bereft him of speech. His whole being had been painfully conscious of his own unworthiness and of God's omniscience.

His confidence might have been restored if his earthly father had given him some encouragement, but old Luther's heart had again hardened and he could only reproach the young priest for leaving home and becoming a monk. When he asked his son what had gone wrong after the opening words of the mass, Martin declared that it had been as if a voice from heaven had addressed him. His father's unhelpful comment was: "God grant it was not an apparition of the devil."

Although Martin's mind was in a turmoil with terror and doubt, he made every effort to perform the duties allotted to him. He practised every form of self-denial, praying and fasting in a genuine pursuit of holiness. He even made a pilgrimage to Rome and spent a month there, seeking out spiritual indulgences for himself and his family. But the more he came into contact with the Italian priests, the more he was convinced that many of them were ignorant charlatans living in vice and lechery. On the other hand, he also met a large number of sincere ecclesiastics who practised goodness and morality. His own faith, therefore, was not entirely shattered. He was disillusioned on several counts, but he still believed that through God alone could he hope to be spiritually regenerated.

A second visit to Rome still left Luther in a state of uncertainty, but soon afterwards he went to Wittenberg where he had the good fortune to meet Johann von Staupitz, a vicar of the Augustinian order, who was to give the doubter some of the reassurance he needed.

In those days Wittenberg was famed for its newly founded university. In 1511 the Elector of Saxony, Frederick the Wise, determined to equal the achievements of the University of Leipzig, had approached the Augustinians and Franciscans with a request for three additional professors. Martin Luther was one of the three appointed.

Not even in the cultural and intellectual atmosphere of the university did Martin find real relief for his troubled spirit. He tried long periods of confession as a remedy, taking upon himself the impossible task of confessing every sin he had ever committed. It appeared to him that the whole nature of man was essentially corrupt and had to undergo a complete change.

Aided by von Staupitz, Luther next plunged into mysticism. He attained to the feeling of exaltation he sought, but he could not long remain on such a lofty spiritual plane. Frustrated and tormented, he experienced that "dark night of the soul" through which the English Jesuit poet Gerard Manley Hopkins was to pass almost four centuries later. To his own disgust he realized that in spite of his insignificance in the scheme of things, he was actually rebelling against his Creator.

To save his friend from the mental and spiritual crises that were racking him, von Staupitz urged Luther to take his Doctor's degree with a view to becoming a preacher and lecturing on the Bible at the university. The work involved would surely take his mind off his personal problems.

Thus Luther began an intensive study of the Scriptures. He was particularly impressed by Christ's desperate invocation before he died: "My God, my God, why hast thou forsaken me?" That Christ too had known alienation from God came as a revelation to him and from that moment Luther's conception of the Almighty underwent a profound transformation. God had indeed allowed His Son to die, but He had also resurrected Him. By the same token, if man kept himself free from sin, God would grant him everlasting life. Perhaps Luther's own words best express the significance of his discovery: "I grasped that the justice of God is that righteousness by which through grace and sheer mercy God justifies us through faith. Thereupon I felt myself to be reborn. . . ."

Until 1516 von Staupitz's cure appeared to have been effective. Luther had been kept busy preaching, lecturing and writing. All the time, however, something had been worrying him. The citizens of Wittenberg, many of whom belonged to Luther's flock, were in the habit of seeking forgiveness of sins by purchasing indulgences, a Church practice that had long commended itself to popes anxious to swell their revenues. Luther had already preached twice in condemnation of indulgences. On Halloween, the Eve of All Saints, 1516, he again spoke out against these papal promises, drawing everyone's attention to his revolutionary view that the Pope could *not* free souls from purgatory. He condemned the very idea that money payments could wash away sins as pernicious. Logically it simply meant that the wealthy could sin with impunity.

Not only did Luther's broadside threaten the Church; it also alarmed the Elector of Saxony, many of whose revenues came from the sale of indulgences. The Castle Church at Wittenberg and even the university where Luther was employed were both dependent to a large extent on the same lucrative source of revenue.

Luther's battle against indulgences flared up again in 1517. Albert of Brandenburg was seeking to add the archbishopric of Mainz to the sees he already controlled and had to pay Pope Leo X a large "fee" for his co-operation. To compensate Albert, the Pope gave him permission to sell indulgences in his dominions for the next eight years. Luther's parish lay outside the affected area, but his parishioners crossed the border to take advantage of the concessions that were offered. To boost sales a Dominican friar named Tetzel had been specially authorized by the Pope to preach about the pains of hell and how they could be avoided by buying indulgences.

Incensed by such sharp practice, Luther nailed to the door of Wittenberg church a list of 95 theses, denying Pope Leo's right to forgive sins in such a manner and offering to support his arguments in open forum. He also sent a copy of the document to Albert of Brandenburg who in turn passed it on to Pope Leo X. It is not difficult to imagine the latter's reactions to extracts such as the following: "The pope would do better to appoint one good pastor to a church than to confer indulgences upon them all. Why doesn't the pope build the basilica of St. Peter out of his own money? He is richer than Croesus. He would do better to sell St. Peter's and give the money to the poor folk who are being fleeced by the hawkers of indulgences.... Papal indulgences do not remove guilt.... He who is contrite has plenary remission of guilt and penalty without indulgences.... I claim that the pope has no jurisdiction over purgatory.... To say that souls are liberated from purgatory is audacious. To say they are released as soon as the coin rings in the coffer is to incite avarice."

All good fighting talk, of course, but up to that point Luther was more or less echoing the complaints of financial extortion as voiced by the people for more than a hundred years. The seeds of rebellion were sown by other passages in which the author condemned indulgences as blasphemy against God's mercy. He wrote: "Indulgences are positively harmful to the recipient because they impede salvation by diverting charity and inducing a false sense of security. Christians should be taught that he who gives to the poor is better than he who receives a pardon.... Indulgences are most pernicious because they induce complacency and thereby imperil salvation. Those persons are damned who think that letters of indulgence make them certain of salvation.... When a man believes himself to be utterly lost, light breaks. Peace comes in the word of Christ through faith. .... He who is baptized into Christ must be as a sheep for the slaughter. The merits of Christ are vastly more potent when they bring crosses than when they bring remissions."

Pope Leo acted swiftly. He took immediate steps to have Luther suppressed, appointing a new general of the Augustinians whose orders were to "quench a monk of his order, Martin Luther by name, and thus smother the fire before it should become a conflagration".

Luther's enemies were confident that the rebel would be burned in less than a month. They rubbed their hands gleefully when he was summoned to Heidelberg to appear before a meeting of the chapter. When he went there, however, no mention was made of indulgences. He was merely asked to report on his work in the parish of Wittenberg and to put up a sound defence for Augustinian theology. He was shown every honour, was highly praised by the younger brothers, and after carrying out his instructions returned safely to Wittenberg.

In any event, it was too late to "smother the fire". Luther's theses had been surreptitiously printed and were being read all over Germany. A storm of controversy ensued. Luther was ordered to proceed to Rome to answer charges of heresy and contumacy. After various negotiations, it was at last agreed that the rebel should state his case before the Diet of Worms. Then the Elector Frederick intervened, and in the end Luther attended a private hearing at Augsburg. With the Emperor, the Pope and Cardinal Cajetan, the papal legate, ranged against him Luther's chances of survival looked decidedly slender.

The papal legate's task was to persuade Luther to recant and become reconciled to the Church. Otherwise he was responsible for delivering the heretic to Rome as a prisoner. Not only did Cardinal Cajetan fail to get anywhere. After three appearances before the Augsburg Diet, Luther heard that his arrest was imminent, so he fled under cover of darkness and went back to Wittenberg.

The situation changed in 1519 when the Emperor Maximilian died. His successor, Charles V of Spain, was too busy in his own country to deal with a religious controversy in Saxony, so fortunately for Luther the matter was not taken beyond the authority of his Saxon Elector Frederick. Although the Elector dared not openly endorse a condemned heretic's opinions, he was not prepared to throw Luther to the papal lions. On the other hand, Pope Leo could not afford to alienate so important a ruler as Frederick. For a time at least Luther felt reasonably safe in Wittenberg.

No doubt encouraged by the improved circumstances, Luther launched a fresh attack at a conference in Leipzig. He was accused of falling into the same sort of errors as the English reformer John Wycliffe and of "espousing the pestilent errors of John Hus, who claimed that Peter neither was nor is the head of the Holy Catholic Church". After a good deal of argument, Luther decided to make his position absolutely clear; and he declared "I am a Christian theologian and I am bound, not only to assert, but to defend the truth with my blood and death. I want to believe freely and be a slave to the authority of no one, whether council, university, or pope. I will confidently confess what appears to me to be true, whether it has been asserted by a Catholic or a heretic. . . ."

After a protracted debate of eighteen days, Luther was branded as a "son of iniquity", a Hussite and an insurgent heretic. Through his writings he was also building up a reputation both at home and abroad as the leader of a movement that was to develop into the Reformation.

For a year or so Luther enjoyed a period of relative calm, but the Pope had by no means forgotten him. When another appeal to the Augustinian order failed to keep him quiet, Leo wrote to Frederick complaining of Luther's rebellious attitude and begging him either to do something about it or to have him arrested. The following extract from his letter indicates how strongly the Pope felt on the subject:

"This Luther favours the Bohemians and the Turks, deplores the punishment of heretics, spurns the writings of the holy doctors, the decrees of the ecumenical councils, and the ordnances of the Roman pontiffs, and gives credence to the opinions of none save himself alone, which no heretic before ever presumed to do."

The resumed papal persecution came to a head with the arrival of a bull on 10 October, 1520. Exactly one month later, in the presence of the faculty and students of the University of Wittenberg, Luther consigned the document to the flames together with other papal publications. After this decisive gesture there was no turning back. Excommunication of the heretic and revolutionary was inevitable.

In response to an invitation from the Emperor, Luther presented himself before the Diet of Worms. Urged to renounce all or at least part of what he had written, he replied first in German, then in Latin:

"Unless I am convicted by Scripture and plain reason – I do not accept the authority of popes and councils, for they have contradicted each other – my conscience is captive to the Word of God. I cannot and I will not recant anything."

Four of the six Electors present signed a document pronouncing Luther a notorious heretic, but Frederick of Saxony and Ludwig of the Palatinate abstained. The tense situation was aggravated when posters depicting the symbol of the peasants' revolt (a sandal clog) appeared during the night on the doors of the town hall and other prominent buildings in the city. Possibly as a result of this ominous warning, another attempt was made to extract a partial recantation from the rebel, but he obstinately refused to give way.

The next move was to accuse him of an attack on the seven sacraments. Some of the wording in the charge was unnecessarily vicious. "His teaching makes for rebellion, division, war, murder, robbery, arson and the collapse of Christendom." Although the bull of excommunication had yet to be promulgated, Luther was henceforth to be considered a convicted heretic. His writings, together with a picture of their author, were formally burned by the Diet and his arrest seemed to be a matter of time.

Once again, however, the Elector of Saxony came to the rescue. He made arrangements for Luther to go to ground in Wartburg Castle. The fugitive shed his monkish garb, went about dressed as a knight, and as an additional disguise grew a long beard. At first the solitude, inactivity and unvaried diet affected his health, but he found an outlet in writing. It was during his stay at Wartburg that Luther translated the whole of the New Testament into his native language.

Meanwhile the Reformation continued to flourish. Priests married, monks and nuns renounced their vows of celibacy, the tonsure was no longer compulsory. Other innovations included the celebration of the sacrament by priests in ordinary clothes, the elimination of vespers and masses for the dead, permission to eat meat on fast days and modifications in the vespers.

Then in 1522 Luther paid a surreptitious visit to Wittenberg in connection with a number of tracts he had written. He returned to Wartburg fully convinced that the Reformation was developing along the right lines but not as rapidly as he would have liked. On the other hand, he was not in favour of the reforms he had envisaged being brought about by violence. The abuses had to go, but they had to be tackled constitutionally. As he himself put it:

"If the peasant is in open rebellion, then he is outside the law of God, for rebellion is not simply murder, but it is like a great fire which attacks and lays waste a whole land. Thus, rebellion brings with it a land full of murders and bloodshed, makes widows and orphans, and turns everything upside-down like a great disaster. Therefore, let everyone who can, smite, slay and stab, secretly or openly, remembering that nothing can be more poisonous, hurtful or devilish than a rebel."

Although Frederick advised him to remain in hiding, Luther decided to brave the imperial and papal bans and return to Wittenberg. If he hoped that the new pope, Hadrian VI, would have a more tolerant attitude towards the Reformation, he was doomed to disappointment. No pope, however large his views, could be expected to approve of what was tantamount to a new denomination. Consequently nobody was surprised when Hadrian asked Frederick to put a stop to Luther's revolutionary activities. As usual Frederick's reply was polite but evasive.

Despite Luther's efforts to check the excesses of his more irresponsible followers, the whole of Germany was convulsed with riots, vandalism and upheavals of every description. Mobs of restless serfs stormed the parish churches and expelled the priests, pillaged castles and monasteries, broke into game preserves and generally made nuisances of themselves. The culmination of all this lawlessness was the Peasants' Revolt of 1525. Much of the blame for this abortive affair was laid at Luther's door and yet the reformer had already made it abundantly clear that he had no sympathy for the citizen in arms. The end of it was that thousands of peasants were cruelly butchered, and any hope that the German people would be freed from tyranny was crushed for a further three hundred years.

During the disturbances many monks and nuns left their cloisters to take refuge in remote villages. Luther played a leading role in the escape plans of a dozen nuns, making it his business to find them husbands in their new homes. Two years later one of them, Katharina von Bora, was still unprovided for, so he decided to marry her himself. He took this step, according to his own version of the affair, to satisfy his father, to annoy the Pope and the Devil, and "to seal his witness before martyrdom". Although neither he nor Katharina had any money, they were assisted financially by the Elector and other influential admirers. They lived happily together for the rest of Luther's life. Katharina bore him six children and over the years they adopted four orphans. He had been married only a year when he told a

Galileo, in his villa at Arcetri near Florence, standing behind the telescope he invented (*top*). Looking through the "optic glass" is John Milton. (From the painting in the Pisani gallery, Florence.) – When hostilities broke out between King and Parliament, John Hampden (*above*) took a colonel's commission and raised a regiment of infantry to support the Parliamentary cause. – Toussaint L'Ouverture (*left*), one of the liberators of Santo Domingo. His struggle against radical prejudice has a special significance today.

Alexander Hamilton (*top*), the American statesman who played a leading part in drawing up the present American Constitution (from the original painting by Chappel). When the American War of Independence broke out, Hamilton joined the rebel army and served on General Washington's staff. After distinguishing himself at Yorktown, he concentrated on legal studies and became one of the most eminent lawyers in New York. When the new government was established in 1789, Hamilton was appointed Secretary of the Treasury, but his attempts to win greater authority for the central government led to several clashes with Thomas Jefferson.

The ablest and most sincere of the leaders of the French Revolution, Georges-Jacques Danton (*centre*), played an important part in the rising that led to the deposition of the King, and was rewarded by being appointed Minister of Justice. In the Convention he bent his giant strength to crush the moderate Girondists, and after they were expelled from office Danton shared the leadership of the Assembly with Robespierre. Henceforth all his energies were devoted to firing the hearts of Frenchmen against his country's enemies and to conciliating domestic hatreds.

Mary Wollstonecraft (*bottom*), the protagonist of the rights of women, left home at the age of nineteen to earn her own livelihood. She was in turn a companion, a schoolmistress and governess in Lord Kingsborough's family. Her *Vindication of the Rights of Women*, published in 1791, was a work of genius, advocating equality of the sexes and the main doctrines of the modern women's movement. After an unhappy liaison with the American Captain Gilbert Imlay, she lived with, and eventually married, the revolutionary philosopher, William Godwin. This illustration of her is an aquatint from a painting by Opie.

friend: "My Katie is in all things so obliging and pleasing to me that I would not exchange my poverty for the riches of Croesus." Throughout twenty-one years of marriage Katharina never gave him cause to revise his opinion.

Domesticity changed Luther's mode of living, but he continued with his preaching and teaching, constantly advocating resistance to the Pope and sometimes to the Emperor as well. Many of the German States accepted his reformed doctrines; others remained Catholic and all attempts to effect a union only seemed to widen the gulf. The brash defiance of Luther's younger days frequently degenerated into irascibility and petulance, but it must be remembered that during the last quarter of his life he was plagued by a variety of maladies including catarrh, stone, gout, insomnia and fits of dizziness. Moreover, banned as he was by Church and State, he could never feel entirely secure. If the Diet or the Emperor decided to pounce, not even his friend and patron Frederick could have offered him protection.

If his poor state of health rendered him peevish and spiteful, it did not prevent Luther from fighting the abuses of the papacy wherever he saw them. Although he was often racked with pain, he never shirked his duties as a preacher and as a teacher. It was his insistence on going personally to Eisleben to act as mediator in a quarrel between the counts of Mansfeld that most certainly hastened his death. The journey was made in winter, the weather was bitterly cold and Luther was in no fit state to travel. He successfully reconciled the disputants, but on his way home he was taken seriously ill and a few days later the old rebel was dead.

Throughout his eventful life Luther had oscillated between exaltation and depression, between burning faith and harrowing doubt. His God was both terrible in his wrath and most merciful in his infinite compassion, but despite his rebellious nature, the chains that bound him to his Maker had been forged seven times in the fire. At the end he could indeed claim: "Thou wilt crown me at last with honour. If only I have that, I will not ask for earth or heaven. When body and soul fail me, thou art ever God, my heart's comfort and my portion."

Chapter 6
Galileo
1564–1642

The first truly modern scientist whose outlook and methods would not be out of place in the present century, Galileo was born on 15 February, 1564 at Pisa. The city, then under the domination of Florence, had known independence until 1406. Five years after the birth of Galileo it was to be incorporated into the Medicean Grand Duchy of Tuscany, thus accounting for Milton's reference in *Paradise Lost* to "the Tuscan artist".

He was the son of Vincenzo Galilei, a Florentine cloth merchant, who could afford to have the boy educated at the monastery school of Vallombrosa. Disturbed by the fact that his son was developing a sense of vocation, Vincenzo, who was a clever mathematician, musician and composer, decided to instruct him personally at Florence. The curriculum he devised embraced Latin, Greek, Logic and Mathematics. Under such expert guidance, Galileo soon displayed a special aptitude for mathematics and was particularly interested in music. He had an acute intelligence, a more than average ability at drawing, and the temperament of a poet. One of his admirers, Rudolf Thiel, described him as "bellicose, passionate, spiteful, ruthlessly determined and unscrupulous in his choice of methods". His favourite hobby was the manufacture of mechanical toys. His subsequent passion for astronomy may well have been roused when, as a boy in Florence, he saw what was then believed to be a "new" star in the constellation of Cassiopeia.

At the age of twenty-three, Galileo was sufficiently ambitious to set his heart on the chair of mathematics at Bologna University, but despite the many strings that were pulled on his behalf, he was not granted the appointment. As an alternative he devoted himself to medicine. At that time the great authority on medicine at the University of Pisa was Claudius Galen. Galileo who found Galen unimaginative and uninspiring sought relief from the monotony of the lecture theatre in a barrage of questions, thus earning for himself the soubriquet "the Wrangler".

Eventually, in response to his father's entreaties, Galileo abandoned medicine. Once again outside influence was brought to bear to secure him a university post, this time successfully. Through the good offices of the Marchese Guido Ubaldo del Monte, the young man was installed in the chair of mathematics at Pisa. His salary was by no means impressive, but at least he was working at something he enjoyed doing. At the age of twenty-five Galileo had thus become a university professor.

According to the records of that period, Galileo had already made an important scientific discovery. One day, while he was in the cathedral of Pisa, he noticed a bronze sanctuary lamp swinging on its chain. Using his pulse as a chronometer, he found that the swing of a suspended object takes the same time whether it moves in a large arc or a small one. From this simple experiment he went on to design an instrument for timing pulse-beats, an invention that could be used for medical purposes.

His mathematical studies at Pisa led him to challenge the universally accepted teachings of Aristotle. This Greek philosopher had believed, among other things, that the earth was stationary and the centre of the universe, and that a heavy body would fall to the ground a good deal faster than a light one. Galileo began by questioning this second dogma. In his opinion, two objects of unequal weights ought to fall at the same speed (always allowing for the effect of air resistance). He is supposed to have supported his theory by publicly dropping simultaneously a cannon ball and a bullet from the leaning tower of Pisa. They struck the earth almost at the same instant. If the demonstration could have taken place in a vacuum, Galileo maintained, they would have fallen side by side and landed together.

Galileo's rebellious views made him most unpopular in Pisa, especially after he had inspected a newly invented machine intended to dredge Leghorn harbour and had condemned it as quite useless. In 1592, as a result of the hostility shown him, Galileo felt that the time had come for him to quit Florence and her dependencies. Supported once more by the Marchese, he moved to the chair of mathematics at the university of Padua, a city governed by the Republic of Venice.

It had not been only his unpopularity that had prompted Galileo to try his fortunes farther afield. In 1591 his father had died, leaving a wife and family without sufficient financial backing. Galileo therefore had welcomed the opportunity to earn a larger salary in Padua and to work in an environment offering better prospects. Furthermore, he had a useful friend there, Giovanni Francesco Sagredo, who was a member of the influential Council of Ten.

At Padua, Galileo lectured officially on mathematics and astronomy, but he also found time to direct his genius for practical mathematics towards advanced work in mechanics and engineering. Among his discoveries were an air thermometer and an instrument for simplifying the calculations of gunners and military engineers. He called it a "geometric and military compass". Constructed of two straight ruled arms hinged at one end and capable of being set at any angle, the latter gadget could be used to solve a variety of mathematical problems and for enlarging maps and charts.

Two years after his arrival at Padua he became seriously ill and was henceforth a martyr to arthritis. He was taken care of, however, by a good-looking Venetian girl named Marina Gamba who lived with him as his mistress and bore him three children (two daughters, Virginia and Livia, and a son, Vincenzo). Galileo never married this accommodating lady, but when he returned to his native Tuscany in 1610, he sent her money regularly until she married a Venetian three years later. When his daughters grew up, he committed them to a convent where they were underfed and far from happy. One of his former pupils adopted Vincenzo and brought him up in an atmosphere of wealth and luxury.

Meanwhile Galileo's classes were steadily growing and students were beginning to arrive from other countries. To them he imparted his theories about the universe—theories that in those days were considered revolutionary. He told them that the earth belonged to a system of stars and planets which were always on the move. He even went so far as to say, as Copernicus had said before him, that the earth itself moved, revolving daily on its own axis and circling the sun once a year.

In 1609 Galileo was able to confirm many of his beliefs concerning the movement of the earth and of other heavenly bodies, for in that momentous year a Dutchman, Hans Lippershey, had accidentally stumbled on the principle of the refracting telescope. Although he had no actual model of the Dutchman's "spyglass", Galileo made one for himself, and by applying his knowledge of optics, modified and improved the instrument. With it he saw that the moon's surface was diversified by valleys and mountains, that the Milky Way was a vast stretch of countless stars, that the planet Jupiter had four satellites, that on the sun there were dark spots which moved and therefore proved the sun too rotated on its own axis.

In that same *annus mirabilis* (the year when Kepler announced his discovery of the laws of planetary motion), Galileo took his *cannochiale* to Venice to demonstrate its capabilities to the Doge. He set it up on the top of the campanile of St. Mark's, the tallest building in the city, and invited the chief magistrate and his senators to view the surrounding countryside through the contraption. Such was its magnification that they could clearly distinguish citizens strolling in the streets of Padua 25 miles away.

Obviously his *cannochiale* would be of inestimable value in war-time, so Galileo decided to hand it over to the authorities. He took it to the Ducal Palace and formally presented it to the Doge. In return he received a scroll bearing the following proclamation:

"Be it known to all present this 25th day of August in the year of Our Lord 1609, Master Galileo Galilei, having been professor of mathematics in the University of Padua for seventeen years, and having given to the world certain discoveries and inventions such as the thermometer and the military compass and especially having invented an instrument by which far off things are brought close, the Council of the Republic of Venice does hereby make him professor for the rest of his life and gives him a salary of one thousand florins a year."

Galileo's reputation was firmly established. He made more telescopes and sold them; he prepared pamphlets, complete with explanatory diagrams, and sent them to learned men everywhere; he continued to scan the heavens and make new discoveries.

His future seemed assured, but unfortunately he was not only gaining many admirers. He was also arousing the hatred of all those who still claimed that the earth was the centre of the solar system and that everything else went round it.

Elated by his successes, Galileo now made a mistake that was to prove his undoing. He went back to Pisa.

In July 1610 Galileo was given the appointment of chief mathematician and philosopher to the Grand Duke of Tuscany, a post for which he was paid a thousand florins annually. In addition he became head mathematician at Pisa University, although he did not have to live or teach there. In fact he settled down in Florence where he carried on his telescopic observations. At that stage he seemed blissfully unaware that his enemies were plotting his downfall.

The following year Galileo went to Rome, fully intending to launch a one-man crusade in favour of Copernicanism. At first he was greeted enthusiastically wherever he went. He was given an audience by Pope Paul V who gave him every encouragement and a week later he was made a member of the *Accademia dei Lincei*, an honour not easily earned. The professors at the Roman College examined Galileo's discoveries in the field of astronomy and expressed their approval. He was universally lionized and had every reason to believe that his views on the workings of the cosmic system had been generally accepted.

But Galileo had not reckoned on the reactions of the jealous, the ignorant and the fanatical. Many eminent philosophers begrudged him his widespread popularity, while those who still clung to the Aristotelian concept of a centrally fixed earth looked upon Galileo as a dangerous revolutionary. The Jesuit fathers were convinced that they had been ridiculed by some of the arguments in Galileo's discourse, published in 1612, on *Things that Float or Move on Water*.

Towards the end of 1611, one of Galileo's artist friends informed the mathematician that he should beware of a "certain crowd of ill-disposed men" who were only waiting the propitious moment to strike. No doubt Galileo was also reminded of the fate of Giordano Bruno who had taught the Copernican theory in the universities and had been burnt alive in Rome less than fifteen years ago.

One of the first to denounce the Copernican interpretation of the universe publicly in the pulpit was a Florentine Dominican, Fra Tommaso Caccini, a monk who had a reputation for fiery outspokenness. Another Dominican monk to make a hostile move against the rebel was Niccolo Lorini who sent a letter to the Secretary of the Holy Office, pointing out that Galileo's cosmic theories challenged what was written in the divine Scriptures. Immediate action, he insisted, should be taken against the heretic.

On a higher level Galileo's beliefs were obliquely attacked in a letter written by Cardinal Bellarmine on 12 April, 1615. The relevant extract runs:

"To affirm that the sun, in very truth, is at the centre of the universe and only rotates on its own axis without going from east to west, and that the earth is situated in the third sphere and revolves very swiftly around the sun, is a very dangerous attitude and one calculated not only to annoy all scholastic philosophers and theologians, but also to injure our holy faith by contradicting the Scriptures."

In the same epistle the Cardinal emphasized that the Council of Trent had forbidden the scriptures to be interpreted "in a way contrary to the common opinion of the holy fathers".

Then Caccini took the drastic step of denouncing Galileo to the Inquisition. Fortunately for the mathematician, the witnesses produced by Caccini gave conflicting evidence, so the Court of the Holy Inquisition did not on that occasion proceed against Galileo. Undeterred by his failure, however, Caccini continued his campaign and gradually built up a large body of supporters in Rome.

Galileo's admirers, seriously disturbed by the ugly situation that was developing, urged the mathematician to act with moderation, but their advice fell on deaf ears. Galileo refused to suppress what he knew to be the truth. Not only did he repeat his former assertions; he also went out of his way to belabour his enemies with his devastating wit. In the words of one of his friends, Galileo "turns the laugh against all his opponents and answers their objections in such a way as to make them look perfectly ridiculous".

Eventually the ecclesiastical authorities felt compelled to deal with the rebel once and for all. In February 1616 the cardinals of the Holy See drew up two propositions, both of which they held were absurd and heretical. The first was that the sun was the centre of the universe and devoid of local motion; the second stated that the earth was not the centre of the world but moved as a whole and also with a diurnal motion. Both of these propositions were read out to Galileo and he was ordered in the name of the Pope to abandon them except as hypotheses. With regard to Copernicanism as a physical fact, he had to "abstain altogether from teaching, defending, or discussing this opinion and doctrine". If he remained obdurate, then he was to be cast into prison.

Galileo behaved reasonably and agreed to accept the papal ruling. Since he was allowed to discuss the controversial topic of Copernicanism as a hypothesis, he was not particularly put out by his appearance before the Inquisition. He remained in Rome for a few months, during which time he was again received in audience by the Pope. Paul V, Galileo tells us, "bore me the greatest goodwill and was ready to show his affection and favour towards me on all occasions". On the face of it, the rebel had got away lightly with his heresy.

After his return to Florence, he kept fairly quiet for the next two years. Then, unable to maintain complete silence on the subject nearest his heart, he hit on an indirect way of disseminating his views on Copernicanism. He brushed up and published a paper he had written before the ban. Ostensibly the subject was the phenomenon of tides, but by suggesting that the combined axial and orbital movements of the globe produced the alternate rise and fall of the sea's surface, he was also proving that the earth was in motion. When he sent a copy of this document to Cardinal Orsini and there were no repercussions, Galileo began to feel less restricted.

Later on in the year, when a Jesuit named Grassi used the appearance of three successive comets as an argument against Copernicanism, Galileo reacted sharply. In an angry attack on the Jesuit he referred to him as an "unmannerly poltroon, swindler, ungrateful boor, shameless creature, rude ruffian". He followed up this diatribe with his *Discourse on the Comets* to which Grassi replied with *The Astronomical and Philosophical Balance,* and there for a time the matter lay in abeyance.

The final word, however, rested with Galileo. In 1623 he published what has been described as "the greatest polemic ever written in physical science". Under the title *The Assayer,* the book brilliantly and succinctly examined Grassi's specious arguments, proved them erroneous and contemptuously dismissed their author as an ignoramus. All poor Grassi could do at that stage was to withdraw from an unequal contest.

Galileo's triumph was further enhanced in so far as *The Assayer* came off the press at the same time as his old friend Matteo Barberini became Pope Urban VIII. Never one to let an opportunity slip, Galileo dedicated the book to the new pope. But although Urban praised the work fulsomely, he could not be persuaded to repeal the sentence of his predecessor. Galileo was still denied the right to propagate his views on heliocentrism.

Yet the ageing rebel was not to be silenced after all. Between 1625 and 1630 he wrote his *Dialogue Concerning the Two Chief World Systems – Ptolemaic and Copernican.* This long, leisurely masterpiece, published in 1632, is nothing more or less than a powerful defence of Copernicanism expressed in the form of a conversation between two characters. The case against heliocentrism is put forward foolishly and ineptly by a third character called Simplicio. Unfortunately for Galileo, his enemies saw Simplicio as a caricature of the Pope himself and were not slow to draw Urban's attention to such a deliberate insult.

The book was an immediate success, especially among Galileo's friends. One of them had this to say: "I hardly had time to glance at it before it was snatched from me and lent to another. Today no sooner did I get it back by main force than I was begged by a host of others to let them have it."

To the Pope and to Galileo's opponents the new publication was anathema. The former friendship between Urban and Galileo counted for nothing. Sales of the book were promptly stopped, and after an interview with the Inquisitor in Florence, the author was given a month in which to report to the Commissary General of the Inquisition in Rome. As he was very ill at the time, Galileo appealed for the hearing to take place in Florence, but so incensed was Urban VIII that all he would consent to was a postponement until the end of the year.

When the day of departure dawned, not even a trebly certified medical chit was allowed to stand in the way of Galileo's 23-day journey to the capital. The rebel could have crossed the frontier into Switzerland or rejoined his many friends on Venetian territory, but his obstinate nature would not let him run away from the Holy Inquisition. Besides, he had already convinced himself that he could make the Inquisitors see reason.

After he had voluntarily surrendered to the Inquisition, he was treated with unusual consideration and tolerance. Instead of lingering in a common prison, he was comfortably lodged in a suite of rooms in the headquarters of the Holy Office. "My health is good," he told a friend, "for which, next to God, I have to thank the great care of the ambassador and his wife."

Then began a series of interrogations. The case against him was proved beyond all doubt, and according to the Dominican Commissary of the Inquisition, Galileo "clearly recognized he had gone too far and erred in his book, and he was ready to make this confession before his judges".

On 21 June, 1633, the day of the final examination, Galileo deliberately lied, maintaining under oath that after the decree of 1616 he had rejected heliocentrism and had firmly believed that an unmoving earth was the centre of the universe. Although his judges knew he was lying, they took no action against him for perjury. Next day, in the great hall of the Inquisition, in the presence of the cardinals the court's sentence was pronounced. Galileo had to abandon for ever his belief in the Copernican theory; he was to suffer imprisonment for a term to be decided by the Holy Office; for the following three years he had to recite every week the seven penitential psalms.

This sick old man of seventy then had to go down on his knees and intone the formula of abjuration.

After spending the next five months at Siena with his friend the Archbishop, he was allowed to go back to his house in Arcetri so that he could be near his daughter Virginia who, under the name of Sister Maria Celeste, was still living in the convent next door. When she died in 1634, her heart-broken father drew what consolation he could from working at his latest and greatest book, *Dialogues Concerning Two New Sciences.*

Published by a Dutch firm in Leyden, the new *Dialogues* dealt with dynamics and statics, and once more the old rebellious streak was evident, for he again made use of the three characters who had appeared in the volume that had so offended Pope Urban VIII. Simplicio, of course, figured in the book, but this time Galileo wisely refrained from dangerous polemics. Instead he concentrated on scientific truths and created an experimental-mathematical method that has been the basis of all progress in physical science since his death.

Worn out and totally blind, he passed away peacefully in his bed on 8 January, 1642. His life-long battle against bigotry, ignorance and the abuses of authority was over. His rebellions against established opinions had brought him into conflct with the full weight of the Holy Inquisition. In a physical sense, Galileo had been "cabin'd, cribb'd, confin'd". In another sense, he had triumphed. He had, as he himself said, "discovered in the heavens many things that had not been seen before our age", and in the teeth of his oppressors, his observations had led him to transform physics into an exact science.

Chapter 7
John Hampden
1594–1643

A political leader who preferred to remain in the background, a debater and a committee man rather than a great orator, the most single-minded member of the Long Parliament, John Hampden will always be remembered as one of King Charles I's subtlest and most dangerous enemies. Although John Pym played a more prominent part in the Great Rebellion, it was largely due to Hampden's operations behind the scenes that the liberties of England were so ably defended by the Parliamentary party. It was also Hampden's personal resistance to the infamous Ship Money levy that helped to make Parliament an effective guardian of the people's privileges against the king's prerogatives.

Eldest son of William Hampden of Hampden, in Buckinghamshire, and Elizabeth Cromwell, John was born in London in 1594. He spent very little of his childhood in the Manor House at Hampden, for his parents sent him to the Free Grammar School at Thame where he was a boarder living in the headmaster's house. He studied Greek and Latin as part of a crammed curriculum, working from six in the morning until five in the evening. The basis of the school's educational programme was essentially religious.

The emphasis still lay on religion when John matriculated to Magdalen College, Oxford, at the age of fifteen. During his four years' residence the teachings of Arminius appealed to many students, and Calvinism was also attractive to the young Puritans who were growing up to fear God and believe that in His sight all men were equal.

Young Hampden's next move was to the Inner Temple to study law. There he came under the influence of Sir Edward Coke, an unpleasant character in many ways, but one who was not afraid to voice his opposition even to the highest authority in the land, the king himself. Hampden probably agreed with Coke's rejection of the royal principle that it was illegal to dispute "that which concerns the mystery of the king's power" and most likely shared the famous jurist's non-acceptance of Charles's other well-known dictum, "Encroach not on the prerogative of the crown". Naturally Coke was subsequently dismissed, but his resistance had been admired by many law students.

John then went to settle in the ancestral home in Hampden. In due course he married a girl named Elizabeth Symeon and for the next twelve months he led a quiet country life. Although his mother, who was ambitious for her son, kept insisting that there were "multitudes of lords a-making" in London, John was not tempted to explore the possibilities of the capital. Peerages could be bought, but John was too upright a man to seek preferment in that way.

It was not until the end of January 1621 that he forsook his rural retreat, and as a member of parliament for Grampound, began his political career at Westminster. He was never outstanding as an orator, but his honesty, directness and zeal soon earned him a prominent position in the opposition party. He attended sittings with unfailing regularity and performed his various duties with understanding and conscientiousness. So far he had given no indication that beneath his deceptively placid and self-effacing exterior lurked an uncompromising rebel.

At that time the Commons were especially concerned about the system of monopolies from which a number of eminent courtiers, notably the king's favourite, Buckingham, were profiteering on an unprecedented scale. They were even more worried about the Catholic question and the unhealthy influence of Spain. Sir Edward Coke, who since his dismissal from the King's Bench had gone into politics, gave a powerful speech in the House condemning Spain, but John Hampden was much more impressed by a penetrating analysis of Catholic motives delivered by a comparative newcomer to politics, John Pym. Pym's main point was that the Catholics were interested only in the ultimate ascendancy of their creed over all others. They would never tolerate Protestants. The king, therefore, should abandon all ideas of marrying his son Charles to the king of Spain's daughter and seek a more suitable match with a Protestant.

The king's reactions were fully predictable. He ordered the Commons not to meddle with matters that did not concern them. Indeed he was so furious that he only stopped short of accusing them of treason. But the Commons were not to be brow-beaten. Pointing out that "the liberties, franchises, privileges and jurisdictions of parliament are the ancient and undoubted birthright and inheritance of the subjects of England", they firmly declared their right to discuss whatever policies they chose without fear of arrest. To underline their determination, their protests were entered in the House of Commons' journals. James's swift reply was to tear the pages out and to dissolve parliament. To show that he meant business, he sent Coke to the Tower and John Pym was put under house arrest. As the royal revenues stopped with the dissolution of parliament, the king imposed a special "Benevolence" tax whereby men were expected to pay out of the goodness of their own hearts. Quite clearly such a tax was unconstitutional and quite illegal.

John Hampden calmly studied the situation and decided that the only defence against royalist irregularities would be a Commons capable of opposing court policies. He therefore pressed for the restoration of the ancient privileges of Wendover, Amersham and Marlow, three Buckinghamshire boroughs that used to be represented three hundred years ago. As each would be entitled to two members, the opposition vote would be increased by six, should anti-court candidates be elected. Hampden himself proposed to resign as member for Grampound (far away in Cornwall), and stand for Wendover.

Meanwhile negotiations were going ahead for the Spanish marriage. Prince Charles, with the ubiquitous Buckingham in attendance, went to Madrid to pay court to the Infanta. Buckingham's arrogant attitude, however, so disgusted the Spaniards that the visit came to nothing. The people of England rejoiced when the young prince came home a bachelor and a Protestant.

With a continental war in the offing, James naturally wanted money, so he recalled Parliament early in 1624 and even addressed the Commons courteously and inoffensively. Hampden was not present on that occasion, but on 4 March, when the three Buckinghamshire boroughs were ready to send along their newly elected members (with Hampden one of the two representatives for Wendover), James prorogued Parliament, and as it was then constituted it never reassembled.

In the summer of that year an English "army" crossed the Channel to support the Palatinate against the Spanish invaders. Owing to inadequate preparations, maladministration and peculation, the whole venture proved disastrous. More than half of the expeditionary force, ex-gaol-birds or press-ganged into service, were interested only in plundering and attacking the harmless civilians in the Dover area; there was a shortage of ships and the French at Calais refused to co-operate; food-stocks were practically non-existent and deaths from the plague ran into thousands. Within a week of this military fiasco, James died of a tertiary ague. John Hampden, gloomily watching these events, could only hope that his successor would govern England more wisely.

Charles I certainly seemed to be a considerable improvement on his father, but it soon became apparent that such virtues as he possessed were all negative. For a start he was excessively religious. Then again he set too much store in the "divinity that doth hedge a king". Thirdly, shortly before James's funeral, he had married the French princess Henrietta Maria, a Catholic. Worst of all, his spiritual guide was the hated Doctor William Laud, while his mentor and model in everything else was none other than George Villiers, Duke of Buckingham.

When the new parliament met, John Hampden took his

seat as member for Wendover. He soon discovered that nothing had changed. Tonnage and poundage (the duties paid on imports and exports) were granted to Charles for twelve months only, whereas previous kings had benefited for the duration of their reigns. The Commons passed a Bill to this effect, but it was blocked by the Lords. Two weeks later, when the members reassembled at Oxford, they were still not prepared to yield to royal pressure. So Charles took precisely the same step as his father would have taken. He dissolved parliament.

Profoundly disturbed by the king's autocratic attitude, John Hampden went home to Buckinghamshire. England had a different monarch, but the country was no better off than before. In Hampden's opinion, there was no hope whatsoever of reconciling the views of King and Commons. The member for Wendover could see no way out of the *impasse*. But by that time he had come to admire Sir John Eliot, a born leader and a more striking personality than Pym. Before long Hampden began to see that there was an answer to all their problems.

After another costly defeat (an abortive attack on the Spanish fortifications at Cadiz), Eliot decided that the man responsible for his country's ruin had to be brought down.

That man was Buckingham....

Accordingly Eliot asked John Hampden to prepare a list of points for impeachment. Under the heading *The Causes*, Hampden set out no fewer than ten reasons including such obvious ones as Buckingham's support of the Papists, plurality of offices, sale of honours and misuse of the king's revenue. When the charges were ready, they were discussed in the House of Lords and each one was clarified in great detail. These proceedings extended over a period of three days.

The immediate outcome was the arrest of Sir John Eliot and of Sir Dudley Digges who had opened the case against the king's favourite. The latter was set free the same day, but Eliot was imprisoned in the Tower for a week. Charles further antagonized the Commons by making Buckingham Chancellor of the University of Cambridge. As a final gesture he dissolved Parliament and burned the list of charges drawn up by Hampden.

As far as Hampden was concerned, matters came to a

head when Charles, desperate for money as usual, imposed a forced loan on his subjects and appointed a group of commissioners to act as collectors. Hampden resolved not to pay. He boldly stated his objection to the loan when he appeared before the Privy Council on 29 January, 1627. "I could be content to lend as well as others," he said, "but I fear to draw upon myself that curse in Magna Carta which is to be read twice a year against those who infringe it."

Thrown into prison, he was soon joined by his friend Sir John Eliot and by Sir Thomas Wentworth, the member for Yorkshire. Many others who refused payment were conscripted and sent off to the wars, for men were needed on the continent to fight against England's latest enemy, France.

More than anything else Charles needed money, so he was reluctantly compelled to recall Parliament. In an obvious attempt to win over the Commons, he released a batch of political prisoners including Hampden, Eliot and Wentworth. All three, together with other candidates who had stood out against the forced loan, gained seats in the parliamentary elections and at an informal meeting it was agreed that a new law was necessary, clearly setting out the limits of the royal prerogative.

By his resistance to the loan, Hampden had suddenly sprung into prominence as a forceful politician. He was invited to serve on a number of important committees, occasions which gave him the opportunity to extend his knowledge of constitutional law and practice. Much of his work went into the Petition of Right which was approved by both Lords and Commons on 28 May, 1628. This uncompromising document dealt with such grievances as imprisonment without just cause, unpaid billeting of soldiers and illegal taxation.

A week later the Petition was followed by a Remonstrance to which was appended a final clause accusing Buckingham as the root cause of the prevailing chaos. Charles tried to help his favourite by proroguing Parliament, but other forces than the Commons had been unleashed. The whole country was out for Buckingham's blood. Nobody was surprised when he was assassinated by a disgruntled subaltern of Suffolk, John Felton by name, on 23 August.

When Parliament reassembled, John Hampden was again

kept busy on committee work. One of his tasks was to look into the operations of the infamous Star Chamber court, an institution which enabled the king to bypass the House of Commons on constitutional and religious issues. He was also briefed "to search the course and precedents in the Exchequer concerning the injunction against merchants' goods detained for the non-payment of duties". On this question of confiscation Hampden supported Eliot whose opinion was that customs officers had been exceeding their rights.

The struggle between King and Commons came to a head when Eliot, with the inevitable dissolution of Parliament only a few minutes away, arranged for the doors of the House to be locked and read out his personal protest against the confiscations. He then crossed over to the Chair, moved his own resolutions and set fire to the incriminating document.

Events moved quickly. There was a thunderous knock at the door. The king had sent for the ultimate symbol of authority, the Mace. The Commons to a man defied anybody to touch it. Shortly afterwards they were informed by one of the king's messengers that the guard was coming to batter down the door and drive all the members out of the building. Whereupon the rebels opened the doors themselves and rushed out to tell the people exactly what had happened. As Hampden was leaving, he was shocked to see that the military had already arrived. He had a grim foreboding that he was witnessing the eclipse of constitutional government in England.

Hampden was right. Within twenty-four hours the so-called ringleaders of the revolt were imprisoned and Eliot had to pay a £2,000 fine. Hampden himself retired to his country residence. He assumed full responsibility for the education and welfare of Eliot's two sons and invited them to treat Hampden House as a second home. As long as correspondence was allowed between them, he wrote regularly to the prisoner, giving him the news and assuring him that the boys were making good progress at Oxford. He never abandoned hope that one day the king would relent and order Eliot's release, but as the long years passed his friend's health gradually deteriorated. Deprived of exercise and fresh air, poor Eliot became consumptive. When he died on 27 November, 1632, Hampden was inconsolable. From that moment on he was a dedicated man. He was determined that his friend's murderers should meet their just deserts.

Henceforth Hampden's avowed aim was to incite the people of England to rebel against their oppressors. It would take time and the right leaders would have to be found, but he was a patient man and he knew there was a number of outstanding personalities in the anti-royalist party. Precipitate action would have been disastrous, and as far as he was concerned he thought it advisable to remain in the background. He passed his days looking after his estate, attending to any repairs that were necessary and performing his duties as a Justice of the Peace. To his tenants he seemed harmless enough, but underneath the superfical equanimity lurked Eliot's avenger. He was committed and the family motto was *vestigia nulla retrorsum* ("no way back").

Hampden had to support yet another cruel blow in the summer of 1634. After fifteen years of domestic happiness during which she had borne him nine children, his wife Elizabeth died. He felt her loss keenly and thereafter was rarely to be found in Hampden House. It was too full of memories.

Apart from a successful brush with Laud concerning church attendance, Hampden made no significant move until the following summer. Then came the opportunity he had been praying for. Basing his demand on the principle that all counties, inland as well as coastal, should contribute towards the upkeep of the navy, Charles called upon the county of Buckinghamshire to supply him with a war ship, its crew and its armaments. The alternative was to pay a fine of £4,500. Confronted with this dubious request, Hampden and his fellow land-owners realized at once that the king was interested not so much in ships as in adding to the royal revenues. They were also very much aware that in giving money to Charles they would virtually be cutting their own throats, for the sums collected would enable him to exist without a parliament. Charles might even take it into his head to build up a private army and thus be in a position to rule the country by force. The payment of "Ship Money", Hampden decided, would inevitably lead to the loss of every true-born Englishman's rightful heritage – his civil liberties.

He resolved to resist the levy no matter what happened.

In Hampden's case the amount involved was a small one. On his Stoke Mandeville property he was expected to pay a mere twenty shillings. Not even his worst enemies would be able to accuse him of acting from self-interest. The whole country would know that a man in Hampden's position would be challenging "Ship Money" solely because he denied the king's right to impose such an iniquitous levy.

Hampden's case against the Crown opened on 6 November, 1637. His lawyer, Oliver St. John, stated categorically that if the king wanted money, he should stick to the normal constitutional procedure and ask for it through Parliament. If Charles was allowed to mulct his subjects as and when he pleased, then every man's property was threatened. Going back through the records of previous reigns, the lawyer could find no precedent for the "Ship Money" demands. On what grounds were the present ruler's exactions based?

For three days St. John argued on his client's behalf, and then Sir Edward Lyttelton, the Solicitor-General, put forward the case for the Crown. His main point was that the amount collected would be used to strengthen England's navy which afforded protection to the lives and property of all. He added that if Charles had approached Parliament for the money, the result would have been interminable and frustrating delays, thus endangering the country.

When the case had reached its twenty-seventh day, Robert Holbourne addressed the court in support of Hampden. He contended that in the original claims for "Ship Money" there was no reference whatsoever to any danger that threatened the country as a whole. The additional vessels were wanted, according to the wording of the levy, to protect merchant shipping from pirates. In any event, it was not for the king to decide whether or not there was a national emergency. On such important issues, Parliament alone was the final arbiter.

The Attorney-General wound up for the Crown and six months later the court passed judgment. Under the circumstances nobody was surprised to hear seven of the twelve judges declare that Charles had acted well within his powers. Their verdict was philosophically accepted by John Hampden who did not expect to win anyhow. The object of the exercise had been accomplished. His countrymen were now fully cognizant of their king's shaky principles. Better still, they realized that parliamentary government stood at the crossroads. Hampden's one-man rebellion had demonstrated to the voters that their duly elected representatives were engaged in a life-or-death struggle.

Venerated throughout England as the *Pater Patriae,* Hampden now felt he could safely leave other anti-royalists to complete the work he had begun. He withdrew from public life, put his personal affairs in order and in April 1638 joined a group of Puritan families who proposed to set sail for America. With his cousin Oliver Cromwell he boarded one of the eight ships that were scheduled to take the emigrants, but at the last minute the scheme was blocked by a royal edict prohibiting emigration. Hampden and Cromwell, obliged to disembark, returned to London more determined than ever to bring Parliament's fight against Charles to a successful conclusion.

Rebellion in Scotland, arising from Charles's introduction of a new Prayer Book, forced the king to summon Parliament. As representative for Buckinghamshire, Hampden took his seat in an unusually full House. Charles was confident that, faced with a common danger, the Commons would furnish him with cash and provisions for the war against the Scots. Hampden's view was that Parliament would be more interested in shielding the people against abuses of the royal prerogative. He knew that the Commons' trump card was the control of money and supplies.

Speaking for the king, the Lord Keeper informed the House that members could debate their own grievances *after* they had granted essential subsidies to Charles and had entered the Tonnage and Poundage Bill safely in the Statute Book. Significantly no mention was made of "Ship Money". The Commons' reactions were decidedly cool.

A week went by, a week during which Hampden skilfully steered the debaters in what he considered to be the right direction, and at the end of it Charles had not gained an inch of ground. The Commons' attitude was clearly expressed in the resolution: "Till the liberties of the House and Kingdom were cleared, they knew not whether they had anything to give or no."

The king brought pressure to bear through the medium of the Upper House, but the Commons stood firm. He threatened them with dissolution and then, two days later, he tried bargaining, offering to waive "Ship Money" if they would grant him £840,000. Urged by Hampden who saw that opposition to the proposed grant would only divide the House, the Commons agreed that the debate should be restricted to the original request for subsidies. The manoeuvre proved effective. Charles had to reconcile himself to the fact that neither money nor supplies were forthcoming.

On the following day the king dissolved Parliament. Hampden was held in custody long enough for his study to be searched for incriminating evidence, but nothing was found and he was released. Despite the obvious dangers, he remained in the capital to keep an eye on developments, sometimes staying at his son-in-law's house, sometimes operating from his own London residence, from Pym's lodgings or from the homes of his fellow members. All the time he worked indefatigably, hammering out a practical policy. On the one hand the Commons were too patriotic to help the Scots; on the other, they wanted them to know that the people of England sympathized with their cause. When a Scottish army crossed the border and routed Charles's army, Hampden privately rejoiced. Along with Pym and St. John, he prepared petitions asking Charles to come to terms with the Scots, to summon Parliament and to iron out the grievances that had alienated his subjects. These petitions were brought to the king's notice by a delegation of peers from the Upper House. Harassed by financial difficulties, Charles agreed that Parliament should be recalled on 3 November.

Hampden snatched at this golden opportunity of packing the House with Puritan members. During the next four days he and Pym visited as many constituencies as possible, putting the electorate in the picture, presenting their policies, and above all canvassing for candidates who shared their views.

The "Father of the Country" found himself in a delicate situation when the new Parliament assembled. As the man who had refused to pay "Ship Money", he could depend on the support of all members, but as a Puritan he was bound to meet with a certain amount of opposition. He knew he would have to tread warily.

His most dangerous opponent was the Earl of Strafford who aimed to make his master "the most absolute prince in

Christendom". As the king's principal adviser, Strafford recommended that Hampden and his friends should be arrested for collaborating with the Scots. Anticipating such a move, however, Hampden was instrumental in having Strafford impeached and lodged in the Tower.

On 12 May, 1641, before a crowd of two hundred thousand, Strafford was executed on Tower Hill. Within a week of this show of strength by the Commons, Charles decided that his only salvation now lay in Scotland which after all was his native land. He knew he could rely on the support of Montrose, the leader of the Covenanters. With such a powerful backing, he fancied he could drive a wedge between the Commons and their numerous friends north of the border.

Such were the king's plans when he went to Edinburgh in the summer of that same year. Hampden, sent to the Scottish capital to assist with the peace negotiations, kept a close watch on Charles, but the ill-starred monarch's schemes collapsed as a result of a plot to murder the Covenanting lords.

Back in London both the king and Hampden admitted to themselves that the chances of avoiding a head-on collision were indeed slender. Charles's "cavaliers" were roaming the city streets and generally making a nuisance of themselves. The capital's trained bands were springing to the defence of the government.

The crunch came at the beginning of the New Year. Hampden, Pym and three other members of the House were impeached. The indictment said that they had "traitorously endeavoured to subvert the fundamental laws and government of the kingdom of England". Other charges included slander, incitement to revolt, collaboration with a foreign power (Scotland), and unparliamentary conduct. A Serjeant-at-arms was sent to the House to make the arrests, but the Commons would not hand over the five members. Charles himself, escorted by 400 cavaliers, fared no better when he went to seize the "criminals" by force. Hampden and the other four had gone to ground in a house in Coleman Street.

A week later, having aroused the hostility of the whole country, Charles fled from London and headed for York. His flight was the signal for the five members to come out of hiding and take their rightful places in the House.

Hampden who had married again settled down at Coley near Reading. After his impeachment he was a changed man. His character seemed to have hardened and he was no longer prepared to tolerate waverers and ditherers. He was unashamedly in conflict with the king and the king's men and did not care who knew it. His *raison d'être* was to wage war ruthlessly on the monarchy as it was then constituted and he had no intention of relaxing until victory was achieved.

With a civil war imminent, Hampden rode to Buckinghamshire to rally his constituents, for he knew that men and money would be needed if the parliamentary cause was to survive. Thanks to his vigorous campaigning, his relatively small county collected £6,000 for the government's defence funds. The man who had once refused to pay out twenty shillings in "Ship Money" willingly subscribed £1,000 towards the Buckinghamshire contribution.

Meanwhile Charles was massing his troops on Heyworth Moor near York. He sent part of his forces to lay siege to Hull, for he planned to gain control of its magazine and warlike stores. He had already made arrangements for his Danish allies to land an army of between thirty and forty thousand men at the port. At that stage it was a recruiting race between the King's Commissioners and the Parliamentary Lieutenants appointed by the Militia Ordinance (a measure passed by both Houses to further defence preparations in all counties).

After the failure of a last desperate bid by the Commons to avoid a civil war, Hampden was called upon to play an active military role. He visited various centres of resistance to ensure that the militia was properly trained and equipped, and then returned to Buckinghamshire where he raised a regiment of a thousand foot-soldiers. Men from all walks of life converged on Chalgrove Field. They were issued with arms and uniforms and throughout that hot summer they marched and drilled under the eye of Hampden's second-in-command, Sir Richard Ingoldsby. The regimental standard of the "Buckinghamshire Greencoats" bore Hampden's famous crest, *Vestigia Nulla Retrorsum.*

Hampden had his first real taste of battle at Coventry where the king had marched with his troops. The Royalists had settled down to besiege the city when Hampden arrived with his greencoats. He had no experience as a military tactician, but his courage and his remarkable leadership qualities stood him in good stead. In a brisk engagement just outside the city, the Royalists were utterly routed.

The tide of battle swept from Coventry by way of Nottingham, Worcester, Shrewsbury and Edgehill until on 29 October, 1642, Charles established his headquarters at Oxford. The Parliamentary forces had their successes, but aided by the dashing Prince Rupert, Charles continued his advance towards the capital. It seemed that a Royalist victory was inevitable, especially when it was learned that over on the continent the Queen had collected £1,000,000 to be used on her husband's behalf. The rumour was that the king of France would ship an invasion force across the Channel and march on London from the south.

Hampden, quick to detect the Parliamentarians' weaknesses, did all he could to knit together the independent county organizations by amalgamating small district contingents into larger and more effective units. Despite his advancing years, he dashed from place to place, giving practical help and advice wherever they were needed. One day he was at Windsor preparing to occupy Reading; another day he was elsewhere quelling a mutiny.

But in spite of all Hampden's efforts, the year 1643 was one of Royalist triumph. It was the year, too, when in response to an attack launched by Prince Rupert on Chalgrove Field, John Hampden was responsible for the powerful counter-attack that followed. Unfortunately he was shot twice in the shoulder, so he was forced to quit the field. He managed to get as far as Thame, where he was carried into the town hall more or less unconscious. The surgeons who examined his wounds said he was beyond all mortal aid.

Hampden died during the morning of 24 June, before the Royalist-Parliamentary struggle reached its climax. It is on record that his last words were: "O Lord, save my bleeding country!" Almost another three years were to elapse, however, before Cromwell's Ironsides completed the work to which Hampden's whole life had been dedicated, but if this plain Buckinghamshire squire had not inspired his fellow countrymen to rebel against tyranny, Parliament's stand against the king might have been crushed at the outset.

Perhaps the fairest assessment of the celebrated Puritan leader is to be found in Macaulay's essay on *Lord Nugent's Memorials of Hampden.* After referring to the other great figures in the parliamentary party, the essayist goes on: "But in Hampden, and in Hampden alone, were united all the qualities which, at such a crisis, were necessary to save the state . . . others could conquer; he alone could reconcile."

John Hampden was certainly a rebel, but after the Great Rebellion had succeeded, England undoubtedly missed "the sobriety, the self-command, the perfect soundness of judgment, the perfect rectitude of intention, to which the history of revolutions furnishes no parallel. . . ."

Chapter 8
Toussaint L'Ouverture
1743–1803

The negro slave who became the first governor of what is now known as the Dominican Republic in the West Indies was born probably in 1743 on the Bréda plantation at Haut du Cap. Various explanations have been given for the second part of his name, Toussaint L'Ouverture. One story goes that after the rebel leader had successfully stormed Dondon, the French Civil Commissioner's comment was, "*Cet homme fait l'ouverture partout.*" ("That man makes an opening everywhere.") Another version has it that Toussaint acquired the nickname L'Ouverture because there was a very noticeable gap in his front teeth. Then again, one of his friends relates that Toussaint adopted the name L'Ouverture because he initiated the movement that led to the slaves' uprising in the north of the island. It seems more likely that he was called L'Ouverture simply because of his bravery in breaking open the enemy's ranks in battle.

But in order to understand Toussaint L'Ouverture and the rebellion he led, it is first necessary to know something of the history of the turtle-shaped island where he performed his memorable exploits. Only by examining the changes brought about on the island through successive invasions by European powers is it possible to appreciate the environment that transformed a simple herdsman into a soldier, a statesman and finally a martyr.

To begin with, before the blessings of civilization reached them, the inhabitants formed a cheerful, unspoilt, sociable community that was entirely self-supporting. The islanders cultivated their own vegetable gardens. Sometimes they hunted; sometimes they went fishing. When they were not concerned with producing food, they made nets and hammocks. They enjoyed smoking their home-grown tobacco, went about naked and practised polygamy. There was not a scrap of harm in them.

Then, in 1492, three Spanish ships under the command of Christopher Columbus sailed into one of the northern bays of the island. After Columbus had moved on, his compatriots initiated a systematic programme of pillage and rape. Their brutal excesses provoked the hitherto peace-loving natives to retaliate. The first batch of Spaniards were all killed, but others soon followed and before long both sides were killing each other on sight. Many of the islanders who fell into the hands of their oppressors were employed as slaves, but the Spaniards usually preferred to massacre their victims wholesale. So vast was the scale of the slaughter that by 1507 only sixty thousand of the original million inhabitants were still alive. During the next four years three-quarters of the survivors were put to death, but black slaves from nearby islands and from Africa were brought in. Thereafter there were riots and uprisings until the natives attained a measure of independence. As for the Spaniards, their incompetence as administrators gradually brought the colony to the verge of ruin.

Then came other colonists – the French who occupied part of the island and called it Saint-Domingue. They, too, were plunderers and persecutors and were as merciless towards the natives as the Spaniards had been. As might have been expected, the two Occupying Powers were soon at each other's throats. In 1697 when peace was declared, Louis XIV of France was granted possession of the western end of the island.

Those who suffered most from these early attempts at

colonization were, of course, the poor natives. The white people looked upon them as little better than animals and treated them accordingly, subjecting them to the most hideous forms of torture. Some of the punishments meted out to slaves were: burying them alive, pouring boiling wax into their ears, sewing them up inside the skins of dead animals, nailing them to walls by their ears, burying them up to their necks and using the heads as skittles in the game of nine-pins, throwing them alive into hot ovens, fitting iron masks over their faces and thus starving them to death.

Under such abominable conditions it is not surprising that the black slaves revolted. A major insurrection was quickly crushed and the ringleaders were summarily dealt with in the most barbaric fashion, but other risings followed in a number of localities.

It is at this stage in the island's bloody history that Toussaint L'Ouverture's name began to be heard. To start with, he was content to remain in the background, leaving the control of affairs in the hands of his friend Jean-François. But he was intelligent, reliable and full of courage. It was immediately apparent that Toussaint was a force to be reckoned with.

Little or nothing is known about Toussaint's childhood and boyhood. He certainly became a herdsman and subsequently a coachman for the manager of the Bréda plantation. During his leisure hours he picked up reading and writing and a sound knowledge of the medicinal plants on the island. He had a strong personality and was held in high regard by the men of his own race. Through the tremendous influence he wielded over his fellow slaves, he was able to organize a large-scale rebellion in 1791. It was thanks to Toussaint's tireless efforts that the slaves had axes, pikes, knives, spears and other weapons. Their angry demonstrations against the colonists should have warned the white men that the blacks and mulattos had reached breaking-point.

Just over three weeks later the islanders were defeated. The atrocities to which they were subjected served only to fan the flames of rebellion, and before long the freedmen at the Diègue plantation rose up against their oppressors. When the wealthy planters were forced to flee, they realized for the first time that the despised blacks were fast learning the arts of war. An appeal to England, requesting military aid from Jamaica, was turned down, so the whites had to accept a treaty in which the coloured freemen were granted equality of status in the Colonial and other Assemblies. Unfortunately the peace that followed was short-lived, for at the earliest opportunity the Constituent Assembly cancelled all concessions gained by the blacks and mulattos. Soon the island once again presented the familiar pattern of oppression, fighting, massacres and attempts at vengeance.

This unhappy state of affairs continued until 1793, the year when France, celebrating the anniversary of the Republic, announced the abolition of slavery in all her western possessions. By that time a number of English troops had arrived, ostensibly to protect the colonists against the rebellious natives. They occupied part of the territory that was under French rule. The Spaniards, too, were doing their share of land-grabbing, and when the English marched into Port-au-Prince on 4 June, 1794, it was beginning to look as if France was going to lose possession of Saint-Domingue.

Toussaint L'Ouverture had followed all these manoeuvres with interest. While operating with the rebels against the French, he had called himself "Doctor of the King's Armies", a title he later amended to "General of the King's Armies". Although Toussaint had been largely instrumental in moulding the blacks and mulattos into a useful fighting force, he had his enemies within the rebel army and was rapidly coming to the conclusion that even his friend Jean-François was jealous of his success. He had also been studying both the Spaniards and French as colonists and had been impressed by the recent French pronouncement on slavery. The Spaniards had always kept the natives in subjection, whereas the French had brought liberty and political rights.

After careful consideration Toussaint L'Ouverture decided to join the French cause against the Spaniards and English.

His opening move was against the English soldiers holding Saint-Marc. This attack was repulsed, but Toussaint met with better fortune against the Spanish troops, driving them out of such places as Saint Raphaël, Saint Michel and Dondon. Towards the end of 1794, as a result of Toussaint's vigorous prosecution of the war, practically all the northern province was under French control, and in a second battle against the defenders of Saint-Marc, the English were beaten and their commander, Major Brisbane, was badly wounded.

Nevertheless the English continued to flourish on the island, extending their authority to other areas. More troops arrived during April 1795, but three months later, by the treaty of Basle, their Spanish allies ceded their Saint-Domingue territory to France. Within twenty-four hours the French National Convention acknowledged their indebtedness to Toussaint L'Ouverture by appointing him a brigadier-general.

Now the Governor of Saint-Domingue, Major-General Laveaux, relied for his authority on the support of Toussaint and his coloured army. When a revolution broke out in Cap-Français on 20 March, 1796, the rebels arrested Laveaux and flung him into prison, but in less than forty-eight hours he was released as a result of Toussaint's forceful intervention. Toussaint again had to be summoned to quell a riot in Petite-Anse a week later. Finally, after the black leader had dealt with another ugly situation in Cap-Français, Laveaux had no alternative but to make him Lieutenant-Governor.

Alarmed by Toussaint's growing power, French agents did their best to discredit him, accusing him of stirring up the conflict and inspiring "hatred in the heart of both parties". Despite all their machinations, however, Toussaint was made Commandant of the western province. He was at last well on the way to the fulfilment of his ambitions. The next important step was to have Laveaux removed from the scene.

Laveaux's departure was easily organized, for Toussaint was in a position to influence the election of Deputies to the French Legislative Assembly. He had no trouble in ensuring that the Governor of Saint-Domingue was duly elected. For the proper performance of his duties, the new Deputy was obliged to set sail for France. He left in October, 1796, and the following month Toussaint received a sword and a pistol of honour to go with his promotion to Major-General. Five months later the former slave had become Commander-in-Chief of the armed forces of Saint-Domingue.

Toussaint had worked miracles, but he was still not quite satisfied. There was still one man standing between him and supreme command – the French agent Southonex. For him, too, a seat in the Legislative Assembly was obtained by devious means and in due course away went the agent, leaving Toussaint without a rival.

Wholly committed now to the French cause, Toussaint thought that the best way of pleasing the authorities in France would be to expel the English from Saint-Domingue. Accordingly he assembled his army and launched a series of crippling attacks. For once he over-reached himself. The French Government, impressed by his generalship but suspicious of his motives, sent out another agent, General Hédonville, with instructions to keep a wary eye on Toussaint L'Ouverture's activities.

But Toussaint's campaign was racing swiftly to its conclusion, and shortly after the new agent's arrival, the commander-in-chief of the British forces on the island offered to pull out of a number of places including Port-au-Prince. Although it was a great victory for the French, Hédonville was seriously disturbed by the fact that the man who had won it had become a national hero. If all the praise and adulation were to turn his head, his very presence in Saint-Domingue could threaten the security of the French colony there. Toussaint's arrival at Port-au-Prince had caused enough stir. Contemporary records tell how "magnificently dressed white women showered flowers on him. Some colonists even prostrated themselves before him." That the rich French planters had to be protected by a black man shocked and disgusted the patriotic Hédonville. It was a blow, he felt, to his own prestige.

Unwilling to risk an open breach, the French agent made a clandestine attempt to topple Toussaint from power. He persuaded young officers fresh from France to poke fun at the Commander-in-Chief's flamboyant taste in clothes and to ridicule his religious fanaticism. He encouraged them to spread rumours that Toussaint's position as head of the army was in jeopardy. In Toussaint's presence he went out of his way to flatter Rigaud, a mulatto general.

The subject of these subtle attacks, however, remained essentially calm and dignified. He completed his self-imposed task of subduing the English, and his triumphant entry into the last stronghold, Môle, marked the end of England's bid to settle in Saint-Domingue. A lesser man might have been tempted by the English Commander-in-Chief's suggestion that Toussaint should assume the title of king, but the black liberator was too intelligent to swallow such an apparently attractive bait. He knew that any move in that direction would have to be backed by the British fleet and would have to be paid for by granting England exclusive trading rights with the island.

Then, on 5 September, 1798, Hédonville came out into the open as Toussaint's enemy. He wrote to him condemning his behaviour and his policies, but he soon discovered he had started something he could not handle. Harassed by a series of local riots, driven to despair by his own inadequacies, humiliated by the sight of Frenchmen kowtowing to a black upstart, Hédonville decided to go back to France. Before he left he sent General Rigaud a letter full of lies and subversion: "Compelled to quit the colony through the ambition and perfidy of General Toussaint L'Ouverture, who has sold himself to the English, the emigrants, and the Americans, – and has violated his most solemn oaths – I release you entirely from the authority intrusted to him as C.-in-C., and I entreat you to assume the command of the Southern Department...."

When the contents of this letter were made known to Toussaint, he asked Rigaud to tender his resignation. The discredited General was offered the usual sop – a deputyship in the Legislative Assembly. – But the new French agent, Roume, refused to let him go. Acting on the assumption that Rigaud's presence on the island would be a source of irritation to Toussaint, he restricted his sphere of influence and kept him in Saint-Domingue.

Thereafter Roume's policy was to stir up trouble between Toussaint and Rigaud, hoping that in the end the two generals would destroy each other. When the time was ripe, he accused Rigaud of being a danger to the government and invited Toussaint to discipline him. This cunning move brought matters to a head. Rigaud, faced with the choice of flight or war, decided to give battle. His soldiers fought courageously, but they could do nothing against Toussaint's superior forces. On 29 July, 1800, Rigaud boarded a Danish ship and sailed away from Saint-Domingue. Toussaint had again demonstrated his ability in the field, but as Roume had foreseen, his harsh treatment of Rigaud lost him thousands of supporters.

Toussaint's power was now so great that he was to a

D

large extent independent of France, although he always tried to act in accordance with the wishes of the French authorities. As a legislator and administrator, he introduced many reforms that the French themselves had to admit were sound and beneficial. He dealt in turn with absentee landlords, the postal service, the navy, imports and exports, rents and revenues, agriculture, road works, licences, police, customs-houses and gambling. He was especially concerned about the secret ceremonies and dances that went on at night and about the mysterious powers of those who practised *vadoux* or voodoo. Because he believed that these nocturnal gatherings were often occasions when conspirators met to plot against the government, he issued a decree banning such meetings. Here again his ruthless attitude towards offenders cost him a great deal of popularity.

During this period Napoleon despatched three major-generals to his West Indian colony, but their presence did not deter Toussaint from pressing on with his constitutional and social changes. They were no doubt astonished to learn that a white woman had actually crowned the black leader with laurels and compared him to their beloved Bonaparte. Planters who only a few years previously had viewed black men and mulattos with loathing and contempt were vying for Toussaint's favours. The visiting generals were soon convinced that Toussaint was getting too big for his boots.

When the new constitution for Saint-Domingue was adopted on 9 May, 1801, Toussaint was invested with the title of Governor-General for life. He was also granted the inestimable privilege of nominating his successor. He alone was responsible for selecting suitable candidates for civil and military posts and to him was entrusted the command of the army. Other clauses of the 1801 constitution covered agriculture, legal questions, courts-martial, religion and divorce. The main point was that slavery was abolished for all time. The programme as a whole was calculated to bring peace and prosperity to the island.

Although everything seemed to be running smoothly, Toussaint was uneasy about Napoleon's possible reactions, and not without reason. The Master of France had been informed of Toussaint's independent attitude and had made his dispositions. He was determined to crush the black usurper and to restore slavery to Saint-Domingue.

Under the leadership of Napoleon's brother-in-law, a French fleet carrying an army 45,000 strong set out on 14 December, 1801, bound for the West Indies. The object of the expedition was simply to seek out and destroy Toussaint L'Ouverture. The thoughtful Napoleon had even put Toussaint's two sons, who were then in France, on one of the ships, hoping they would be able to talk their father into a more reasonable frame of mind.

After the expeditionary force had landed at Saint-Domingue, events moved quickly. Many native soldiers were rounded up and savagely done to death. Then, the French troops advanced on Port-au-Prince, occupying the town on 5 February, 1802. They only just missed Toussaint L'Ouverture who had got wind of their approach and had fled to Grand Boucan. The negro leader had moved on almost immediately, heading for d'Héricourt, but *en route* he and his escort had been fired at and Toussaint's horse had been badly wounded. With his former supporters falling away from him on all sides, he took to the open country with the remnants of his army. The very colonists whose welfare he had so ardently fought for and the priests whose benefices he had secured, all deserted him in his hour of need.

Even though he must have known that his cause was doomed, Toussaint was not yet ready to come to terms. When his two sons brought him a message from General Leclerc to the effect that if he surrendered, the General would make him his second-in-command, the indomitable rebel refused to co-operate. In a brilliantly organized fighting retreat, Toussaint foiled his pursuers again and again. Confident that they had him trapped, the French marched on Gouaives, only to learn that their quarry had escaped. Rochambeau's army tried to pin him down at La Ravine-à-Couleuvres, but Toussaint got the better of the engagement. An attempt was made to besiege him in the fort of La Crête-à-Pierrot, southwest of La Petite Rivière, but his men resisted stubbornly and succeeded in smashing their way through the French lines.

Compelled to retire to Les Cahos, Toussaint at last admitted to himself that he had reached the end of the road. On 6 May, 1802 he set out for Cap Français to surrender formally to General Leclerc. Cannons firing from the forts and war ships in the harbour thundered out a welcome befitting his rank, while the French Commander-in-Chief received him with feigned affability and flattery. Two days after his arrival Toussaint was graciously permitted to go to one of his plantations where he proposed to settle down and devote his remaining years to agricultural pursuits.

Unfortunately for Toussaint, Leclerc had other views. Although the former rebel leader was without weapons, without an army and would soon be sixty years old, the Frenchman still saw him as the possible focal point of another black rising against the French authorities. To leave Toussaint at large, in Leclerc's opinion, was to run an unnecessary risk. On the other hand, to imprison him without any real justification would certainly lead to all manner of disturbances on the island. His best plan was to persuade Toussaint to break the law and then have him arrested and legally confined.

Leclerc therefore instigated some of his soldiers to carry out a series of raids on Toussaint's plantation and to steal whatever they could lay their hands on. He hoped that eventually Toussaint would catch one of the robbers in the act and use violence against him. But once again the wily native out-smarted his persecutor. Whenever he caught a man plundering, he kept himself under control and merely reported the offender to his superiors. For some time he endured these and other minor irritations, but finally Leclerc's vicious campaign wore him down. He first moved to Beaumont, but when he found no respite there he informed the French Commander-in-Chief that he intended to seek refuge in one of his ranches in the Spanish part of the island.

This was the opportunity Leclerc had been waiting for. He and another major-general named Brunet wrote to Toussaint telling him they were content to let bygones be bygones. Henceforth the negro leader could expect nothing but friendship and respect from the French authorities. While his letter was on the way to Toussaint, Leclerc was making arrangements to have the old rebel picked up as soon as he arrived at the Georges plantation.

Brunet and a posse of soldiers were standing by to receive Toussaint. They seized him, trussed him up like a common criminal and put him on board the frigate *La Créole.*

Later, when his captors transferred him to the *Héros* which was sailing for Brest, Toussaint is reported to have said: "By my overthrow the trunk of the tree of negro liberty at Saint-Domingue is laid low – but only the trunk; it will shoot out again from the roots, for they are many and deep."

At the end of his voyage to Brest, Toussaint was flung into a damp cell at the Fort de Joux. His wife and children, brought to France on another ship, were also imprisoned at Bayonne.

During the first few weeks of his incarceration, Toussaint was permitted to retain one of his servants to cook for him and perform such domestic duties as were necessary. Later, this amenity was denied him, and the man who had once been the governor of Saint-Domingue was left in solitude to suffer from the penetrating cold of the Jura, from hunger and from whatever insults and humiliations his guards chose to heap on him.

On 27 April, 1803, when one of the prison guards entered Toussaint's cell, he discovered the prisoner sitting in his chair near the fireplace. His dark hands seemed to be gripping his knees and the fine grizzled head was slightly inclined to the right. We shall never know what the greatest of all black warriors was thinking about before the end, but it would not be unreasonable to suppose that his imagination had transported him back to the West Indian island where he had rebelled so successfully against the tyranny of white over black.

In these days Toussaint L'Ouverture's long struggle against intolerance and racial prejudice has a special significance. The prophetic words he uttered before being shipped into captivity can be applied to places other than Saint-Domingue. And as for those who have taken up the torch borne so nobly by Toussaint L'Ouverture, there is comfort in Wordsworth's splendid tribute to the great liberator:

> "There's not a breathing of the common wind
> That will forget thee; thou hast great allies;
> Thy friends are exultations, agonies,
> And love, and man's unconquerable mind."

Chapter 9
Alexander Hamilton
1757–1804

The great American statesman who was to play a leading part in drawing up the present American Constitution was actually a British subject by birth. He was born on 11 January, 1757, on the small sugar island of Nevis in the Leeward Group. His father, James Hamilton, was a merchant with a pleasant disposition and a happy-go-lucky attitude towards business. Young Alexander, however, had far more in common with his mother (née Rachel Fausette) who was as brilliant as she was beautiful. From her he no doubt inherited his quick intelligence, his deep sensitivity and his warmly affectionate nature. Her relatives were responsible for his upbringing practically from infancy, for his parents were poor and everybody on the island knew it. Nevertheless he grew up with a fierce love of independence. Even as a child he resented any form of patronage. Alexander Hamilton preferred to rely on his own unaided efforts.

The boy was soon launched into the world of getting and spending. He was not yet sixteen when he completed his apprenticeship in the warehouse at St. Croix. He was given plenty of opportunities to visit other islands on business and his employer was so impressed by Alexander's strong sense of responsibility that he often left the youth to run the office while he was away. Alexander Hamilton's rare talent for dealing with correspondence undoubtedly dates from his spell in the St. Croix warehouse.

His facility with the pen was by no means limited to the formal phraseology of business letters, for in 1722 after the Leeward Islands had been blasted by a hurricane, Alexander was moved to literary composition. His description of the devastation was considered good enough for publication. Although the article appeared anonymously, it soon got around that young Alexander Hamilton was the author. This unexpected leap into print persuaded his relatives that the boy had ability and deserved a college education, so they put up the money and away went Alexander to New York.

Twelve months at a grammar school paved the way for his entry into Princeton College. When Alexander insisted that he should race through the curriculum at his own pace, the trustees refused to co-operate. The whole situation was reviewed and instead of going to Princeton the young man spent two very full years at King's College, Columbia.

The turning point of his life came in the autumn of 1773. He happened to be in Boston on that memorable day when, as a protest against the Townshend duty on tea, a party of Bostonians disguised as Indians tipped a cargo of that useful commodity into the sea. The incident instilled in Hamilton the principle of resistance. He had started out in life, as he himself tells us, as a loyalist. After the Boston Tea Party, he became a rebel.

In the following year he discovered to his surprise that he was no mean orator. After matriculating in July, he attended a large open-air political meeting in New York. He listened to a number of vote-catching speeches and then he decided to address the audience himself. He spoke on a subject dear to his own heart – oppression of the colonies by the Mother Country. It was, he assured the crowd, the duty of every honest American to resist British exploitation whereever it manifested itself. Everybody listened spellbound to the youthful enthusiast who was at that time only seventeen years old.

Resolved to help push his fellow countrymen towards a

full-scale rebellion against British governmental interference in America, Hamilton next turned his attention to pamphleteering. In such documents as *Full Vindication, The Farmer Refuted* and *Remarks upon the Quebec Bill*, he dealt with a variety of topics, but the basis of all his political thinking was that the American colonists should deny Britain's right either to tax them or to give them the laws they lived by. The only choice patriots had was between spineless subservience and a popular uprising. Although he claimed to be fundamentally an aristocrat and a traditionalist, there can be no doubt that his pamphlets contained the seeds of rebellion.

To prepare himself for the stiff fighting that lay ahead, Hamilton joined a volunteer organization called the Hearts of Oak. Dressed in his smart green uniform, he attended drills and began to learn something about weapons. Some months previously he had set out to acquire a thorough knowledge of constitutional law, but he now devoted all his spare time to studying strategy and tactics. If he was going to be a soldier, he was determined to be a good one.

Hamilton was now fully committed as an active rebel against the British parliament. He had already been approached by the loyalists with a view to enrolling him as a supporter, but although his sympathies lay with the monarch, he could not join an organization that wanted to perpetuate the system whereby decisions made by a body of men in London were affecting the lives of American citizens. The only logical answer to it all was for America to become independent.

And so for six long years Alexander Hamilton did battle for an ideal. As might have been expected in so versatile a young man, he turned out to be a highly efficient and coolly courageous soldier. At nineteen he became captain of an artillery company, and thanks to his keenness and leadership qualities he was noticed first by General Greene and later by Washington. After effectively helping to slow down the British attack at White Plains, Hamilton's battery also behaved with conspicuous gallantry during the autumn retreat through New Jersey.

Hamilton's promotion to lieutenant-colonel came at the beginning of March 1777 when he was appointed Washington's A.D.C. He found his duties were mainly secretarial, copying out (and sometimes anticipating) his chief's battle orders, but he was also given other assignments that called for tact, firmness and all the qualities that go to the making of a good staff officer. On one occasion, shortly after Burgoyne's surrender, he had to tackle General Gates on the thorny subject of reinforcements. Asked to release two of his brigades, Gates went off like a fire-cracker. Few lieutenant-colonels would have had the temerity to argue with a notoriously stubborn general, but Hamilton would not budge an inch until Gates agreed to let the two brigades leave his command.

Then again, in 1779 somebody thought up a wild plan which entailed the kidnapping of the British general Sir Henry Clinton. It was Hamilton who strongly advised Washington not to go ahead with the hare-brained scheme. He objected on the grounds that after long experience of Clinton's fairly predictable behaviour on the field of battle, it would not be to America's advantage if he was replaced by an unknown commander with whose military tricks and stratagems they were unfamiliar.

In the winter of 1780 Hamilton took time off from his various commitments to get married. The lady of his choice had great charm and a lively mind. Although she was the daughter of General Schuyler, the young lieutenant-colonel had not viewed the match as a stepping-stone in his military career. He genuinely loved his Betsy and the marriage turned out to be a happy and successful one.

Two months after his matrimonial venture, Hamilton suddenly changed direction within the army framework. He had convinced himself that in the military profession he had found his true *métier*, but ambitious as always, he now saw himself in the role of a great commander in the field. In the belief that his secretarial appointment would not further his plans, he resigned his staff job and in the summer took over the command of a light corps as a full colonel. He distinguished himself shortly afterwards at Yorktown and in a brilliant action was instrumental in capturing one of the redoubts there. Washington's comment on Hamilton's exploit was: "Few cases have exhibited greater proofs of intrepidity, coolness, and firmness than were shown on this occasion."

But it was not after all as an army commander that Alexander Hamilton was to achieve greatness. Although he had all the attributes of a first-class soldier and leader of men, he had something else that was destined to lead him into a new sphere of activity. He had an extraordinary flair for statesmanship.

His interest in affairs of state had blossomed during the sixth year of the War of Independence. Uncomfortably aware of Washington's dissatisfaction with the way in which Congress had been handling the country's military machine, Hamilton had gone carefully into the question of cause and effect and had come up with a solution. The trouble lay in the fact that the Federal Government comprised thirteen states all pulling in different directions. Congress consequently lacked the authority and the business-like efficiency that were necessary if the war against England was to be prosecuted with any hope of success. The individual states had not yet learned to act together. As long as each one continued to cling jealously to its own laws and its own rights, and refused to acknowledge that the whole was greater than the sum of the parts, a stable central government with one voice speaking for all would never be established. In short, Hamilton had reluctantly arrived at the conclusion that the *United* States of America was, in the late eighteenth century, a misnomer.

These ideas and others he set down in a series of papers, penned during those weeks that bridged the gap between his resignation as a military secretary and his transfer to a fighting unit. No biographical sketch of Alexander Hamilton would be complete without a glance at some of his theories on the evolution of the Federal Government and its subsequent development.

According to Hamilton, the thirteen states of America, each of which took a pride in its sovereign power, had simply united in opposition to the common enemy, England. His greatest fear was that after they had beaten the English and had created an American nation, the loose federation of states would revert to the old pre-Revolutionary system of individual legislatures. If that happened, the country would again fall under the domination of one of the European powers (not necessarily England). The remedy, Hamilton concluded, lay in the hands of Congress, but not the weak, shilly-shallying, indecisive and powerless Congress they had known so far. Only a strong, impartial, truly sovereign central government could save America. As Hamilton wrote:

"There is something noble and magnificent in the perspective of a great Federal Republic, closely linked in the pursuit of a common interest, tranquil and prosperous at home, respected abroad."

To give Congress its due, it had done its best during the war and many of its shortcomings could be attributed to its lack of experience in the arts of government and to the small-mindedness of some of its members. Called upon to perform the duties usually associated with a country's ruler, Congress had built up an army and navy, produced paper money, handled finance and established alliances. On the other hand, once the American Revolution was under way, much of its impetus came from the patriotic fervour of ordinary citizens and from the selfless devotion, purposeful energy and high idealism of a handful of born leaders.

Two of those leaders – men who knew that America's whole future depended on union – were George Washington and Alexander Hamilton.

When peace came in 1783 Congress was still the sovereign power in name, but the thirteen states were already drifting apart, obeying Congress's decrees only when it suited them. Their worst sins, however, were sins of omission. In the peace treaty, in return for considerable concessions made by Britain, Congress had agreed that all amounts owed to British subjects by American citizens would be paid, that existing acts of confiscation against loyalists would be repealed, and that all loyalist persecutions should cease. But as soon as the English had gone, the states ignored those promises given by Congress on their behalf. Loyalists who tried to collect outstanding debts from Americans were laughed at or abused; property taken from them was not restored; their persecutors started a new wave of oppression.

This flagrant disregard for justice and humane principles shocked all fundamentally decent Americans. Many had the courage to voice their protests and were prepared to fight for their beliefs. The acknowledged spokesman of those rebels was Alexander Hamilton.

After Yorktown Hamilton had gone back to Albany fully determined to become a barrister. For a few months he worked as receiver of continental taxes for the State of

New York. Then he was elected to Congress, and at the age of twenty-five he was admitted to the bar. He was now in a position to press for a federal government that America could be proud of and one that other nations would respect. As he pointed out to Washington: "It now only remains to make solid establishments within, to perpetuate our Union, to prevent our being a ball in the hands of European Powers, bandied against each other at their pleasure; in fine, to make our independence truly a blessing."

As a lawyer Hamilton was an immediate success and quickly built up a considerable clientele, but public affairs began to claim more and more of his time. His first big opportunity to air his revolutionary views on a suitable constitution for America came at the Convention of Philadelphia on 14 May, 1787. Two opposing schemes were put forward – the Virginia Plan and the New Jersey Plan. The former recommended a democratically elected government with an upper and a lower house, a president for a limited term only, and supreme court judges appointed by the legislature. The latter advocated a government based on state boundaries. One system favoured the Rights of Man; the other gave priority to State Rights.

Neither plan satisfied Hamilton who spent five hours explaining his own proposals to the Convention. After demolishing the New Jersey Plan as fundamentally unworkable in so far as it was merely an extension of the shaky doctrines on which the present government was based, he rejected the Virginia Plan on the grounds that complete extinction of the States was unacceptable to the American people. He then went on to maintain that the best government for America would be one modelled on that of Britain where national strength was united with individual security. In other words, he wanted a compromise between the two plans already submitted. The legislature would consist of two chambers, an Assembly elected by popular vote and a Senate elected by the States, and at the top of the structure would be a strong president who would also act as Commander-in-Chief of the armed forces. The triple aim of such a constitution would be a financial policy independent of European bankers, a commercial policy based on national self-sufficiency, and a foreign policy that brooked no interference from the Old World.

Hamilton's main problem was to convince the American people that the constitution he envisaged was a sound proposition. His solution was to initiate a series of newspaper articles under the title *The Federalist.* The aim of these 85 essays, most of which were written by Hamilton, was to win support for the new Constitution of the United States.

A month or so after the Philadelphia Convention, the draft resolution put forward by Hamilton came up for consideration by the Convention of New York State. In spite of powerful opposition the young lawyer's plan was eventually approved. In the spring of the following year, by a unanimous vote, General Washington was elected first President of the United States. Five months later Alexander Hamilton was appointed to what was probably the most demanding of governmental posts, the secretaryship of the Treasury Department. At the age of thirty-two he had to handle all the financial problems of a nation on the verge of bankruptcy whose commercial credit had almost reached rock bottom.

Although he had not been trained for such a responsible position, Hamilton created out of chaos a monetary system that worked and augured well for the future. He met with innumerable obstacles in his efforts to collect state debts, but when it came to national debts, whether they were foreign or domestic, he ruthlessly brushed aside all excuses and delaying tactics. He allowed nothing to divert him from his avowed intention – to put the American economy back on its feet both at home and abroad. During his busy years in the Treasury Department, the public credit soared to heights that even Hamilton's most ardent admirers would never have thought possible.

Everything Hamilton concerned himself with seemed to be running smoothly. Then, in 1790 Thomas Jefferson of Virginia, author of America's Declaration of Independence, came to New York to be Washington's Secretary of State. As one who was strongly opposed to giving greater power to the central government, he clashed with Hamilton right from the beginning. In Jefferson's eyes the Secretary of the Treasury Department was working against the Republic with a view to establishing a monarchy. He even suspected Hamilton of secretly pursuing the possibility of an alliance with Britain.

Within a year of his arrival in New York, Jefferson had launched his Democratic Party, a political group that jealously resented any infringement of state rights. The Democrats fought the Republicans at every turn, charging their leaders with dishonesty, peculation and misappropriation of public funds. Hamilton himself was falsely accused of treason and of cooking the books, so in reply he prepared a detailed statement of his accounts and presented it to Congress. Not even his worst enemy dared to say that the Treasurer had been anything other than scrupulously correct.

Another important question on which Hamilton and Jefferson could not see eye to eye was America's foreign policy. Hamilton viewed with misgiving the progress of the French Revolution, and when France declared war on Britain on 1 February, 1793, his hopes of improving Anglo-American relations were irrevocably shattered. Although Hamilton persuaded the government to endorse a Declaration of Neutrality, Jefferson and his party opposed his plan to send a mission to England. The Democrats were clearly resolved to make political capital out of the situation. America might be neutral on paper, but it was always possible to apply commercial pressure and to repudiate outstanding debts to British citizens.

His failure to forge closer links with the country he so much admired was a great disappointment to Hamilton, but he was soon busy with a new problem, ostensibly connected with excise duties in Pennsylvania. Refusal to pay the duty on whisky triggered off a number of prosecutions and they in turn provoked riots and disturbances. In July 1794 agitators were fanning the flames of rebellion into what looked like developing into a dangerous conflagration. Ironically Hamilton, a rebel himself, was the man who did most to bring the Pennsylvanian rebels to order. He was one of those who advised that the army should be brought in and by a demonstration of force compel the trouble-makers to disperse.

In the autumn of that same year, at a meeting of Congress, Hamilton let it be known that he would shortly be retiring. His reasons for such a step were twofold. He had run into debt, and in order to protect his children's interests he wanted to discharge his obligations. Then again, as he looked round him and saw a strong, independent, peaceful nation, he realized that his task was done. Consequently he handed in his resignation at the end of January. In his reply Washington wrote these words: "In every relation which you have borne to me, I have found that my confidence in your talents, exertions, and integrity has been well placed."

After his retirement, Hamilton continued to practice law for a further six years and was frequently consulted by Washington. He saw the President withdraw from public life in the autumn of 1796 and the installation of his successor, John Adams, who was elected by a very narrow majority.

The Adams administration sowed dissension among the Federalist party leaders. Adams tended to be jealous of Hamilton, while Hamilton had scant respect for Adams. Both hated anarchy and lawlessness, but in all other matters their outlooks were poles apart. Hamilton, as we have seen, loved his country more than he loved his fellow countrymen whereas Adams's patriotism rarely rose above personal considerations. In any event, it was unlikely that the new head of the state would have relished a situation where an outsider had so much influence over the cabinet. As Adams so bitterly declared, although he was supposed to govern the country, it was really Hamilton who was "the commander-in-chief of the House of Representatives, of the Senate, of the heads of Department, of General Washington, and last, and least, if you will, of the President of the United States!"

In the 1800 election, with Jefferson pitching for the presidency, Hamilton and his Republicans were opposed by Aaron Burr, a ruthless party organizer, and the Democrats. Out-manoeuvred by Burr's unorthodox electioneering techniques, Hamilton was defeated. Later on, when it was a question of choosing between Jefferson and Burr as President, Hamilton backed Jefferson and thus contributed to the victory of one he hated as a man and despised as a statesman. Burr became Vice-President.

Thereafter, although he had little or nothing to do with the Jefferson administration, Hamilton snatched at every opportunity to oppose Aaron Burr whom he abhorred as a political adventurer of the worst type. In the end Burr decided that Hamilton's attacks had gone too far, so he challenged his enemy to a duel. Hamilton was pleased to accept, but he said he first needed a few weeks in which to wind up his affairs. Burr agreed to the delay and the next time the two met was at a banquet on 4 July, 1804. Contemporary records state that Burr was taciturn and unsociable, but Hamilton appeared to be in a gay, festive mood.

A week later, "under the heights of Weehawken, upon a grassy platform overlooking the Hudson River", the duellists faced each other. At the first exchange of fire, Hamilton dropped. The great statesman who at forty-seven had achieved so much that one wonders what he might have accomplished had he lived another twenty years died the following day.

In retrospect Hamilton's whole life was cast in the mould of a rebel, for he began by "rebelling" against the circumscribed island existence into which he had been born; at the Boston Tea Party he felt a close kinship with the rebels who dumped the tea into the harbour; in the War of Independence he fought for the rebel cause; when he got into politics, he rebelled against the prevalent views on government; the pamphlets he wrote breathe the spirit of rebellion. After they had beaten the English, he even rebelled against those rebels who went on persecuting the loyalists.

But Hamilton's most significant rebellion was his uncompromising rejection of the American constitution as it then existed, for he was rebelling not only against his political opponents but also against the people of America. The task he undertook was the tremendous one of convincing men from thirteen separate territories that their prosperity, their security and their future felicity lay outside State boundaries. First he fought to make the States independent; then he fought to unite them. It is because he won both battles that America in 1788 could at last claim to be a nation.

Chapter 10
Danton
1759–94

Generally acknowledged to have been the most able and sincere leader of the French Revolution, Georges-Jacques Danton was born on 26 October, 1759, in Arcis-sur-Aube, right in the heart of the desolate Champagne district. He was of good yeoman stock, but in view of what happened later to Georges-Jacques, mention must be made of his father's reasonable success as an advocate before the local court at Arcis.

As might have been expected in a sleepy French hamlet in the latter half of the eighteenth century, Georges-Jacques's early education was a casual affair in which any knowledge the boy acquired would be largely due to his own efforts. As the greater part of these formative years was spent outdoors, he developed into a healthy, energetic youth well able to take care of himself physically. But he was awkward and ill-mannered in company. So when he was thirteen his parents arranged for the rough surfaces to be smoothed and polished in the nearby city of Troyes, the capital of the *département*.

Young Danton found this thoroughly bourgeois city with its population of 30,000 full of variety and interest. His quick eye noted the colourful costumes of the citizens, the prevalence of cassocks, and the panache of the new "nobility" (most of whom owed their titles to tradesmen ancestors who had bought them). After the strictly conventional and closely circumscribed life of Arcis-sur-Aube, Troyes seemed to offer Danton liberty, urbanity and wider horizons.

The country scholar first completed two years' lower seminary training and then moved into the *Catalogus Scholasticorum* of the Collegium Trecense, an establishment staffed by secular clerics. The instructional programme was inspired by Jansenism, a doctrine that repudiated the ordinary Catholic dogma of the freedom of the will and encouraged attacks, both religious and political, on orthodox beliefs. No doubt some of the heresy and rebelliousness rubbed off on the impressionable Danton.

Quite apart from religious training, the students covered a wide range of academic subjects including the two classical languages, Latin and Greek, history and French. The broadly based curriculum also embraced mathematics, mechanics, practical physics, cosmography, and anatomy. Then again, Danton was interested in the college's approach to the drama.

He attended the college as a day pupil, so outside the normal time-table he was more or less left to organize his leisure hours. Although he derived a great deal of pleasure from wandering round the city and seeking adventure, Danton also found time to learn the rudiments of English and Italian. On the whole his college days passed happily and agreeably, while his extra-mural experiences of life in a provincial capital left him with an urge to explore further afield.

The opportunity came shortly after his return to Arcis-sur-Aube, for his parents decided to send him to Paris as a law student. Accordingly, at the age of twenty, Danton found himself in the offices of the *procureur du parlement,* Maître Vinot, in St. Germain-des-Près which was, with its large working-class population, one of the most revolutionary districts in the capital. The object of the exercise was to study jurisprudence, but once again the young man was fascinated by his environment, yielding to the subtle spell of a city that was even then seething with revolution. He went everywhere, absorbing the heady atmosphere of the Paris scene, meeting the people and acquiring a first-hand knowledge of their day-to-day problems. He was already a well-known figure, distinguished by his bulk, his broad shoulders, his pock-marked features and his powerful voice. His humble origins and inspiring speeches appealed to the Parisians and earned Danton an immediate popularity.

Despite his casual attitude towards intellectual labours, Danton was awarded his diploma of *Licencié-en-Droit.* He took an office in the Rue des Mauvaises-Paroles, which was nothing but a back-alley in a depressing neighbourhood on the left bank of the Seine. Few clients visited him there, so he had plenty of time to think about what was happening around him in Paris.

Back in Arcis he had been conscious of a hard-working peasant class scraping a bare living out of the soil and trying to exist on what remained after they had been bled white by their feudal overlords. The situation in Paris, as Danton saw it, was equally iniquitous. He could see that the *bourgeoisie,* although a force to be reckoned with financially, was allowed no say in the way the country was being run. Just like the peasants they were crippled with heavy taxes, contributing towards a system of government that benefited only the nobility and clergy, neither of whom were taxed at all. Remembering the discontented rumblings he had heard in Troyes, Danton took the political pulse of Paris and knew beyond all doubt that changes would have to be made.

One day when he was too ill to leave his bed, he picked up the *Encyclopédie ou Dictionnaire raisonée des Sciences, des Arts et des Métiers,* a book which contained a series of well-written articles set out in alphabetical order, presenting the sum total of universal knowledge. He was astonished to discover, when he read the definitions of such words as "power", "authority", "legislator", that he had in his hands an open incitement to revolution. In bold and unequivocal language the reader was more or less invited to rebel against the twin tyrannies of Church and State.

The subversive ideas whirling in Danton's head might

have induced him there and then to enter the political arena, but at the time he was pre-occupied with a possible matrimonial venture, for he had fallen in love with Antoinette-Gabrielle, the daughter of the *patron* of his favourite haunt, the *Café Parnasse*. He had genuinely lost his heart to the girl, but he was practical enough to accept her father's offer to set him up in practice as an *avocat aux conseils du roi.* Two days after his appointment was officially confirmed, he and Gabrielle were married.

Thanks to his father-in-law's generosity (which was not altogether disinterested) Danton left the sinister Rue des Mauvaises-Paroles and moved into a large comfortable house in a more salubrious quarter. There, attracted doubtless by his imposing establishment, all manner of clients flocked to him with their legal troubles. He got on well with his colleagues, and his two clerks were delighted to be working for so considerate an employer. Gabrielle was happy and soon presented her husband with a son. Apparently Danton had decided to settle down as a well-to-do family man and respectable official of the law courts.

His future career, however, was shaped by the stirring times in which he lived. With the country's financial position getting more and more shaky, the rulers of France were compelled to convoke the States-General for 1 May, 1789. In the elections that followed, the people freely expressed their dissatisfaction with the régime and demanded an end to privileges and oppression. Danton whose infant son had just died was too upset to show concern when his district did not include him among the elected deputies, but after he had recovered from the first shock of grief he realized that the revolution he had read about in the encyclopaedia was not far from becoming a reality. He knew too that destiny had chosen him to play a leading role in the drama that was about to unfold. Meanwhile, all he had to do was to wait patiently in the wings.

Then, in July the Paris mob exploded into violence. The night after the fall of the Bastille, Danton led the civic militia of the *Cordeliers* district in a march on the state prison.

From that moment Danton, with his dominating personality and outstanding skill as an orator, became the acknowledged revolutionary leader of his district and was henceforth known as "the man of the *Cordeliers*". Like the roaring of an angry bull, his voice thundered across the Paris streets denouncing France's corrupt rulers and whipping up the people into a frenzy of indignation and hatred. His speeches were always impromptu. As ideas, lines of action, urgent directives flashed into his mind, so he passed them on in that tremendous voice. He was the spokesman of the *Cordeliers,* and *his* district was the hub of the Paris movement. In the *Orateur du peuple* a contributor wrote: "Danton will save the country if you give him the chance to save it. You need men of character who will grow with the danger they have to face and will cause your foes to tremble."

On 6 December, 1791, Danton became public prosecutor for the Commune. At first his new appointment allowed him few opportunities of impressing his colourful personality on the public, but in April of the following year he again stepped into the limelight. For some time he had been campaigning without success for the removal from office of Bailly, the Mayor of Paris, and Lafayette, the commander-in-chief of the civic militia. He now seconded a motion advocating that the busts of these two lukewarm revolutionaries should no longer remain in their places of honour in the *Hôtel de Ville.* Danton seized upon the occasion to deliver an impassioned address affirming his personal and political creed. All hearts were touched by the words: "My whole life has been devoted to the people and no man shall attack and betray them unpunished. If necessary I am ready to die in their defence."

Meanwhile, in the midst of all these events, the King had fled from Paris. The *Cordeliers* had promptly demanded the abolition of the monarchy, but the revolutionary authorities were not yet ready to take such a drastic step. Instead they prepared a petition stating: "The National Assembly is called upon to take note in the name of the nation that Louis XVI on 21 June resigned the crown entrusted to him, and it is requested to find a substitute." (The substitute they had in mind was the Duke of Orléans.)

This moderate approach to the problem did not please Danton. Despising half-measures, the firebrand of the *Cordeliers* made a number of incendiary speeches, most of which emphasized the necessity of doing away with kings and queens and even regencies. As a result of his outspokenness he was forced to lie low for a while, first near Fontenay-sous-Bois, then in Troyes and Arcis, and finally he crossed the Channel to seek refuge in England.

When the hue and cry had died down, Danton returned to Paris. Tactfully he proposed a less revolutionary constitution from which the King would not be excluded, "should the monarchy prove itself a friend to that liberty which is its sovereign". However, the French court took the view that a successful Bourbon restoration would depend on foreign aid. Paradoxically both revolutionaries and royalists wanted war. The former thought that if the whole country united against a common enemy, their movement would take on the nature of a crusade. The latter were of the opinion that France was bound to lose and in defeat the French people would come flocking back to the strength and security of the old régime.

When the war *did* come, the opening engagements were against the Austrian Netherlands. Danton instinctively knew that it was the right moment to strike. He said: "The executive has become bold only because we have been weak. I pledge myself to carry terror into the corrupt court." He began by pressing for taxation concessions for the poorer classes and by urging the National Assembly to pass a law that would force Louis XVI to part from his wife and send her back to Austria. He could see that the other great revolutionary leader, Robespierre, was not yet prepared to make the final break with the monarchy, but he himself was resolved to fight to the bitter end. Unless the King was deposed, the revolutionary machine would grind to a standstill.

Once more the stentorian voice rang out, warning the Parisians that they were being duped and advising them to ignore the rumours that were rife. A manifesto threatening the people of Paris, published by the Duke of Brunswick, added to the confusion. It was not long before nearly everybody in the capital was echoing Danton's demand for Louis's deposition. Already a battalion of volunteers from Marseilles had been clandestinely quartered in the monastery of the *Cordeliers*. The tension was steadily mounting.

Then, at long last, the revolutionaries were on the march.

They stormed the Tuileries; the monarchy was overthrown; tax reforms were immediately proclaimed. As a reward for his tireless activities and unswerving loyalty to the movement, Danton was made Minister of Justice and given an office in the *Hôtel de la Chancellerie.* The farmer's son from Arcis-sur-Aube was the undisputed Dictator of France.

Although Danton has been blamed for the September massacres of 1792, and although he accepted full responsibility for the atrocities, sometimes boasting "They were my work", it was actually Marat, the darling of the scum of Paris, who initiated the butchery. The guilt of Danton (and also of Robespierre) lies in the fact that he did nothing to prevent the slaughter. In January, 1793, he certainly voted for the execution of Louis XVI, and he was one of the original members of the infamous Committee of Public Safety, but on the other hand there is plenty of evidence to show that he tried to curb the Committee's ruthless severity. He is also reported to have said: "I prefer being guillotined to guillotining."

In any event, Danton was, aove all else, a fervent patriot and his country was in danger from foreign foes. Once before, under the inspiration of Joan of Arc, Frenchmen had forgotten that they were Bretons or Gascons or Provençals, and had fought together as a nation. Now, after the decree of 15 January, 1790, had created 83 artificial *départments* covering almost equal areas of land with practically identical population densities, 25 million Frenchmen were again swept along on a wave of nationalism. Danton knew that the French artillery was the best in Europe. What he had to do was to ensure that the rest of the army was properly organized, provided with weapons and supplies, backed by adequate reinforcements, and imbued with the will to victory. With a view to boosting morale he addressed the National Assembly and the crowds packing the public gallery. Everyone present rose to his challenging words: *"Il nous faut de l'audace, et encore de l'audace, et toujours de l'audace, et la France est sauvée!"*

While Danton was rallying the country to meet the threat of invasion, France's enemies were gradually closing in on Paris. They had captured Longwy and reached the gates of Verdun. When it seemed that nothing could prevent them from occupying the capital, the Executive Council wanted to move the seat of government to Blois or Tours. Danton, to whom Paris was France, refused to countenance such a withdrawal. Instead he threw all his tremendous energy into restoring the confidence of the War Department.

Then the miracle happened.

With General Dumouriez commanding all forces between Dunkirk and Montmédy, the tide of battle began to turn. The Prussians were held at Valmy and were soon falling back before an unexpectedly savage onslaught. One after the other, Speyer, Worms, Mainz and Frankfort were overrun by the victorious French armies. By 23 October every hostile soldier had been driven from the soil of France.

A fortnight later Dumouriez decisively defeated the Austrian army near Jemappes. This crushing blow opened the way to Antwerp and Danton knew that it would inevitably lead to the very conflict he wanted to avoid. He had no doubt that England would never tolerate the annexation of Belgium. If the French occupied Brabant, they would certainly find themselves at war with England. Danton was almost in despair when the revolutionary government passed a resolution containing the following ominous statement:

"The Executive Council will appoint national commissioners who will forthwith proceed abroad to come to an agreement with the provisional administrations, elected by the people, on the regulations for common defence, and the means for clothing and rationing the armies of the Republic, and for meeting the expenses of the troops." To Danton these words had only one possible interpretation. France fully intended to trample on Belgian sovereignty.

But the annexation of Belgium was not Danton's only worry. Early in the New Year the National Convention voted to decide the fate of the King. The majority vote was in favour of death. Then a second vote was taken to determine whether or not the execution should be postponed and the majority were against any delay. Consequently, on 21 January, 1793, Louis XVI was led out through the mist and rain to the *Place de la Révolution* and guillotined. When the royal head dropped into the basket, Danton abandoned any hopes he might still have had of establishing amicable relations with England. The execution of

Louis XVI meant that the English would never recognize the French Republic.

The repercussions were even worse than Danton had foreseen. Not only did England expel the French Ambassador. In a gesture of protest Naples joined the coalition ranged against France.

Although it seemed as if the whole world was leagued against his mother country, Danton still clung to his dream of a strong and prosperous French Republic playing a leading part among a European system of states. As he himself put it: "The frontiers of France are marked by nature; we shall reach them at four points; the Rhine, the Ocean, the Alps, and the Pyrenees. These must be the borders of our Republic, and no power on earth shall prevent us from reaching them."

While Danton had been in Belgium during the crisis there, news had reached him that his wife was seriously ill. He had rushed back to Paris, but his beloved Gabrielle had died before his arrival. His bereavement was a terrible blow, but it came at a time when he had to shelve his grief and concentrate on his duty to France.

The House of Hapsburg despatched such a powerful army to liberate Belgium that the French were beaten back on all fronts. Even Paris would have panicked had not Georges-Jacques Danton been there to put fresh heart into the Convention with his optimistic appreciation of the situation. Together with Robespierre and Marat he pledged the country's full support of General Dumouriez, but all three soon found that their faith in the general had been sadly misplaced, for Dumouriez suddenly took it into his head to try to bring back the monarchy in the shape of Louis XVII. It was largely due to Danton's intelligent handling of affairs that the attempt was frustrated.

Shortly after this episode other groups in France tried to restore the monarchy and the country was plunged into a civil war. All these troubles at home and abroad were automatically blamed on the Committee of Public Safety in which Danton was still a leading light. When a new Committee was formed, Danton's old supporters turned against him on the grounds that his revolutionary zeal was on the wane and he was not re-elected. Thereafter the

Committee was wholly controlled by the supposedly incorruptible Robespierre.

The summer of 1793 was a disastrous one for France. Agitators in the provinces were stirring up riots and disturbances; the war was going badly; Marat, one of the revolutionary Triumvirate, was murdered in his bath by Charlotte Corday. As far as Danton was concerned, the year 1793 was also a turning-point. Spiritually and physically he was utterly exhausted. So he went to Arcis-sur-Aube to recuperate, with his second wife, a pretty 16-year-old named Louise Gély.

During his absence from the capital the reign of terror went on unabated. Queen Marie-Antoinette, along with many nobles and political prisoners, fell a victim to the guillotine. Danton recognized that those who had risen up against their oppressors were motivated by fear, but he could find no justification for their excesses. He felt that after the first angry and possibly excusable manifestations of their loathing for the régime, the revolutionaries should have directed their energies to social reforms and welfare. It was not enough to free the people from their chains; they had to be given education, food and housing.

And all the time Robespierre was patiently waiting for the propitious moment to dispose of his chief rival. The coldly calculating leader of the extremists had already struck at the *Girondins* (the party of moderates) in 1793, expelling many of them from office, imprisoning others and even condemning some to the guillotine. On 13 March, 1794 he again attacked "the internal foes of the French people", but on this occasion most of his venomous shafts were aimed at Danton.

Danton's friends tried in vain to bring about a reconciliation. They next begged their hero to leave the country until the storm blew over, but it was too late. At the end of the month he was arrested and had to answer a series of trumped-up charges such as conspiracy, deserting the common cause, embezzlement and treason. When he appeared before the Revolutionary Tribune on 2 April, his defence was so sublime in its audacity and its magnificent buffoonery that his embarrassed prosecutor illegally cut him short for "insulting justice". His accusers who produced neither witnesses nor evidence found him guilty and

Danton was guillotined on 5 April. It was typical of the man that on the scaffold he turned to the executioner and said, "You should show my head to the people; it's worth showing!"

It is difficult to decide whether the great revolutionary leader was a fiery democrat or a corrupt politician, a fanatical patriot or a crafty traitor, an eminent statesman or a ruffianly demagogue. Nor can one be quite sure whether he launched the insurrection of 10 August, 1792, or whether he was lurking cautiously in the wings until it was safe to take the centre of the stage. What we *do* know is that the people of Paris worshipped him and that he had a natural sympathy with the man in the street. Even if some of the charges levelled against him are true, revolutions, as Bulwer-Lytton points out, "are not made with rose-water".

Chapter 11
Mary Wollstonecraft
1759–97

In the eighteenth century the only place in which a woman might occasionally be treated as a reasonable human being was the home. She had no rights whatsoever; no say in her country's politics; no education worthy of the name. Even the few who had property of their own lost it as soon as they married. Not only did husbands automatically take possession of their wives' belongings; they also dominated their lives, ordering them about like servants, using them for their pleasure as and when they liked, punishing them for real or imagined offences, disciplining them whenever they stepped out of line, sometimes lashing them with their tongues, at other times resorting to physical violence. Wives had no redress, no means of retaliation. Because they were women, they were considered to be intellectually and morally inferior to men, the undisputed lords of creation.

This relationship, in which man was the master and woman his slave, had existed for so long that it had come to be accepted as normal, practical and final. Man, the provider, naturally saw himself as the head of the household and had no scruples about keeping the woman in a state of subjection. Woman, the weaker vessel, just as naturally believed that her main function was to be decorative, pleasing, and above all subservient. For the former it was an admirable arrangement. For the latter it was just another cross she had to bear.

Clearly such a division of responsibilities was unfair and iniquitous. That women had never rebelled against their miserable lot speaks well for their tolerance but would appear to be a sad reflection on their intelligence. It must be remembered, however, that throughout history they had been carefully conditioned to be second-class citizens. They had, in fact, been exploited by their unscrupulous menfolk who had deliberately withheld from them the advantages of a proper education. There can be no doubt that if women had been better informed, they would have appreciated the injustice of the system and would have demanded their rights earlier.

The average man's attitude towards the opposite sex had been unequivocally expressed by Rousseau. He wrote: "The education of women should always be relative to that of men. To please, to be useful to us, to make us love and esteem them, to educate us when young, to take care of us when grown up, to advise, to console us, to render our lives easy and agreeable; these are the duties of women at all times, and what they should be taught in their infancy."

Treated as "children of a larger growth", women were not expected to have opinions of their own. In so far as theirs was not to reason why, they were not encouraged to question the man-made rules and regulations by which their lives were circumscribed. It is therefore not surprising that the first rumblings of revolt against inequality of the sexes came not from women but from men. Daniel Defoe and Jonathan Swift voiced their disapproval and Helvetius made some pertinent observations concerning women's education, but it was Baron Holbach, in his *Système Social,* who actually dared to advocate a better deal for the weaker sex. Subsequently Condorcet, in his *Progrès de l'Esprit Humain,* insisted on the necessity of establishing a perfect equality of civil and political rights between the individuals of both sexes.

Meanwhile rebellious thoughts had been fermenting in the mind of a remarkable young woman who was not prepared to subscribe to the almost universally held opinion that her sex had been created to play a purely secondary role in the human comedy. Experience had taught her that men had no monopoly as far as intelligence was concerned and that given the opportunity women had the mental agility and strength of character to equal them in most fields of endeavour and, indeed, to surpass them in some. Her approach to the whole subject of women's rights was novel, humanitarian and revolutionary. The name of this daring pioneer was Mary Wollstonecraft.

Born on 27 April, 1759, probably in Hoxton, London, Mary Wollstonecraft was one of the five children of Elizabeth Dixon, an Irishwoman, and Edward John Wollstonecraft, a man of considerable fortune. As a child she watched her father's wealth gradually disappear as he moved about the country trying to set himself up as a gentleman farmer. His spendthrift nature and his reckless incompetence she might have overlooked. What hurt her most was his drunkenness, for once the drink was in him, Mr. Wollstonecraft became a hectoring bully, quarrelling frequently with his wife and generally acting as a brutal domestic tyrant. Mary's unhappy home background certainly left its mark on the sensitive girl. Her efforts to protect her mother from her father's vicious assaults were often physically exhausting, but at least she was learning to challenge masculine authority and resent the conditions that made her interventions necessary.

She was also discovering that any partnership based on inequality was a contradiction in terms. At the age of fifteen she had already resolved that she would never enter into a union which robbed her of her independence.

In Mary's determination to be independent lay the seeds of her rebellion against man's assumption that a woman had no right to a life of her own. Every woman, in Mary's opinion, was entitled to think for herself, to make her own decisions, to take up a career, to enjoy a reasonable measure of freedom, to share the many privileges that man had so far reserved for himself. In her own home and in the houses of friends she had seen her sex degraded by arrogant brutes whose behaviour made a mockery of marriage. Her own father disgusted her. She was repelled by her mother's cringing subservience. If civilization was to develop in any worthwhile sense, then the man-woman relationship had to be drastically reorganized.

Mary's opening move in what was virtually a war of the sexes was to improve her intellectual status. The smattering of education she had received at town day-schools had to be supplemented, so she embarked on a programme of wide reading. At the same time she pestered her parents until at last they yielded to her repeated demands for a room of her own. A small victory, perhaps, but nevertheless a significant one. She had demonstrated that the enemy was vulnerable.

Then in 1777, after the Wollstonecrafts had moved to Walworth, the young rebel reached a momentous decision. Despairing of any amelioration on the domestic front and alarmed by her failing health, Mary knew that there was only one sure way to the independence she craved. She had to sever all family ties and try to support herself by her own efforts. She resolved to leave home.

Reluctant though she was to abandon her mother, she applied for the post of companion to Mrs. Dawson, a rich lady of Bath, was accepted and was soon stepping westwards.

Chez Mrs. Dawson, Mary found herself in a world of fashion and high society with a multitude of diversions to engage her attention and take her mind off family problems. For the first time she was able to study the leisured classes in their natural habitat and she was not impressed. The stratagems and manoeuvres employed by the ladies of Bath, either to trap husbands or to retain those they already had, did not provide a very edifying spectacle. Miss Wollstonecraft was more determined than ever to remain single and independent.

Although she found most of her employer's friends and acquaintances trivial and superficial, Mary liked Mrs. Dawson on sight, admiring her wit and intelligence. With the passage of time, however, she came to realize that the lady had other and less endearing traits. Good-humoured banter gradually gave way to barbed reproof and light-hearted repartee degenerated into bad-tempered vituperation. Like the rest of the domestic staff, Mary had to endure undeserved outbursts of irascibility without answering back. She was forced to admit to herself that in breaking with her family she had merely exchanged one form of domination for another. The freedom she had sought in Bath had somehow eluded her.

Fortunately she was not expected to dance attendance on Mrs. Dawson twenty-four hours a day. She had ample leisure for reading, and in accordance with her original policy she snatched eagerly at every opportunity to extend her mental and cultural horizons. She still believed that the answer to all her problems lay in self-education. If men could be persuaded to accept women as their intellectual equals, the fight against female subjection was as good as won. Quietly then, Mary continued to equip herself for the struggle that lay ahead.

She tolerated Mrs. Dawson's tantrums until she heard from the family in 1780 that her mother's health had broken down under the stress and strain of living with a man she feared and detested. Mary went immediately to Enfield where the Wollstonecrafts were then living, and assumed full responsibility for nursing the dying woman and for running the stricken household. Mrs. Wollstonecraft could do nothing for herself and Mr. Wollstonecraft did not even offer to help, so Mary's services were in constant demand either in the sick-room or in the kitchen. It was a long back-breaking period of thankless drudgery, but Mary managed to cope with her multitudinous tasks right up to the end.

After her mother's death, the 21-year-old girl went to live with the family of her bosom friend, Fanny Blood, at Walham Green near Fulham and there she stayed for the next two years. Her skill in needlework enabled her to contribute her share towards the household expenses. Her spare time she devoted entirely to books and self-instruction, for in spite of all her vicissitudes her objective remained the same – to liberate her sex from man's shameful tyranny. As always with Mary, education was an essential preliminary to the positive action she had in mind.

Faced in 1782 by yet another family crisis, Mary's rebellious nature again brought her into conflict with conventional morality. Her sister Eliza, who had recently married a blustering bully called Bishop, lost her reason after a difficult confinement. Summoned to the rescue, Mary

Percy Bysshe Shelley (*left*), revolutionary and unconventional by nature, protested against religion, hated all forms of tyranny and believed in a new golden age. To escape calumny he eventually abandoned his dream of reforming the world, deciding to pass on his inspiration to others through his poetry. – John Brown, a fanatical supporter of the movement to abolish slavery, was convinced he had a divine mission to free the negroes employed as slaves in the southern states of America. He is here (*below*), in the painting by Thomas Hovenden; seen going to his execution after his ill-fated attempt to seize Harper's Ferry.

Richard Wagner (*below*) revolutionary composer of operas, looking down at Liszt and von Bülow. On his right is Liszt's daughter Cosima, who became Wagner's second wife. (From the painting by W. Beckmann.)

Emmeline Pankhurst (*bottom, third from left*), militant suffragist and co-founder of the Women's Social and Political Union, after one of her many spells in prison. The photograph was taken in 1908.

promptly diagnosed the cause of her sister's derangement. She could see that Eliza was terrified of her sadistic husband and that the only chance of a return to sanity lay in immediate flight. Consequently, disregarding all the popular conceptions appertaining to the sanctity of the marriage vows, Mary convinced her sister that her best plan was to run away from home – a drastic step inviting social ostracism for both of them.

When Eliza fell in with Mary's proposals, the two sisters had to find a means of earning a livelihood. After eliminating a number of possibilities, Mary rented a large house in Islington and converted it into a school. The new venture proved such a success that she subsequently opened a similar establishment at Newington Green. There was nothing revolutionary about the curriculum, but Mary's views on the proper training for young girls were very far from orthodox and were to be expressed later on in a volume of essays.

For a time everything seemed to be going smoothly. Then Mary's friend, Fanny Blood, who had joined the Wollstonecrafts at Newington Green, left to get married in Lisbon in 1785. Towards the end of the same year, Fanny died after a painful confinement. Her death was a bitter blow to Mary who had gone to Lisbon to nurse the young mother during her last days. To add to Mary's general despondency, when she got back from Lisbon she found that the school had run into debt during her absence. Money had to be obtained somewhere, so she tried her hand at authorship.

Her first published work, *Thoughts on the Education of Daughters*, with its somewhat pretentious sub-title, *Reflections on Female Conduct in the More Important Duties of Life*, although little more than a pot-boiler, deserves attention in so far as some of Mary's arguments were to be amplified and reinforced subsequently in her masterpiece, *A Vindication of the Rights of Women*. In any event, her *Thoughts* contain a great deal of controversial matter. She had already committed herself to rebellion against the current order of things. She stated fearlessly that instead of handing them over to wet-nurses, mothers should suckle their own children, that they should treat them with affection and consideration, and that they should bring them up to appreciate the beauties of nature. Furthermore, far too much pressure was being brought to bear on young girls to fit them for fashionable society. Mothers would be better advised to teach their daughters how to handle the problems of motherhood. Most significant of all the author again and again stressed that women concern themselves overmuch with genteel behaviour and polite manners, attaching undue importance to their prospects in the marriage market. Mary urged them to concentrate rather on improving their minds to make themselves worthy of a better place in the social system.

For her *Thoughts on the Education of Daughters* Mary was paid ten guineas by her publisher. When it emerged in 1787, the book appealed to very few readers and passed more or less unnoticed by the reviewers. It was, after all, no more than a loose series of essays, the sort of stuff overworked teachers might have written to unco-operative parents. Nevertheless it was a start. To Mary Wollstonecraft the book meant a good deal more than the mere satisfaction of breaking into print. She had proved that she could write, that her thoughts had been considered interesting enough to be made available for others, that she could earn money by her literary efforts. More gratifying still, she could conduct her own life without having to rely on male support. She felt she had at last attained the independence she had coveted for so long.

Mary's elation, alas, was of brief duration. She still had many outstanding debts and her creditors began to press for payment. Although she knew that the situation was desperate and that she could not afford to wait upon events, she seemed curiously incapable of decisive action. It was as though she had lost all zest for life and had given up the struggle. Then, for no apparent reason she suddenly pulled herself together and demonstrated her intentions to straighten out her financial position by taking a job as governess with Lord Kingsborough's family of Mitchelstone in County Cork. First she would settle her obligations; afterwards she hoped to save enough money to keep herself going while she applied her talents seriously to a literary career.

Mary stayed in Ireland for a year, at the end of which period she was dismissed by Lady Kingsborough who grew jealous because her children became excessively fond of their new governess. In any case, it is doubtful if Mary could have tolerated much more of her employer's wounding superciliousness. Besides, she had taken a strong dislike to Kingsborough Castle which, although it was surrounded by beautiful scenery, gave her the disagreeable sensation of being in a prison.

During her spell with the Kingsboroughs, Mary had again come into fairly frequent contact with society, this time at a particularly high level. The vapid types she met were no different from the wealthy idlers who had attended Mrs. Dawson's parties. Their frivolous attitude towards life served to confirm her belief that the social system was in urgent need of a thorough overhaul. She must have often known disgust and frustration at Kingsborough Castle and would probably never have endured twelve months of such a boring existence had she not escaped occasionally into creative work. She was able to voice her dissatisfaction with the world as it appeared to her in a partly autobiographical novel entitled *Mary, A Fiction.*

The book may not have established Mary's literary reputation, but at least it impressed the publisher sufficiently for him to provide her with steady employment for the next five years as a reader and translator. She was also busy on a volume of children's stories and yet another sentimental novel. For her it was a stimulating time. She was meeting prominent personalities, writers, eccentrics, men who delighted in good talk, friends of freedom and democracy. Above all, she was harnessing her forces for a devastating attack on the inequality of the sexes.

Meanwhile an event was taking place across the Channel that was to arouse Mary's sympathy and to appeal to her rebellious spirit. To her the French Revolution meant the awakening of freedom in Europe. She was confident that the emancipation of Frenchmen would lead inevitably to the liberation of all mankind. Women's independence would soon become a reality.

Mary Wollstonecraft's splendid protest against the unjustified subjection of women by tyrannical men was published in 1792. A highly original book, exploring social problems without bitterness or cynicism, passionately and sincerely stating the woman's point of view, her *Vindication of the Rights of Women* fearlessly exposes the need to "strengthen the female mind by enlarging it". Her main argument is set out quite clearly in the dedication to the book. There she says, "that if woman be not prepared by education to become the companion of man, she will stop the progress of knowledge, for truth must be common to all, or it will be inefficacious with respect to its influence on general practice."

Although the *Vindication* is lacking in organization and bristles with stylistic infelicities (possibly because it was hurriedly put together in six weeks), it is still a significant book, and as far as its central theme is concerned is almost a hundred years ahead of its time. The radical and revolutionary tenets it upheld certainly shocked conventional readers, especially as they came from the pen of a woman. The "hyena in petticoats", as Horace Walpole called her, spared no one in her determination to destroy the smugly complacent man's world and replace it with a system in which no invidious distinctions were drawn between the sexes. Her *Vindication* was a blueprint for all future feminists.

After stressing her belief in liberal principles, she asserted that "arbitrary power" was the root cause of most of the world's troubles. Blind authoritarianism, she pointed out, would eventually create a climate in which the oppressed were bound to rebel. She then went on to examine the miserable plight of women, generally despised by men because of their inferior mentality. Unmarried, a woman was compelled to resort to all sorts of degrading tricks in order to ensnare a husband. Married, she became a domestic drudge whose duty it was to obey her husband's slightest whim. The situation was even worse in so far as women had come to terms with their servitude and were too apathetic to fight for the independence to which they were entitled.

Mary's argument next dealt with a subject that had concerned her for a long time – the need to provide adequate educational facilities for women. Pausing only to take a side-swipe at Rousseau (who had advocated that women should develop only their beauty and subtlety), and to draw critical attention to the treacherous views of Madame de Staël, Mrs. Piozzi and Madame de Genlis, all of whom agreed with the masculine approach to the problem, she then mentioned some of her female contemporaries who had already proved that they were on the same intellectual level as men of education and culture.

Her insistence that a liberal education for women as well as for men would be the basis for a truly progressive partnership and for sound democratic living was not only a *cri du coeur*; it was an impassioned plea for humanity.

Other revolutionary measures she put forward in her *Vindication* included changes in the property laws, political and social reforms that would give women a say in the running of the country, the admission of women to trades and professions that had always been reserved for men. That she attacked neither religion nor the institution of marriage suggests that her pious and orthodox upbringing had left its mark even on her unsubmissive character. Mary Wollstonecraft's protest was directed against the false assumption that woman was created to be man's plaything. Her firm contention was that not only marriage but the entire human race would benefit from an intellectual companionship of the sexes.

Her biographers make much of her unfortunate affairs with Henry Fuseli the artist, and with the materialistic American Gilbert Imlay. Her happy but regrettably short-lived marriage to the philosopher William Godwin, whose unconventionality at least equalled hers, also played a not insignificant part in her life. But here we are concerned with Mary Wollstonecraft the rebel, the most fearlessly intelligent woman of her time. In an age where women were not supposed to have ideas, let alone voice them, she had the courage to speak out. She was accused of immodesty, indecency and wantonness, but this uncompromising lady, without any formal education or literary training, went serenely about her self-imposed task of championing the cause of womankind. Although her views may not have had a profound influence on the nineteenth-century feminist movement, her contribution was recognized and appreciated by those who carried on the fight subsequently. Mary Wollstonecraft's rebellion was only the beginning.

Chapter 12
Shelley
1792–1822

Percy Bysshe Shelley, the famous son of Sir Timothy and Lady Elizabeth Shelley of Field Place House, Wareham, near Horsham, was born on 4 August, 1792. Brought up on a magnificent estate in an environment where there was no shortage of money, young Shelley might have developed into a self-centred prig, but Sir Timothy, a typical country squire, was determined that Percy should not be pampered. He therefore subjected his son to a rigid system of discipline, bearing down heavily on the boy almost to the point of persecution. It was no doubt Sir Timothy's dictatorial approach that provoked the rebelliousness that was to become a dominating trait in Shelley's character.

As part of his programme for turning the child into a scholar and a gentleman, Sir Timothy sent the six-year-old Percy to the curate at Wareham for a daily dose of Latin. This classical training was to stand him in good stead later, but what the lad most enjoyed was riding round the estate in the company of his father's steward. There was so much to see and little Percy was interested in everything. He loved chatting with the servants and farm labourers, all of whom took an immediate liking to the son of their employer. Some of his happiest days were spent with the younger members of the family – Elizabeth, Mary, Helen, Margaret and John. His four sisters worshipped him, especially when he told them the stories he invented. Even at that time Shelley was already mastering the art of narrative, terrifying his spell-bound audience with his tales of horror.

When he was ten, Shelley became a boarder at Sion House Academy, Brentford, a reputable establishment run by a Scotsman, Doctor Greenlaw. The curriculum was a comprehensive one that appealed to Shelley, as did the school library with its numerous thrillers. The worst feature of Sion House, especially for a boy as reserved and as sensitive as Shelley, was the bullying that went on. As a result of constant persecution (which he probably regarded as an extension of his father's treatment at home) the boy tended to avoid his fellow scholars, seeking protection in isolation.

Two years later he moved on to Eton, a school where the educational policy was to develop a pupil's personality through freedom of expression. The headmaster was Doctor Goodall, but before Shelley left, Goodall was replaced by the notorious martinet, John Keate, who despite his lack of inches once flogged 80 boys in succession. So once again the impressionable youth was subjected to the type of discipline that either breaks the spirit or encourages rebellion. In Shelley's case repression affected him in two ways. He stubbornly refused to be browbeaten for any reason whatsoever, and he dedicated himself to the protection of the weak and helpless. He began by trying to liberate his sisters from Sir Timothy's baleful influence. He ended by trying to liberate the world from the "forces of unreason".

At Eton he developed an unusual interest in electricity. He was always experimenting in that particular science and actually had an electrical machine of his own, a contraption that gave rise to many sinister stories concerning "mad Shelley". His other hobbies included chemistry and astronomy. He strongly disapproved of Eton's fagging system and of all the ragging that came his way. When he himself was only a fag, he organized a rebellion against the tradition that forced small boys to become the slaves of their seniors. He was already a sworn enemy of tyrants and of anybody who instigated others to violence.

As far as his academic studies were concerned, Shelley was distinguishing himself in the field of literature, winning prizes for his work and even getting into print. He was fascinated by Pliny and Lucretius, was profoundly influenced by the eighteenth-century sceptical and revolutionary writers, and wrote two crude romances, *Zastrozzi* and *St. Irvyne, or the Rosicrucian.* He also collaborated with his cousin Thomas Medwin in a poem about the Wandering Jew.

Shelley was, however, much too unconventional to fit into the pattern imposed by the energetic Keate, so he left Eton prematurely and in 1810 proceeded to University College, Oxford, where he immediately became friendly with Thomas Jefferson Hogg who was already there. Both were resolved to change the system of society, both were convinced that the world needed enlightenment, and the university careers of both ended in fiasco.

Picking up most of their ideas from the literature of the French Revolution, Shelley and Hogg decided that the religious faiths that men professed were harmful to happiness. Although at that time Oxford was a stronghold of orthodoxy, Shelley, backed by Hogg, rashly voiced the opinion that God did not exist and attempted to launch what really amounted to a theological rebellion. In order to attract people to their cause, the two undergraduates collaborated in the production of a pamphlet entitled *The Necessity of Atheism.* Printed at Worthing, copies of the work were sent to the Oxford and Cambridge authorities, and to a number of bishops and other clergymen. In an even bolder gesture, further copies were displayed in the window of Messrs. Munday and Slatter's book shop in Oxford. Within twenty minutes a Fellow of New College, the Rev. Mr. John Walker, picked up the pamphlet, glanced through the contents and was duly horrified. After administering a sharp rebuke to the book-sellers, he made them burn all copies of the offending pamphlet.

The Necessity of Atheism had been published under a pseudonym, but the authorship was soon traced to Shelley and Hogg. Shelley would admit nothing, but Hogg let slip that they were both to blame. The end of the affair was that the two friends were expelled "for contumacy in refusing to answer certain questions put to them". Thus Shelley who had been at Oxford for only six months forfeited his chance of a first-rate education.

After quitting Oxford the two atheists headed for London where they shared accommodation at 15 Poland Street. Naturally the whole unsavoury episode displeased Sir Timothy who now went out of his way to break off his son's association with the devilish Hogg. He placed three possible alternatives before Percy. He could return to his home at Field Place; or he could make a voyage to the Greek islands; or he could go into politics as the member for Horsham.

Shelley, however, was not interested in any of the proposals, for his mind was fully occupied with other matters. While visiting his sisters at school, he had met and admired Harriet Westbrook, the daughter of a coffee-house owner. The girl who was clearly in love with the handsome youth could not at first go along with his atheistic views. Then she quarrelled with her parents and passed through an unhappy period at home. When news of her distress reached Shelley's ears, he promptly stepped into his favourite role of the "verray parfit gentil knight" bent on rescuing his unfortunate lady. Although Shelley was only nineteen and Miss Westbrook three years younger, he made up his mind to save her from her overbearing parents by marrying her.

Prompted more by feelings of chivalry than by any real sexual attraction, Shelley persuaded Harriet to elope with him. The young couple went to Edinburgh and there they were married in a registry office. They set up home in lodgings in George's Street where they were subsequently joined by Hogg to form a distinctly curious *ménage à trois*. The explanation for the threesome seems to lie in a letter Shelley wrote at that time to Miss Elizabeth Hitchener, a friend of William Godwin the philosopher. He told her that he and Hogg shared everything they owned. A man with Shelley's unconventional outlook might well have considered his wife as part of his property. Anyway, when the newly-weds moved to York, Hogg went with them.

The three of them lived under the same roof harmoniously enough until one day Shelley went to visit an uncle in Sussex with a view to borrowing money on the strength of his expectations. On returning to York he was surprised but not shocked to learn that during his absence the enterprising Hogg had attempted to seduce his wife. His advanced notions on free love persuaded him to forget the incident, but Harriet who had reached the end of her tolerance forced him to break with his best friend. The household, less Hogg, settled in Chestnut Cottage, Keswick, where one of their near neighbours was Robert Southey whom Shelley had admired as a poet and a revolutionary.

It did not take Shelley long to discover that Southey's poetry was dull and his interest in revolution purely academic. Disappointed he sought for a more intellectual relationship by starting a correspondence with William Godwin whose revolutionary ideas had already influenced him. Shelley had read Godwin's *Political Justice* and saw him as the man most likely to initiate a revolution in England. Godwin for his part had read Shelley's letter and saw him as the heir by entail to an estate worth £6,000 per annum.

After the collapse of a quixotic venture in Ireland undertaken to teach the Irish the doctrine of "love and charity to all men" and to help them redress their wrongs by overthrowing the Union, Shelley visited North Wales and then settled down in Lynmouth. There he wrote a pamphlet advocating liberty of printing and started work on his rhetorical, revolutionary, anti-religious poem *Queen Mab.* In that extraordinary work the rebel really let himself go. He protested against royalty, priests, statesmen, wealth, sects and cults, and all forms of tyranny. The only hope for the world lay in reason, virtue and vegetarianism. Man's salvation would be found in a true partnership with Nature and in the realization that inanimate objects have a life of their own –

"... *The block*
That for uncounted ages has remained,
The moveless pillar of a mountain's weight
Is active, living spirit."

Meanwhile Shelley had met William Godwin and his wife. Harriet had presented him with a daughter, Ianthe, and he had travelled a good deal and made many new friends including the satirist Thomas Love Peacock. In March 1814 he went through the ceremony of marriage with

Harriet according to the rites of the Church of England. Three months later, while staying with the Godwins, he fell in love with their 15-year-old daughter Mary, a girl of fine intellect and vigorous character. Her naive suggestion that she and the Shelleys should live together, she as Shelley's sister and Harriet as his wife, appealed neither to Harriet nor to Shelley. The complicated situation was resolved in a more practical manner on 28 July when Mary Godwin, her half-sister Jane or Claire Clairmont, and Shelley took a postchaise to Dover and crossed over to the Continent. Godwin who was about to receive the sum of £3,000 from Shelley viewed the elopement with philosophical detachment. Harriet who was again pregnant and who blamed Godwin as the source of her broken marriage hoped against hope that her husband would come back to her.

After travelling extensively in Europe, Shelley ran into financial difficulties, so he brought Mary and Jane back to England. At the beginning of the New Year his grandfather died, and with a little help from Sir Timothy he paid most of his debts and henceforth could look forward to a steady income of a thousand pounds a year. He and Mary moved into a furnished house at Bishopsgate and for a time he knew genuine happiness. There he wrote the first long poem to reflect his undoubted genius, *Alastor, or the Spirit of Solitude*. There, too, his son William was born on 24 January, 1816.

In the spring of that year, accompanied by Jane Clairmont, the Shelley family travelled to Geneva. On the shores of the lake Shelley met another great rebel against convention – Lord Byron – who had (although neither Shelley nor Mary knew it) already seduced Jane Clairmont. Right from the start the two poets struck up a warm friendship and spent many entertaining hours in each other's company. There were water-parties, sailing, excursions and endless talk. Once, at Byron's lakeside villa, the Shelleys met the famous "Monk" Lewis and the three men discussed the supernatural with special reference to life and death, to galvanism, to bringing the dead back to life. And Mary listened, took it all in and later started to write a horror novel. Its title was *Frankenstein*. . . .

Shelley's solicitor wrote to him in August, urging him to return to England to help unravel certain financial tangles. Consequently the Shelley ménage including Jane Clairmont who was with child by Byron journeyed across France to Le Havre, took ship to Portsmouth and eventually settled in Bath. Apart from Godwin's intermittent sponging, Shelley seemed to have achieved relative tranquillity.

Then his peace of mind was rudely shattered by two successive tragedies. First of all, Fanny, the daughter of Godwin's first wife by a previous lover, Captain Gilbert Imlay, committed suicide in the Mackworth Arms at Swansea. She was not only Mary Godwin's half-sister; she had also, if Godwin was to be believed, been in love with Shelley. Although Shelley's behaviour towards her had always been strictly honourable, he could not altogether free himself from a sense of guilt and had to seek spiritual distraction in the essays of Montaigne. Worse was to follow, however. On 10 December Harriet, who had by that time borne Shelley a second child, was found drowned in the Serpentine. This second calamity initiated a period of abject misery for Shelley. Harriet's suicide affected him deeply, but he was even more depressed when the Court of Chancery decided that his revolutionary character disqualified him from bringing up his two children, Ianthe and Charles.

Shelley passed through a difficult period. Fortunately he found distraction from his grief in literary London, meeting Leigh Hunt and the Hampstead *coterie,* John Keats, Benjamin Haydon, Horace Smith and William Hazlitt. It was Hazlitt who summed him up so admirably by saying that Shelley had "a fire in his eye, a fever in his blood, a maggot in his brain, a hectic flutter in his speech, which mark out the philosophic fanatic".

At the end of that momentous year, Shelley married Mary Godwin, and the family (together with Jane Clairmont and her daughter Allegra) moved into a rented house at Marlow. There he wrote his long narrative poem *Laon and Cythna.* It was a love story, but the rebel in him introduced the theme of human emancipation and the battle against tyranny. Acting on the advice of his publishers, he made various amendments, altered the title to *The Revolt of Islam,* and in the new version the hero and heroine were no longer brother and sister. Unfortunately a number of the unexpurgated copies had already reached the public, so Shelley's enemies were able to claim that the author obviously had no objections to incest.

Early in 1818 the Shelleys let their Marlow residence and set out on a long tour of Italy. The voyage was undertaken for a variety of reasons, but principally because it was feared that Shelley was suffering from a pulmonary disease. The poet was also eager to escape from Godwin's insatiable demands for money. Inevitably Jane Clairmont and Byron's daughter Allegra accompanied them while Mary's second child, Clara, presented an additional problem. (The baby sickened and died after an agonizing journey from Este to Venice.)

There was a significant change in Shelley's outlook during his Italian wanderings. He appears to have realized at last that he would never succeed in reforming the world by direct political action. He therefore resolved to concentrate on his poetry and let it serve as the medium through which he could transmit his inspiration to others. The urge to rehabilitate mankind was still there, but the old revolutionary fires were burning low. Henceforth he would stimulate men's minds by appealing to their imaginations. To this period belong his *Lines Written in the Euganean Hills,* his autobiographical *Julian and Maddalo,* some of his finest lyrics, and the incomparable lyrical drama *Prometheus Unbound.*

The death of his infant son William in Rome affected him so deeply that he moved to Leghorn to escape from scenes that conjured up painful memories of the dead child. He found a measure of relief in literary work, writing the greater part of a blank-verse tragedy in five acts, *The Cenci.*

Shelley's rebellious nature was destined to flame out once again. While he was in Florence, news reached him of the infamous Peterloo massacres and reminded him that the tyrant's power in England had not yet been crushed. He read that a crowd of reformists in Manchester, defying a government ban on illegal assemblies, had been dispersed by a cavalry charge and a number of workers had been wounded or killed. To Shelley the manifestation could only have been the prelude to a revolution, possibly the first ominous rumblings of a civil war. His immediate response was to write *The Mask of Anarchy* in which he appealed to the workers to exercise self-control in their fight against the tyrants but nevertheless to

"Rise like Lions after slumber
In unvanquishable number –
Shake your chains to earth like dew
Which in sleep had fallen on you –
Ye are many – they are few."

Shelley sent this poetical incitement to revolution to *The Examiner,* but the editors found it too hot to handle. (They had already been prosecuted for libelling the Prince Regent and the House of Commons.) Nor dared they print Shelley's subsequent protest in prose submitted when the publisher of Tom Paine's *Age of Reason* had to go to prison for three years and pay a heavy fine for "blasphemous libel".

The Shelleys were still in Italy when Mary's son Percy Florence was born. Shelley himself was busy with his poetry, but he found time to concern himself with social problems, pointing out in *A Philosophical View of Reform* that as long as so many people in England were "destitute and miserable, ill-clothed, ill-fed, ill-educated", living and working conditions would have to be improved. What he wanted was a fairer distribution of wealth and property and the liquidation of the national debt. His *Ode to Liberty* echoes the sentiments expressed in the prose work.

Then came *The Witch of Atlas* and the rebel was once more decrying tyranny and praising liberty. In the ode that followed, inspired by "the intelligence of the proclamation of a constitutional government at Naples", he was again dealing with one of his favourite political themes. But in his *Oedipus Tyrannus, or Swellfoot the Tyrant,* a parody on the Greek drama describing the arrival of Queen Caroline in England and George IV's attempts to dispose of her claims, the poet could really let himself go in his caricatures of George IV, Castlereagh and Eldon.

An incident in Pisa, where the Shelleys had been living since the beginning of 1820, suggests that the poet still retained some of the romantic notions that had prompted him to rescue Harriet Westbrook from the oppressive watchfulness of her parents. He met the 19-year-old Contessina Teresa Emilia Viviani, a beautiful and intelligent girl who completely captivated him. Because her mother's lover had designs on her virtue, Emilia had been obliged to stay as a *pensionnaire* at the St. Anna convent. Shelley's chivalrous impulse to free the captive, as he explained to his jealous wife, was purely altruistic since his attitude towards her was that of a guardian towards his ward. Fortunately for everybody concerned, the girl's request for a considerable sum of money induced Shelley to break off the relationship. In enigmatic terms the poet described the brief episode in *Epipsychidion,* the last of his autobiographical confessions.

In the summer of 1822 the poet and essayist Leigh Hunt set out for Italy with a view to joining the Shelleys. The idea was to gather together a group of convivial people – Shelley, Hunt, Byron, Trelawney (an English eccentric) and others – to launch a new periodical. Meanwhile the Shelleys had moved to Lerici. Always fond of the sea, although he had never learned to swim, Shelley had a new boat, the *Don Juan,* delivered to him there, and he and a friend named Williams were more than pleased with the vessel. "Williams is captain," Shelley wrote, "and we drive along this beautiful bay in the evening wind under the summer moon until earth appears another world."

Hearing that Leigh Hunt had reached Leghorn, Shelley decided to sail across the bay of Spezzia to greet him. On the outward voyage which took seven and a half hours the *Don Juan* lived up to Shelley's enthusiastic description. After meeting Hunt and seeing that he and his family were comfortably accommodated in Pisa, Shelley returned to Leghorn, and in spite of threatening weather he and Williams set sail next day. Neither of them was seen alive again. The *Don Juan* had either capsized in a heavy sea or had been run down accidentally by some other vessel.

When the bodies were eventually washed up on the beach, two books were found in Shelley's pockets – a volume of Keats's poems and a slim edition of Sophocles. In accordance with the Italian regulations graves were dug, and after being covered with quicklime the corpses were buried where they were found, but about a month later the remains were dug up and burned on a funeral pyre. Shelley's ashes now lie next to those of Keats in the Protestant cemetery at Rome.

In his own time and throughout much of the nineteenth century Shelley was considered to be among the top flight of poets, but in recent years critical opinion has hardened towards him. Matthew Arnold rated him as "a beautiful but ineffectual angel, beating in the void his luminous wings in vain". Later literary experts have drawn attention to Shelley's immaturity, his uneven and sometimes unfinished work, his excessive concern for things spiritual, his naivety and so on.

Perhaps in Shelley's case it would be more charitable to remember that he died when he was only thirty. It must also be remembered that, thanks to his father's dragooning methods, he was a rebel all his life and his poetry often reflects his rebelliousness. His verse is sometimes charged to be harsh, strident, extravagant, but then it is revolutionary language. If he ignores rules and flouts conventions, it is because all rebels behave that way. If he occasionally offends the canons of good taste, every youthful apostle of liberty does as much.

No matter where posterity chooses to rank him in the hierarchy of poets, Shelley the man will always appeal to those who believe that much of the evil in the human heart can be eradicated only by drastically reforming the whole sorry scheme of things. Shelley felt strongly that –

> "*Power, like a desolating pestilence,*
> *Pollutes whate'er it touches; and obedience,*
> *Bare of all genius, virtue, freedom, truth,*
> *Makes slaves of men, and, of the human frame,*
> *A mechanized automaton.*"

He knew, too, that tyrants shall not "rule for ever, or the priests of the bloody faith"; that "all spirits are enslaved which serve things evil". As "the friend of the unfriended poor", he was prepared to rebel against any institution that hindered the evolution of a world in which men would be "equal, unclassed, tribeless, and nationless".

Unquestionably Shelley's revolutionary theories had a debatable effect on some of his poetry when he was simply translating the pronouncements of his idol Godwin into verse. He is far more likely to be remembered for such incomparable lines as:

"To suffer woes which Hope thinks infinite;
To forgive wrongs darker than death or night;
To defy Power, which seems omnipotent;
To love, and bear; to hope, till Hope creates
From its own wreck the thing it contemplates;
Neither to change, nor falter, nor repent;
This, like thy glory, Titan, is to be
Good, great and joyous, beautiful and free;
This is alone Life, Joy, Empire, and Victory."

Chapter 13
John Brown
1800–59

A descendant of Peter Brown, who sailed to America in the *Mayflower,* and a grandson of Captain John Brown, who saw service in the American War of Independence, John Brown was born on 9 May, 1800 at Torrington, Connecticut, and was brought up in the "Yankee" occupied territory of Ohio's Western Reserve.

When John was only five his father moved to Hudson, Ohio. Little is known about his boyhood, but at eighteen he had it in mind to become a Congregational minister. This phase soon passed, however, and for a time he showed an interest in land-surveying as a possible career. Before long his restless nature prompted him to change direction, so he transferred his attention to the tanning business. When tanning palled, he tried his hand first as a sheepherder, then as a wool-trader, but he seemed incapable of the sustained effort that might have led him to success, for we next hear of him as a bankrupt in Akron, Ohio. Seven years later, after trying his luck in Pennsylvania and Massachusetts, he settled down as a farmer at North Elba, N.Y., taking advantage of a scheme whereby small tracts of land were being given to negro settlers. By that time he had married, raised a large family, and most important of all, had dedicated himself to do everything in his power to wipe out for ever the hateful institution of slavery.

In the first half of the nineteenth century an acrimonious dispute over slavery had flared up between the northern and southern states. In the North slavery was considered to be morally wrong, and whenever new western territory was being admitted to the Union, the first anxious question asked was invariably based on whether the new state approved or disapproved of slave labour.

It is only fair to add that although the northern states were opposed to slavery as a matter of principle, they recognized that the southern states, with all their commercial interests in tobacco, rice, sugar and cotton, could not conduct business economically without cheap labour. The northerners were not so much concerned with the slavery that already existed in the South as with the possibility of its spreading into the new territories.

A powerful body of men, then, prompted largely by humanitarian feelings, was genuinely interested in restricting the use of slave labour to areas that had found it practical and indispensable. A much smaller group, however, believed passionately that slavery was evil and should therefore be stamped out wherever it flourished. These were the Abolitionists, sincere for the most part but tending towards extremism. On the other hand, the slave-owners in the South, uncomfortably aware that the antislavery contingent was becoming more and more hostile, were prepared to defend the system on which their very livelihoods depended. Under these circumstances clashes were inevitable.

Then, in 1859, following sporadic outbreaks of violence in Kansas, came what amounted to the armed "invasion" of the State of Virginia in an absurd attempt to liberate the slaves and start an insurrection. This wildly ambitious venture was the brain-child of a mentally unbalanced Abolitionist named John Brown.

Brown's fanatical detestation of slavery and slave-owners had undoubtedly been whipped up by his father's abolitionist newspaper *The Liberator* which was usually lying around the house when John was a boy. But in any case he believed that he had specially been sent down to earth by God to destroy slavery by violent means. Wendell Phillips tells us that John Brown was firmly convinced that he had "letters of marque from God". Furthermore he *looked* the part, with his tight thin lips and glittering blue eyes and spare wiry figure. He was once described by the humorist Artemis Ward as one whose appearance suggested he could subdue a yard full of wild cats before breakfast without even removing his jacket.

Five of John's sons, who were almost as wild as their father, headed for the pioneer state of Kansas in 1854. In those days Kansas wanted to have no truck with either slaves or black men, and when the Brown boys went there, the struggle between "free-state" settlers and those who were in favour of slavery was at its height. Naturally the most troublesome area was in the region of the state boundary with Missouri. With a view to bullying Kansas into accepting legalized slavery, desperadoes from Missouri would cross the border to carry out terror raids. These lightning attacks were sometimes restricted to horse-thieving. More often than not they developed into wholesale burnings and killings.

Within twelve months John Brown packed his bags, said farewell to the remaining members of his family, and went to join his five sons in the new Federal Territory of Kansas. Once he was settled in Osawatomie, he flung himself enthusiastically into local affairs, becoming a conspicuous figure in the border fighting. His first major action against the marauding Missourians took place on 25 May, 1856. This ugly episode has gone down in history as the "Pottawatomie massacre".

After there had been an attack on the Kansan capital, Lawrence, John Brown put himself at the head of a gang of his supporters. Armed with rifles, revolvers and cutlasses, the little army of seven (including three of Brown's own sons and a son-in-law) crossed the state line and were absent for at least twenty-four hours. When they returned, bringing a number of stolen horses, they kept quiet about their exploits, but eventually the full story of the raid became known. Acting under Brown's orders, they had hauled five pro-slavery settlers from their homes and had butchered them in cold blood.

Various reasons were given later to account for such a barbaric killing, but the real motive may never come to light. The affair may have been no more than a retaliatory horse-stealing adventure that got out of hand. One explanation given was that some of the victims were members of a Territorial court which the free-staters wanted to intimidate. Brown himself put out two conflicting versions of the incident: that the five settlers had been murdered because they had threatened the lives of certain free-staters; that his squad was simply carrying out orders received from a higher echelon (possibly a secret organization called the "Kansas Regulators").

Whatever dark forces had been operating at Pottawatomie, Brown wasted no time in brooding over the crime. Only a week later he pulled off another supreme coup, on this occasion at Black Jack where he and a band of 30 free-staters ambushed and took prisoner a Captain Pate with 22 pro-slavery henchmen. Brown was obviously learning his business as a leader of men, for at the end of August, although badly outnumbered, his outfit had no trouble in fighting off an attack on Osawatomie.

Encouraged no doubt by these early successes, Brown felt that the time had come for him to put into operation some of the schemes he had been working out for many years. One plan he had for striking a blow at slave-owners involved sending runaways to freedom in Canada. Another idea was that he and his sons should take over the management of a Dixie plantation, staff it with free negroes posing as slaves and then train them as *agents provocateurs* whose job would be to stir up trouble and create unrest among real slaves on neighbouring plantations. He even visualized setting up an operational headquarters in the Virginia mountains where he and other white abolitionists could build up an effective army of runaway slaves.

But in order to give shape and substance to these and similar dreams, John Brown needed capital. Consequently he used to ride through the north-eastern states collecting funds for the abolitionist cause. Making out that he represented the free-staters in the south, he would drop mysterious hints that he was running a sort of "secret service" mission, although he was careful never to define its actual nature. On these forays Brown was helped considerably by a Scottish-born journalist supporter named James Redpath whose duties were akin to those of the present-day public relations officer. According to the imaginative Redpath, John Brown could be favourably compared with Robin Hood. The same romantic image was presented to their readers by two other journalists who were in the abolitionist camp.

During these money-raising sorties Brown invariably played the role of a dashing guerrilla leader, wearing a peaked fur cap, a leather stock and a military-looking overcoat complete with cape. Once he had commanded a militia unit for six days, so he felt entitled to call himself Captain John Brown. On another occasion he had spent nineteen days on the continent, so he saw no reason why he should not inform people that he knew all there was to know about fortifications, siege warfare and Napoleonic strategy.

There was no question that Brown's propaganda fooled most of the anti-slavery faction most of the time, for even eminent writers such as Emerson and Thoreau handed over their contributions. Wherever he went he was winning more and more supporters. For a man who was mentally unbalanced, he was certainly making remarkable headway.

Only a handful of fervent admirers could claim to have shared some of his innermost thoughts. Together with Brown they constituted "The Secret Six". No one else suspected the frenzy of hate that lay behind his personal vendetta against the slave-owners. But even his closest associates – and they were the ones who had contributed most generously to his "secret" funds – would have recoiled in horror if they had known the lengths to which their bloodthirsty leader was prepared to go.

As soon as his finances were in order, Brown set about recruiting his private army. The nucleus comprised eleven white men and twenty-two negroes. At a meeting in Chatham, Canada, their "Provisional Constitution and Ordinance for the People of the United States" was formally adopted and the following appointments were made: a secretary of state, a secretary of war, a secretary of the treasury and members of Congress. Their commander-in-chief, of course, was John Brown.

Influenced by his memories of the jingoistic style of *The Liberator* and by George Bourne's *Picture of Slavery,* Brown produced his "Declaration of Independence by the Representatives of the Slave Population of the United States of America". Ignoring the fact that George Bourne's reference to slave-owners as "a horde of oppressors, presumptuous, past all feeling, without natural affection, implacable, unmerciful, profligate, unrighteous, turbulent, religious persecutors" applied only to a small minority of Dixie planters, Brown directed his vituperation against *all* who employed slaves. Such men were "Cossacks" and "Christ-killers". In wildly extravagant language Brown declared: "The history of slavery in the United States is a history of injustice and cruelties inflicted upon the slave in every conceivable way." The whole document presented a grossly distorted picture of conditions in the slave states, but it was written for a purpose. Brown was seeking to justify the rebellion he had planned.

With his tiny army Brown now approached the battle area. He moved to a farm only five miles from Harper's Ferry, the site of the Federal arsenal.

In 1859 the military installations at Harper's Ferry consisted of a number of armaments factories, a considerable arsenal, and a small works where rifles were made and repaired. Why the authorities had chosen such a location is difficult to understand, for the township was indefensible. Strategically placed guns on the commanding heights overlooking the place could wipe out any defensive force. It is therefore not altogether surprising that Brown had decided to launch his campaign by capturing Harper's Ferry.

Preparations for the coup kept Brown occupied for the next three months or more. After smuggling in his 21 shock troops, he had to bring up his weapons and ammunition. He had at his disposal 200 repeating carbines, the same number of revolvers, and a thousand pike-heads ready to be fitted to as many shafts. The arrangements were that firearms would be given to those who knew how to use them; the pikes were to be distributed to the negroes who would inevitably rise against their oppressors as soon as the battle was joined.

It is incredible that all this activity at the farm passed

more or less unnoticed. Only two men discovered what was going on, but their anonymous warning to John B. Floyd, the Secretary of War, was disregarded. At the beginning of August 1859 they wrote to Floyd actually naming the leader of the forthcoming raid and the place that was to be attacked. Moreover, they referred pointedly to the Federal Armoury. The Secretary of War did not even bother to investigate the matter.

Crazy or not, John Brown clearly had a talent for organization, for the early stages of the operation ran like clockwork. As most of the weapons had to be left in the farm, Brown ordered three of his men to stay there on guard. The main party, armed with carbines, revolvers and knives, set out on foot in the direction of the railway bridge leading into Harper's Ferry. Brown himself also made for the Ferry in a waggon loaded with pikes, torches, a heavy-calibre swivel gun and a crowbar. *En route* the raiders cut the telephone wires running parallel to the river bank.

It was eleven at night when they entered Harper's Ferry by way of the railway bridge. There was a sentry on duty who immediately recognized Brown, but he thought the "invasion" was merely an elaborate hoax. He was swiftly disillusioned when he felt a gun sticking in his ribs and heard a voice say that he was a prisoner.

The next move was to the Armoury gate behind which they could see the panic-stricken gateman, alone and unarmed. Although he was terrified, he was not without courage for he refused to surrender his keys to the intruders. Grabbing the crowbar, however, they soon had the gate open and within a few minutes the entire armoury area was in their hands. Brown's guerrillas seemed to be having things all their own way.

Once the Armoury was occupied, the party split up, two making for the arsenal, three for the rifle works and half a dozen hurried towards Charlestown with instructions to set free negro slaves wherever they were found and to bring back their owners as hostages. Brown had given special orders to the Charlestown contingent. Their main target was to be Colonel Lewis Washington, the great-grand-nephew of America's first president. Brown wanted not only the Colonel; he also wanted two heirlooms in the Colonel's possession – a pair of pistols that had been presented to George Washington by the Marquis de Lafayette, and a dress-sword believed to have been bestowed on the president by Frederick the Great.

Thus far everything had gone smoothly without any undue noise. Then, an Irishman named Higgins went to relieve the watchman on the railway bridge. Brown's son Oliver, who was controlling that important sector, called upon Higgins to surrender, but the Irishman aimed a blow at him and bolted. The bullet Oliver sent after him only grazed his scalp. The local medical practitioner, Doctor Starry, who lived near the bridge, did not hear the shot, so the report must have been muffled by the covered bridge. Higgins, meanwhile, had recovered sufficiently to tell his story to the conductor of the 1.25 a.m. train when it rolled to a standstill at Harper's Ferry station. A second shot, fired at the conductor as he advanced towards the bridge to find out what was happening, also failed to disturb the sleeping doctor. Tipped off by the conductor, the driver backed his train away from the danger zone. By that time most of the passengers were awake, asking questions, peering out of windows, and catching occasional glimpses of a rangy bearded desperado with madly glaring eyes, as Brown darted here and there directing his boys.

Then, with dramatic suddenness the whole situation changed. A local man, Heyward Shepherd, not knowing what was afoot, set out to meet the train as he usually did. When a voice from the darkness commanded him to halt, he continued on his way. A shot rang out and down went Mr. Shepherd with a bullet in his back.

This wanton killing seemed to have a numbing effect on the rebel leader. Instead of pressing home the advantage he had gained, he sat brooding in the Armoury for at least an hour and a half and then gave the train driver permission to pull out. The cautious driver, however, thinking that the Brown gang had sabotaged the bridge, refused to leave until dawn, after he had had a chance to carry out an inspection. By seven in the morning he steamed into the first station equipped with a live telegraph wire. A few minutes later his superiors were in full possession of the facts, but the story that Brown's guerrillas had attacked and occupied Harper's Ferry sounded so fantastic that the railway officials attributed it to a practical joker. It was not until half-past ten that the president of the line realized that the situation might be serious and passed the information on to the federal and state authorities.

Meanwhile, back in the Armoury, for reasons best known to himself, Brown was still waiting. At first light the raiders who had headed for Charlestown turned up. They had followed Brown's instructions to the letter. With them were Colonel Washington, a couple of his white neighbours and ten slaves who had been reluctantly liberated. The three white men were escorted to the watchman's room in the Armoury fire-house to join the prisoners already taken; the slaves were armed with pikes. As far as the slaves were concerned, Brown's calculations had gone sadly astray. They belonged to plantation owners who had treated them reasonably well and had no particular desire to be "freed", especially by the vicious-looking old white man who was clearly in charge of their equally unprepossessing liberators. They eyed their pikes glumly and would never have accepted them if John Brown had not insisted. All without exception slipped quietly away when the opportunity arose and scuttled back home to their plantations.

Brown's men soon discovered why he had hankered after Colonel Washington's dress-sword. As if he were watching a play in which he himself was the hero, he saw himself going into battle girt with the sword of Frederick the Great. At any rate, once he was wearing the valuable heirloom, he seemed to snap out of the stupor that had gripped him since the murder of the inoffensive Mr. Shepherd. He bade five men transfer weapons from the farm to the schoolhouse on the far bank of the Potomac. This move was very much on a par with his release of the train. Just as the driver had passed on news of the coup sooner than it need have been circularized, so did the schoolchildren broadcast their versions when they went home to enjoy their unofficial holiday.

With the passage of time men employed at the Armoury reported as usual for work. Their fate was to be rounded up as hostages and kept in custody with the others. Altogether there must have been 45 prisoners, for Brown asked the hotel proprietors to supply exactly that number of breakfasts on credit. Fearing poison, he ate nothing. Here again he had overlooked an essential item when planning the operation. He had made no provision whatsoever for victualling his warriors.

Eventually the man he had left in control at the rifle works recommended that they should all get out while the going was good, but Brown was determined not to budge. By noon it was too late to take evasive action. A strong militia unit arrived by rail from Charlestown. After being ferried across the Potomac, the troops stormed the railway bridge, scattering the small holding party stationed there by Brown and cutting off the raiders from their base in Maryland.

Matters were also going badly on the Armoury front. A gang of railway men fought their way into one end of the building and Brown's men were forced to withdraw into the firehouse. The end was not far off.

Brown now decided to come to terms with the enemy. He foolishly imagined that in his capacity of commander-in-chief he was entitled to act in accordance with normal military procedure. He therefore sent out envoys to negotiate, assuring them that they would be protected by the flags of truce they were carrying. He was probably as surprised as they were when the militiamen promptly greeted them with a hail of bullets. His second-in-command was shot and, together with another raider, fell into enemy hands. His own son, Watson Brown, dragged himself back to the security of the fire-house, but he was mortally wounded.

The battle for Harper's Ferry was not quite over. Doctor Starry, very much awake by that time, led a heroic charge on the rifle works and quickly rendered its three defenders *hors de combat* by killing two and taking the third one a prisoner. Desultory firing into the fire-house accounted for the death of Brown's son Oliver and another man. A deserter from the Armoury contingent was shot dead while trying to escape across the Potomac. The two raiders in the arsenal got away under cover of darkness, but the ragged remnants of John Brown's guerrillas stuck it out bravely until the fire house party was reduced to five effectives.

Resistance continued until nightfall when the commander of the militia called upon Brown to lay down his arms, but the arrogant abolitionist still expected concessions that the military were not prepared to grant. Although his last redoubt was surrounded and every man in the fire-house was cold, hungry and thirsty, Brown would not yield an inch. He spoke with the hostages, trying to convince them that his cause was just, but one bold spirit called out that he was a traitor. Two of Brown's men who happened to be within earshot asked their leader if they had really committed an act of treason. When Brown frankly admitted that they had, both men announced that they would fight no more.

Round about midnight a small detachment of United States marines arrived. Their commander was Lieutenant Israel Green, but his superior officer was Colonel Robert E. Lee. Lest the hostages should be harmed, Lee had issued orders that the storming detail should rely entirely on their bayonets to winkle out the defenders. Using a ladder as a battering-ram, Green and a dozen soldiers at last burst into the fire-house. With the heavy hilt of his dress-sword Lieutenant Green managed to batter the wild-eyed bearded guerrilla chief to the ground. A few professional bayonet thrusts accounted for the remaining raiders.

Several days later Brown was fit enough to stand trial in Charlestown. The stubborn old rebel would not let his counsel plead insanity among Brown's relatives in mitigation of sentence, although the evidence was overwhelming, as the following extract from Villard's biography indicates: "Brown's grandmother on the maternal side... six years in hopeless insanity... died insane... of (her) children, Brown's uncles and aunts, two sons and two daughters were intermittently insane... a third daughter had died hopelessly lunatic; (his) only sister, her daughter and one of his brothers were at intervals deranged... of six first cousins, two were occasionally mad, two... frequent commitments (to an asylum)... two more were at the time under close restraint."

On the last day of October 1859, Brown was found guilty of "treason, and conspiring and advising with slaves and other rebels, and murder in the first degree". The Appeal Court subsequently ruled out the treason charge, but there was enough left to hang him.

Throughout November Brown was kept busy with correspondence and interviews, all of which contributed to the new image that was being created of a popular hero and an internationally famous martyr to the abolitionist cause. His last speech in which he denied all the charges brought against him made a vivid impression on all who heard it and on those who read it afterwards. That his attack on Harper's Ferry was more than ordinarily hare-brained cannot be denied. That he fought like a lion for a principle in which he wholeheartedly believed must be conceded even by his worst enemies.

Once described as "a Bible-soaked mistruster of churches who had identified himself with truth", John Brown undoubtedly acted throughout from what he considered to be the purest of motives. Obsessed as he was with the evils of slavery, he felt justified in trying to destroy his enemies by violent means. As he said himself: "Without blood, there is no remission of sins." Inspired by such rebels as Spartacus who had led the great slave rising against Rome, and Toussaint L'Ouverture who had liberated the slaves in Saint-Domingue, he was firmly convinced that he had God on his side.

John Brown made two memorable predictions before his body was left to lie "a-mouldering in the grave". He said that his execution would make him a martyr and would thus benefit the anti-slavery cause more than he could have done if he had lived on. He also said that his country would assuredly experience a bloody catastrophe. There is ample evidence in the racial disturbances in America today not only that he was a notable prophet, but also that "his soul goes marching on. . . ."

Chapter 14
Wagner
1813–83

A contemporary of the other great "romantics", Berlioz, Mendelssohn, Chopin, Schumann, Liszt, Verdi and Brahms, Richard Wagner was born at Leipzig on 22 May, 1813, immediately after the battle of Bautzen. He was the tenth and last child of Friedrich Wagner, Secretary to the Chief Commissioner of Police, and Johanna Rosina Bertz, an artistic lady from Weissenfels. Although his clerical duties often kept Friedrich in the city police courts, he devoted his leisure hours to poetry and other mentally stimulating pursuits including amateur theatricals.

Five months after Richard's birth, Napoleon launched the battle of Leipzig. There can be no doubt that the appalling living conditions within the city helped bring on the fever that killed Friedrich Wagner in the November of that year. The widow was left in such straitened circumstances that in 1815 she decided to marry again. The man she chose, Ludwig Geyer, was largely responsible for opening his stepson's eyes to the possibilities of the colourful world of the public entertainer. Painter, singer, playwright and actor,

Geyer took the Wagner family to Dresden where he had a regular theatrical engagement. Richard's greatest delight was to attend play rehearsals.

Geyer would have liked his stepson to have turned towards painting, but Richard had little talent in that direction. The boy's great love was for the drama and for anything connected with the theatre. He was also learning to tap out little tunes on the piano. It was beginning to look as if Richard was heading for a stage or musical career. Brought up as he was in an artistic atmosphere, he was already devoting himself to music and stagecraft and tending to neglect his lessons.

After boarding for almost a year with a country pastor at Possendorf near Dresden, Richard had to return to base because his stepfather was dying. The occasion was a solemn one for the boy, but it also marked a turning-point in his life. The day before Geyer died, he heard Richard playing the piano in an adjacent room. He remarked to his wife, "Do you think he's got a talent for music?" The young pianist heard those words and he never forgot them. He said nothing to his mother, but he was sure he had the answer to his stepfather's question.

In December 1822 Richard was sent to the *Kreuzschule* in Dresden and there he worked industriously for the next four years. He cared little for mathematics, but he plunged with avidity into creative writing, mythology and history. When one of his poems was published in the school magazine, he resolved to become a poet. Such was his enthusiasm that he spent two years writing a tragedy that was a curious mixture of the "Hamlet" and "King Lear" themes. This ambitious effort was still unfinished when his mother moved from Dresden to Leipzig and Richard was transferred to the *Nicolaischule* in the city of his birth.

To his great mortification the boy had to start in a lower form. He was so disgusted that his whole attitude towards his studies underwent a drastic change. He saw little point in repeating the academic course he had pursued at the *Kreuzschule,* so he made up his mind to concentrate exclusively on music. He thought that by attaining a high standard in that particular subject he would regain his lost prestige.

In the evenings he was still working on his tragedy, but

he had also begun to attend performances at the Gewandhaus, the Leipzig concert hall. For the first time in his life he heard the music of Beethoven – the Symphony in A and the "Egmont" overture. He later described the experience as "overpowering". He made it his business to find out all he could about the great composer. Henceforth Beethoven became the young Wagner's god. Furthermore, with a view to creating his own music, he hired a copy of Logier's *Method of Thorough-Base.* It was his inability to keep up the credit payments that led to his mother's discovery that her son had set his heart on becoming a musician.

After a number of sessions with a music master, Richard picked up some knowledge of violin and organ playing and learned the rudiments of counterpoint and harmony. These lessons, however, were soon discontinued on account of the hot-headed youth's fondness for argument. His teacher kept drawing his attention to the rules and conventions that applied to music; Richard insisted they were unnecessary. Beethoven disregarded all rules with magnificent impartiality, and what was good enough for Ludwig van Beethoven was good enough for Richard Wagner.

Young Wagner was now such a slave to music that he no longer bothered to attend school. Instead he was listening to what was supposed to be the extravagantly incomprehensible Ninth Symphony of Beethoven. He was so enchanted by it that he copied it out and also produced a simplified version for the pianoforte.

There was a brief interlude in 1830 when he forgot music and became interested in a popular rebellion that had attracted the students in Saxony. He actually played an active part in raids on gaols and local brothels, releasing prisoners from the former and surprising shame-faced bigwigs in the latter. It was an exciting period while it lasted, but the municipal guards and soldiers soon stepped in and the insurrection petered out.

Wagner, then sixteen, was enrolled at the *Thomasschule,* but it was obvious that any form of regular education was intolerable to him. All he wanted was his beloved music. He studied the works of other musicians, read mediaeval legends and composed a revolutionary overture in B flat major. His *New Overture* was given a public performance under Heinrich Dorn at the theatre as an interlude. Although

Lenin speaking to the people (*top*). Under his leadership they overthrew the Kerensky Government in 1917 to create the first Communist state. – Jacob Epstein revolted "against convention, against the insincerity of sculpture in England". Here (*above left*) he stands beside his sculpture *The Visitation* (now in the Tate). –

Bertrand Russell (*above right*), philosopher, mathematician and writer. At ninety-seven he is still an incorrigible rebel. In 1914, his protest against the war cost him his fellowship. Shortly before his ninetieth birthday he was sentenced to a week's imprisonment for publicly demonstrating against nuclear weapons.

Michael Collins, the great Irish patriot, (*top*, *marching left*). – The novelist D. H. Lawrence (*above left*) revolted against the "rational intellect", for a richer life. – Aneurin Bevan (*above right*), the Welsh miner's son who became deputy leader of the Labour Party.

the main theme of the *Allegro* was in four-time, Wagner introduced a startling innovation which is perhaps best described in his own words. "After every measure I had put in a fifth beat, quite independent of the melody, which interpolation was emphasized by a tap on the big drum." The persistent reiteration of the *fortissimo* thud excited first astonishment, then outbursts of laughter.

Unmoved by this hostile demonstration, Wagner placidly went on composing for a while and then once again he was gripped by the typical iconoclasm of the frustrated student. He and other revolutionary idealists formed a club in which they could voice their political protests, wear weird clothes and drink beer. None of these practices pleased the authorities, and when Wagner added absenteeism from lectures to his other "crimes", they did not hesitate to dismiss him.

After leaving school, Wagner matriculated at the ancient university of Leipzig, not with the intention of studying for a particular profession but simply in order to attend lectures on philosophy and aesthetics. Once more he found the illicit pleasures and excesses of student life irresistible. In his pursuit of sensationalism he even neglected his music, indulging in rowdy singsongs, duelling, orgies of beer-swilling and his latest vice – gambling.

Eventually he realized that he had to make a genuine effort to break away from the aimless life he was leading and to establish himself as a serious musician. Under the expert tuition of the organist Theodor Weinlig he acquired a thorough knowledge of harmony and counterpoint and developed an acute critical faculty. His compositions were being performed occasionally at the Gewandhaus. Although some of the critics still reacted sharply to Wagner's musical innovations, the public on the whole was gradually falling under his spell.

In 1832 Wagner wrote his first Symphony, a terse vigorous work, and then set out for the famed city of music, Vienna. He was disgusted to find that the Viennese preferred Johann Strauss to Beethoven, so he did not stay very long. Filled with righteous indignation, he made for Prague where several of his compositions were performed by the director of the *Conservatorium*. He also tried his hand at writing a libretto for his first opera, *Die Hochzeit,* and he asked his sister Rosalie to give her opinion about it. Rosalie frankly confessed that she found the whole thing dull and uninspiring. Wagner accepted her judgment and promptly ripped up the manuscript. By destroying something that he had created, he learned a valuable lesson. He could not tolerate inferior music any more than the meaningless routine of a humdrum existence. There was something in him that compelled him to rebel against mediocrity in all its manifestations.

His mother would have liked him to have stayed in Leipzig. But Wagner knew that the time had come for him to go out into the world and stand on his own two feet. At the age of twenty, then, he left for the quiet old town of Würzburg to take up the appointment of chorus-master at the local theatre. His beggarly salary worked out at ten florins a month, yet his duties were far from arduous, and consequently Wagner was free to concentrate on his own compositions.

The following year he was back in Leipzig, vainly trying to arrange a theatre performance for his new opera, *Die Feen.* The manager found it too revolutionary. This disappointment brought out all the young composer's rebelliousness. He voiced his resentment in the ensuing passage taken from an article he sent to a fashionable review: "We are not going to write like Italians, or Frenchmen, or even Germans. No more German stiffness, no more science, no more deceptive Fugues. What may be noble verities in Bach or Handel, we've got to look on as absurdities in ourselves. We've got to take our own times by the shoulders and pound them into shape."

He moved on to Magdeburg to take up a conductor's job. He would not have stayed there long if he had not met the handsome, elegant Wilhelmina Planer, one of the members of the theatrical company. Not only did he fall in love with "Minna"; he was also inspired by her singing to write an opera in two acts, *Das Liebesverbot,* in which he gave new values to vocal melody, action and scenic effect. The first performance, however, proved a lamentable fiasco. The company went bankrupt and Wagner was left almost penniless.

The Leipzig and then the Berlin theatre rejected *Das Liebesverbot,* but Wagner somehow managed to keep his head above water. For a time he pinned his faith on the manager of the Königstädter Theatre in Berlin who fed the composer with vague promises. Then, losing his patience, he set out in search of his "Minna". He finally caught up with her in Königsberg, and they were married on 24 November, 1836. Six months later, without any explanation, she packed her bags and left him.

Wagner pursued her to Dresden, effected a reconciliation and took her to Riga where he had been offered the appointment of First Music-Director of a new theatre. Still worried about all the debts that had been piling up since the Magdeburg disaster, he frenziedly set to work on his latest conception, *Rienzi,* an opera based on the novel by Bulwer Lytton. He became so engrossed with the project that when Minna deserted him again, this time running away with a business man, he was not excessively disturbed, although for form's sake he put on a show of grief.

He liked neither Riga nor its theatre manager, but his youthful vigour and lively personality earned him an encouraging popularity and the box-office receipts shot up accordingly. What *did* impress Wagner was the lay-out of the theatre; the pit was built in tiers, the auditorium kept dark and the orchestra placed in a sort of trench. Using the same formula later, Wagner was to be largely responsible for a large-scale architectural revolution in theatre construction.

Tiring of her lover, the mercurial Minna begged Wagner to overlook her temporary fall from grace and take her back as his wife. He readily forgave her. Until the summer of 1839 they settled down peacefully enough in the Faubourg de St. Petersburg. Wagner was beginning to weary of the provincial stage and to hanker after the amenities of a large capital. Paris was beckoning and he felt that in that city he would achieve the fulfilment of his ideals.

After a roundabout trip which included a week or so in London, the Wagners reached Paris in September and put up in the Rue de la Tonnellerie in a dingy out-of-the-way neighbourhood. He had been given a number of so-called useful contacts, but nobody was willing to help him. Even the boulevard theatres refused to employ him and his attempts at song-writing brought in a few francs only. His one source of comfort was the wife who had twice deserted him, for Minna looked after him with touching devotion.

His financial situation, however, steadily deteriorated until at last he had to depend on the results of visits to the pawnshops.

The spirit of revolt still stirred in him and he automatically rebelled against any notion that suggested his work was below standard. Better than anybody else he knew the true value of his art and nothing would induce him to prostitute his genius. He was confident that one day his run of ill-luck would end. Always sanguine, he moved into more expensive accommodation on the strength of a theatre director's promise. When the arrangements fell through, Wagner's struggles to make ends meet became really painful. On 28 October he was imprisoned for debt. Fortunately a friend came to the rescue and he was quickly released.

More determined than ever to press on with his musical rebellion, he carried on composing in the same revolutionary idiom, ignoring the rules and defying existing conventional patterns. Within seven weeks he completed the libretto and music for *The Flying Dutchman.* Then came some heartening news. *Rienzi* had been accepted for production in Dresden.

His character mellowed by his experiences in Paris, Wagner returned to Leipzig in the spring of 1842. After a short holiday in the Bohemian Hills he went to Dresden to attend the *Rienzi* rehearsals. Everybody in the theatre cooperated and Wagner worked like a demon. For once there were no unexpected delays, no last-minute hitches, no temperamental clashes. The curtain went up as scheduled on 20 October. *Rienzi* was performed before a packed house.

It was an unforgettable evening. From six o'clock until midnight the audience sat enthralled. The applause at the end was deafening. Although Wagner had made free with history, although his technique was novel, although the world he had created on the stage was strange and unfamiliar, *Rienzi* was an overwhelming success. Its comparatively young composer became famous overnight.

Early in the New Year his *Flying Dutchman,* a far superior work in Wagner's opinion, was also reasonably well received, but this time his unorthodox methods left the audience and some of the critics who were present frankly bewildered. "A chaos of sounds," wrote one reviewer. "A puzzle," was another's brief comment. "A step further and there would have been no music at all," quipped a third. A fourth, writing at greater length, had this to say: "Richard Wagner has ushered in a new era in music; an ebb and flow of violent volumes of sound which are seldom rounded off into a satisfying and comprehensible melody."

There could be no doubt that Wagner had created a new kind of opera. His theory was that the spoken word, even when accompanied by significant gestures, appealed principally to the intellect. To stir up the emotional side of human nature, music had to be added. By combining the two arts in what he called "music-drama" he eliminated the old distinction between recitative and aria.

Then again, he wrote the libretti for his operas himself. Not until the words were ready could the music evolve from the action. Unity was achieved by his use of the *leitmotiv,* a device by which different recurring musical themes could represent a character or an idea. The advantage was that once a musical phrase had been linked with a verbal passage describing a certain emotion, the orchestra was able to conjure up the same emotion simply by a repetition of that particular sequence of notes. In the same way the music could intensify and explain an actor's gestures. Consequently there were occasions when not even words were necessary. The orchestra on its own could recall feelings of joy or sorrow, anticipation or foreboding. Wagner's strength thus lay in his emphasis on the natural and his repudiation of the artificial. His music went hand in hand with the ups and downs of the dramatic situation. Deceptively simple though they were, his *leitmotivs* could be powerfully evocative.

Unrepentant and uncompromising, the rebellious composer offered the public his *Tannhäuser* on 19 October, 1845. The storm of criticism it provoked confirmed one fact: his audience was not yet ready for his revolutionary musical and dramatic theories. Press hostility was especially vicious. Wagner was disappointed but far from discouraged. The failure of *Tannhäuser,* however, had disastrous repercussions. For one thing it exacerbated the persecution complex he had been suffering from since the *Flying Dutchman* notices; for another, it made him more of a rebel than ever before and, worse still, revived his interest in the political unrest of the time. He started to associate with agitators, a move that did not escape the attention of his enemies. It was not long before theatrical managers, even in other towns, were reluctant to have dealings with him. Many people were beginning to look upon Wagner as a dangerous revolutionary.

Not even his most intimate friends realized to what extent Wagner was prepared to go as a rebel. He wanted an artistic revolution that would establish the excellence of his work, a political revolution that would eliminate bumbling officialdom and create a world fit for geniuses to live in, and an economic revolution that would enable him to meet his outstanding debts.

Although politics as such held little attraction for him, Wagner believed that the interests of art depended to a large extent on the strength or weakness of the current political system, and that reform in the widest sense would naturally lead to a Utopian environment in which art would flourish. Whatever his motives, at this period he decided to join in the fight for a New Germany; to involve himself more actively in the national campaign for better education, for better living and working conditions, for better government policies. He had to help his countrymen free themselves from the ancient abuses that were destroying civilization. He was, in short, ready for the 1848 Revolution.

The movement was born in Paris, but it soon spread to Germany and rumours of the popular unrest quickly reached Dresden. Wagner attended the sittings of the *Vaterlandsverein* or Patriotic Club, a notable political organization, and even delivered an inflammatory speech there to an audience of three thousand. Three suggestions of his which were put before the Frankfurt Assembly were that the old *Bundestag* should be dissolved and a new parliament elected, that Germany should adopt the same militia system as was operating in Switzerland, and that Germany should form an alliance with France. His revolutionary poem beginning "Hail, People of Vienna" appeared in the *Austrian Gazette,* while his leader advocating a republican monarchy was published in a Dresden newspaper. He boldly censured royalty, the nobility, the government, Communism and included a plea for universal suffrage.

Shortly after the outbreak of the Revolution, orders were issued for Wagner's arrest, so he very wisely slipped away to Weimar. He stayed at the Hotel Erbprinz where he was befriended by one of the guests, Franz Liszt, who eventually helped his fellow composer escape to Paris. There Wagner had hoped to publish a series of articles dealing with the prospects of art under the Revolution, but when he arrived in the French capital, all the excitement had died down and nobody was interested in his theories, so he moved on to Zurich. His wife joined him there and in October he became a citizen of the town.

The rebel was destined to remain in exile for the next ten years – probably the most important years of his life. The articles he had planned emerged in the form of a brochure, *Art and the Revolution,* in which Wagner acted as an unofficial mouthpiece for contemporary artists. He clearly had great faith in the Revolution and wanted to steer it in the right direction. His creed was that Art and Life are inextricably bound together in spite of superficial differences. He wrote: "Modern art is individualist, at enmity with the people and revolutionary in its tendencies. But out of that very revolution a new love shall spring up...."

Literary work kept Wagner busy until 1853, but he found time to develop his friendship with Liszt, to travel occasionally, to superintend a number of theatrical performances, and to fall in love with Jessie Taylor Laussot, the English wife of a wealthy French merchant. Then music again claimed his attention, and at a little watering-place not far from Zurich he prepared the framework of his superb masterpiece, *The Ring.* Richard Wagner outlined the project to Liszt in a letter: "My plan is to have three plays: (1) The Valkyrie, (2) Young Siegfried, (3) The Death of Siegfried, (later to be known as *The Twilight of the Gods*)". As an introduction to the whole he would write *The Theft of the Rhinegold* (which became simply *The Rhinegold*).

Resigned to the fact that the time was not yet ripe for the glorious revolution in which he had hoped to play a leading part, Wagner retired into a legendary world of his own devising. It was a formidable task he had set himself, but it was a labour of love. The theme was one with which he was only too familiar – the eternal battle for power and domination. He felt that when the record was completed all his personal problems would be solved. The gigantic tetralogy would help him to come to terms with himself.

Wagner made many friends in Zurich. Among them were Otto and Mathilda Wesendonck. Otto, a prosperous silk merchant from the Rhineland, was interested in Wagner's music; Wagner was interested in Otto's pretty wife. The merchant, unsuspecting at first, placed a villa at the composer's disposal and often gave him financial assistance when his debtors became too pressing. Inevitably, for a man of Wagner's temperament, his friendship with Mathilda developed into an all-consuming passion, and quite as inevitably Otto and Minna found out what was going on. Otto took his erring wife away to Piedmont, while Minna said she was going away and Wagner could lead his own life. Neither of these arrangements broke Wagner's volatile heart. He had been in search of a woman who would free him from servitude and Mathilda had filled the bill. As for his relationship with Minna, it had been deteriorating for several years. A separation would be a blessing for both of them.

His affair with Mathilda and his domestic upheavals had not affected Wagner's output. Apart from his work on the *Ring,* he had started to compose *Tristan and Isolde* and had roughed out a draft of *Parsifal.* In 1855 he had even visited England to conduct a series of eight concerts given by the Philharmonic orchestra.

Always in search of peace, Wagner tried Geneva, then Venice, returned to Switzerland (Lucerne), and 15 September, 1859, found him in Paris where he rented a small house in the Champs-Elysées district. He was running short of money and he was craving to be back in the public eye. His first intention had been to have *Tannhäuser* produced at the *Théâtre Lyrique,* but when the venture came to nothing he arranged instead to give three orchestral and choral concerts at the *Théâtre Imperial Italien.*

Although the opening concert was given to a packed and enthusiastic house, the newspaper critics were deliberately hostile or ironic. Their reports were shot with such comments as "All formulas and diagrams", "Music without melody" and "A revolutionary, a musical Marat". The effect of this spiteful press campaign was that relatively few Parisians attended the other two concerts. The reviewers were again vitriolic, but this time a group of prominent people came to the rescue. Thinking no doubt they were doing the composer a service, they persuaded the Emperor to demand a performance of *Tannhäuser*. Rehearsals began at once, money was no object, and the lavish production, in spite of one or two setbacks, was ready for presentation on 13 March, 1861.

The first act passed off smoothly enough, but laughter, hisses and catcalls, organized by the aristocratic Jockey Club, completely ruined the rest of the evening. The "Jockeys" repeated their attacks for the next two nights, so the work had to be withdrawn.

Not long after this unsavoury episode, Wagner was given permission to go back to Germany. He chose the city that had always appreciated him, Vienna, and there he had the pleasure of sitting among a wildly enthusiastic crowd of theatre-goers to watch a performance of *Lohengrin*. He was so touched by the occasion that when the curtains closed he expressed his gratitude both to the artists and to the audience.

Wagner's old friend Liszt arranged a grand reception in his honour in Weimar, and after visiting other friends and other cities, Wagner went back to Paris and spent the winter of 1861 writing the serenest of his creations, *Die Meistersinger*, which celebrates the famous craftsmen of Nuremberg. In the spring of the following year he hid himself away in the peaceful little town of Biebrich-am-Rhein to compose the music, returning to Vienna at the end of the year.

Then followed a brief friendship with Mathilde Maier, a lawyer's daughter, an even briefer visit from Minna, meetings with artists and actresses, occasional concerts and passing flirtations. One particular encounter made a lasting impression on the susceptible Wagner. At a concert in Leipzig where her husband was giving a piano recital, Cosima von Bülow, daughter of Franz Liszt, caught his roving eye and from that moment he was lost. He felt at once that they were made for each other.

But before he found happiness with Cosima, Wagner

passed through the most agonizing period of his life. To start with, his health was bad. Then again, despite his concert appearances in Germany and abroad, his financial affairs were in a sorry state. At one stage he owed 30,000 crowns and it was beginning to look as if he would end his days in the debtors' prison. He had sunk to such depths of despair that he was actually contemplating suicide.

Towards the end of April 1864 Wagner was lodging in a hired room in Stuttgart. His intention was to finish the first act of *Die Meistersinger* and afterwards take his own life.

Then a miracle happened. Quite out of the blue came a message from King Ludwig II of Bavaria inviting Wagner to Munich, where under the royal patronage he could work in peace and seclusion and enrich the world with new masterpieces. He would be provided with living quarters near the castle, the necessities of life and a small allowance from the privy purse. It seemed that Wagner's run of bad luck had come to an end. With royalty as his sponsor he could surely forget all his vicissitudes and pursue the ideals he had cherished for so long.

There were no strings attached to Ludwig's offer. A dreamer himself, he had been struck by the composer's vision of the future. He had understood that Wagner's revolutionary programme was concerned, not with the destruction of existing institutions, but with the regeneration of mankind. Besides, he genuinely appreciated his protégé's artistic aims.

Alas for poor Wagner, he was not allowed to enjoy the king's bounty and protection for very long. The honest citizens of Munich were soon telling each other that they had a revolutionary in their midst. All manner of disturbing rumours were spread by jealous musicians, poets and conductors. The newspaper critics renewed their venomous attacks, accusing the composer of trying to undermine the constitution, of driving a wedge between Ludwig and his faithful subjects, of stirring up revolution and preaching treason. Turning aside to moral issues, they even blamed him for allowing his wife to starve.

Towards the end of 1865 Ludwig was forced to choose between his loyal, affectionate people and the notoriously revolutionary Wagner. So powerful was the pressure put upon him that the king could do no other than terminate the unwritten contract between himself and his favourite. Sad and disillusioned, Wagner sought refuge in Switzerland, first at Vevey, then in Geneva. During that bitter winter he made his way across France as far as Marseilles. He was staying at the Grand Hotel when a telegram was handed to him. It had come from Dresden and it bore the simple message that his wife Minna had died of heart disease. After five years of separation, Wagner probably did not grieve overmuch.

His next move was to Geneva where he was joined by Cosima who had evidently decided to defy the conventions. At any rate they settled down together at "Tribschen", a large estate not far from Lucerne on the Lake of the Four Cantons. The lady's husband, obstinately refusing to believe that Cosima had been unfaithful to him, reluctantly agreed to a separation. As for a divorce, he was prepared to consider the possibility in two years' time on condition that she stayed with her father in Rome.

In the meantime Wagner finished *Die Meistersinger* and accepted an invitation from his former patron, King Ludwig, to return to Munich. On 21 June, 1867, the curtains parted to reveal the opening scene of this the latest development of the ageing composer's genius. For Wagner it was indeed a moment of triumph, for his revolutionary aims had finally been achieved after a struggle that had been waged over a period of at least thirty years. At last he could see the Germanic nations marching side by side under the protection of his art. At one stride the revolutionary had become an imperialist. He actually welcomed the outbreak of the Franco-German War in 1870 as yet another factor in the creation of the United Germany of his dreams.

He had another good reason for rejoicing. Von Bülow had divorced Cosima for desertion and she was now free to marry again. The wedding ceremony took place on 25 August in the Protestant church in Lucerne. The bride was twenty-three years younger than the groom, but she knew how to handle a husband who was temperamental, extravagant, impulsive and not the easiest of men to live with. She also knew that his creed was Love, and she was sensible enough to appreciate that she was not its only tenet.

It was Cosima who had conceived the idea of building a

festival theatre in Bayreuth as a lasting tribute to Wagner's musical achievements. The project was a tremendous one, for even in the design and construction of the building, Wagner was a revolutionary. Money came in slowly and at one stage it looked as if the whole scheme would have to be shelved, but fortunately the composer had a friend in court. Ludwig provided 300,000 marks from the royal treasury and the Festival Hall was ready for rehearsals to begin in the summer of 1875. A year later the first performance of *The Ring* was presented to a thrilled audience which included Wagner's old comrades and supporters and, after a lapse of eight years, his friend and benefactor King Ludwig II.

At the end of the third and last cycle, Wagner stepped on to the stage and addressed the audience. "What I should like to say to you," he said, "may be summed up in a few words, put into the form of an axiom. You have just seen what we can do. It is for you, now, to make up your minds to do it. If you do so, we shall have an art."

In the few years that remained to him, Wagner completed two other major works, *The Twilight of the Gods* and *Parsifal*. He travelled a good deal in Europe, gave occasional concerts, quarrelled with Ludwig, enjoyed an unprecedented success in Berlin when *Der Ring* was presented in its entirety for the first time outside Bayreuth. He even found time to record his revolutionary theories on art, religion and philosophy.

He was in Venice, the city he loved, when the end came. Torrential rain was streaming down the windows of the palace he had rented on the Grand Canal and the very date was ominous – 13 February. In the afternoon his overworked heart faltered, slowed down and stopped beating. The seventy-year-old creator of a revolutionary kind of opera was dead.

Chapter 15
Emmeline Pankhurst
1858–1928

Whereas Mary Wollstonecraft's was a lone voice crying in the wilderness, Emmeline Pankhurst was a cheer leader commanding a formidable team of protesters. Miss Wollstonecraft was in effect a one-woman resistance movement; Mrs. Pankhurst led a "monstrous regiment of women" into battle. Then again, the author of *A Vindication of the Rights of Women* relied on the pen as her weapon, backing up her literary assault by her own personal example. Mrs. Pankhurst, on the other hand, believed that violent action by *all* women was most likely to achieve positive results. Another fundamental difference between the two feminists lay in the fact that Mary Wollstonecraft concentrated largely on equality of education as the gateway to women's rights. Mrs. Pankhurst however launched her main attack against the political system that denied her sex the vote, but she was always ready to strike out in any direction when women's rights were at stake.

Eldest of the five daughters of a wealthy cotton manufacturer, Emmeline Goulden was brought up in Manchester in an atmosphere of bustling Liberalism. It was in that tough northern city that Doctor Richard Pankhurst, an inveterate rebel, had co-operated in the founding of the Women's Suffrage Society in 1865. Emmeline was only seven years old at the time.

Unlike Mary Wollstonecraft, Emmeline Goulden enjoyed all the advantages of an expensive education, and it was soon after her return to England from her finishing school in Paris that the slender, elegant, good-looking young lady of twenty first met the 40-year-old doctor and promptly fell in love with him. Recognizing each other's sterling qualities as ardent reformers, they were married at the end of a whirlwind courtship. Emmeline, indeed, had proposed that they should dispense with any form of wedding ceremony, but Doctor Pankhurst as a professional man could not afford to waive that particular convention.

Already interested in the question of women's suffrage, Mrs. Pankhurst started out, under her husband's wise direction, to read existing literature on the subject and at the same time to acquaint herself with the historical background of feminism. For the next few years she studied hard, although she was forced to forsake her books during her four confinements. Her son died in babyhood, but her three daughters, Christabel, Sylvia and Adela, survived and showed later that they had inherited some of their parents' fighting qualities.

Emmeline first manifested her involvement with her husband's political plans when she pressed him to stand as a parliamentary candidate in the Liberal camp. After he was defeated she persuaded him to move to London with a view to keeping his finger on the nation's pulse. There she was able to add her modest contribution to the family income by going into business. While Doctor Pankhurst laboured over the handful of briefs that came his way, his wife opened a fancy-goods shop in the West End. Between them they had sufficient money to rent a large house in Russell Square and at her *salons* her political education was considerably extended, for the Pankhursts entertained all shades of radical opinion. Their home also served as a meeting-place for the Women's Franchise League they had founded together in 1889.

The subsequent failure of the shop as a financial venture,

coupled with the fact that Doctor Pankhurst's health was suffering through overwork, led to the family's return to Manchester early in the 1890s. Despite his poor physical condition, Doctor Pankhurst was as determined as ever to set the world to rights, joining the Independent Labour Party in 1894 and, as the I.L.P. candidate for West Gorton, fighting and losing his third political campaign. Naturally Emmeline threw herself vigorously into all this socialist activity, persevering in her rebellion against her conservative upbringing. Once again she played hostess to her husband's friends and associates, most of whom belonged to the small, but energetic Labour movement.

It was during this period that she became a member of the Chorlton Board of Guardians and joined battle with the district workhouse officials. Infuriated by their antiquated views on the garments suitable for the little girls committed to their care, Emmeline realized that there was only one way to combat such inhumane conditions. Women were far more likely to insist on reforms where their own sex was concerned. Women, then, had to be given the vote.

At that stage in her career Emmeline had not yet visualized a political system in which *all* women would be entitled to figure on electoral rolls. She was thinking rather in terms of the middle and upper classes only. To extend the franchise to women from decent social *milieux*, in Emmeline's opinion, would breathe fresh life into the body politic and would revitalize the public conscience. Their moral and spiritual superiority alone would have a cleansing effect.

When her husband died in 1898, the family fortunes were at a low ebb. Consequently Emmeline took a job as Registrar of Births and Deaths in the Rusholme district of Manchester. With her sister Mary she had also opened a shop similar to the one she had run in London. The combined income from these two sources, supplemented by the amount she saved by moving into a smaller house, enabled her to pay off her creditors and cope with the family budget. Such leisure hours as were left she devoted entirely to politics and public work. An implacable enemy of the Liberal Party machine that had, in her eyes, been largely responsible for her husband's death, she opposed all government measures to which Doctor Pankhurst had taken or would have taken exception. Her main aim, however, remained unchanged. Everything else was secondary to the vital cause of women's suffrage.

Although Mrs. Pankhurst had joined the Socialist camp, she was under no illusions with regard to the Party's attitude towards votes for women. Two or three members sympathized with the feminists, but as for the rest she could expect no more support from them than she would get from either the Conservatives or the Liberals. As her daughter Christabel pointed out, there would be little advantage to be gained by backing *any* political party, for private members' bills would lead precisely nowhere. The best way to tackle the suffrage problem would be on a sex-war basis.

In 1903, then, Mrs. Pankhurst founded the Women's Social and Political Union. At the inaugural meeting she made the following declaration of intent: "We shall work not by means of any outworn missionary methods but by political action."

The first step would be to draw up a programme that would appeal to all working-class women. Once the crusade was properly under way, whatever government was in power would be compelled either to give serious consideration to the claims of the "suffragettes" or to lose face by refusing to do so. The odds were that no party could afford to ignore a vast body of women clamouring for "immediate enfranchisement".

For the next two years Mrs. Pankhurst, with her family solidly behind her, conducted a vigorous propaganda campaign. She built up a formidable team of lecturers who addressed meetings up and down the country, winning recruits for the W.S.P.U. and preparing the ground for the work that lay ahead. As the leader of all this agitation, Mrs. Pankhurst soon found her commitments so burdensome that she was obliged to resign her registrarship in order to work full time for the Union. For her services she was paid a modest four guineas a week, plus incidental travelling expenses. The W.S.P.U.'s car was placed at her disposal.

Under her capable direction the movement steadily gained strength and momentum, but no significant advance was made until the suffrage issue was debated in the House in 1904. Although the Bill was passed by a fairly substantial majority, parliamentary procrastination ensured that it never reached the Statute Book. In the year following, another Bill, this time advocating that in all acts referring to voting qualifications, the general term "man" should be deemed to include both sexes, was sabotaged by M.P.s deliberately wasting time on a preceding question concerning rear lights on carts.

Incensed by such scurvy treatment, Mrs. Pankhurst took immediate reprisals. She led her supporters outside the House and started an open-air demonstration. Prompt intervention by the police ensured that the affair was given the minimum of publicity, but this minor "rebellion" marked the beginning of a new phase in the battle of the sexes. It was Mrs. Pankhurst's first act of militancy and thereafter her followers were transformed into a real fighting unit. Their brief clash with the forces of law and order achieved nothing, but the suffragette leader was quick to recognize its possibilities. By organizing more effective protests of a similar nature, she could at least draw people's attention to what was clearly a monstrous social injustice. Since a rational approach had failed, she would use every means at her disposal to rouse the public conscience.

With a General Election imminent, Mrs. Pankhurst contented herself with desultory campaigning. She was present, for instance, at the Free Trade Hall, Manchester, on 31 October, 1905, when Winston Churchill was addressing the electorate as a Liberal Party candidate. One of her followers demanded point-blank, "If you are elected, will you do your best to make women's suffrage a government measure?"

Not only did the question remain unanswered; the suffragettes were unceremoniously removed and several were arrested when they attempted to state their case outside the hall. Faced with the alternative between fines or prison, they chose the latter, welcoming the inevitable newspaper accounts as free publicity for their cause.

After the Liberal landslide in 1906, the Manchester suffragettes staged a mass demonstration in London at the Caxton Hall, and Mrs. Pankhurst headed a protest march on a wet and windy day to the House of Commons to ask why there had been no mention of women's suffrage in the

King's Speech. The indefatigable lady's next move was to disrupt procedure in the House by shouts of "Divide! Divide!" from the Ladies' Gallery. She and her band of rebels kept up their chanting until they were forcibly ejected. There were no arrests on that occasion, but the incident did not pass unnoticed by the reporters present.

The suffragettes were evidently warming up to their work. Within the space of a few days, public order was threatened first by yet another march (from Hyde Park to Exeter Hall in the Strand), and then by a "Women's Parliament" summoned and presided over by Mrs. Pankhurst at the Caxton Hall and followed by a militant procession from the Hall to the House of Commons. Obviously acting under orders, the police barred the route near Westminster Abbey and urged the demonstrators to turn back. The women, not to be diverted, pressed on until the arrival of mounted police forced them to break ranks. After a long and bitter struggle in which a number of the marchers were punched and pummelled, some women were arrested and the remainder dispersed. The suffragettes had indeed been routed, but in a sense the movement had gained considerable ground. Police brutality had come as a shock to all those who had watched the unequal contest and highly coloured newspaper stories won a great deal of sympathy for the losers. Not only the government but also the whole country was now aware that the question of women's suffrage could not be shelved much longer.

Spurred on by Mrs. Pankhurst, the militants kept up their protests and demonstrations, their marches and their counter-marches, continually harassing and embarrassing the obstinate politicians who were denying them the vote. Arrests were more frequent, but in the relentless war they were waging imprisonment was accepted as a calculated risk. Mrs. Pankhurst and her supporters simply mocked at deterrents and refused to be suppressed. After every battle they licked their wounds and returned to the attack. Thwarted in one direction, they would strike out in another. Rallying to the slogan "Keep the Government out", they were soon showing their claws at by-elections.

At open-air meetings Mrs. Pankhurst and other leaders made inflammatory speeches denouncing the Liberal Party programme and urged electors to give their votes to men who were in favour of women's suffrage. Moreover, the pressure they brought to bear was not without effect. In several constituencies Liberal candidates trembled for their majorities. Nor were their apprehensions groundless, for at a by-election in Peckham a Conservative won the previously government-held seat.

Mrs. Pankhurst's fame as a rebel was rapidly spreading. At one of her meetings in Yorkshire, for example, she was called upon to address an audience of about a hundred thousand. Whatever she said or did was news. She certainly stepped into the limelight in 1908 when she led a deputation to the House of Commons with a view to a confrontation with the Prime Minister. She was arrested and sentenced to six weeks' imprisonment. Her observations on the experience indicate to what extent she had flung herself into the conflict. She wrote: "My first sensations when the door was locked upon me were not wholly disagreeable. I was desperately weary, for I had been working hard, perhaps a little too hard, for several strenuous months. . . . I was glad to throw myself on my hard prison bed and close my eyes."

Later in the year there was further convincing evidence of Mrs. Pankhurst's drawing power. A crowd of 500,000 gathered in Hyde Park to watch her organize a typical suffragette demonstration. It was a memorable occasion for the movement as the women were displaying their colours of purple, white and green for the first time.

It was during this period that Mrs. Pankhurst must have decided to increase the pace, for in the autumn she was back in gaol for inciting the public to co-operate with the suffragettes in a physical attack on the House of Commons. The three months she served struck her as being a modest price to pay for the wealth of publicity this particular exploit earned for itself. Her incarceration certainly did not curb her rebellious spirit. Within six months of her release she was again in the hands of the law. Her offence was a serious one. Having talked her way into the House of Commons, she slapped the face of a police inspector who informed her that the Prime Minister refused to see her.

Her jubilation knew no bounds after the General Election of 1910 when the Liberal Party lost a hundred seats. Her claim, however, that the swing away from the government was largely due to the efforts of the suffragettes had little foundation. No doubt the insurgent women had influenced the voting to a certain extent in some constituencies, but many other factors had contributed to the Liberal decline. In any event, the changed political structure, with two more or less equal parties constantly jockeying for position, was no matter for rejoicing as far as women's suffrage was concerned. In her blind hatred of the Liberal Party, Mrs. Pankhurst had failed to realize that many of its members were broadly sympathetic towards an extension of the franchise to include both sexes.

In pursuing her programme of militancy, Mrs. Pankhurst lost not only much of the support she had already won within the government; she also alienated many of the less aggressive suffragettes, some of whom broke away from the W.S.P.U. to form a separate group. They felt that her violent methods carried rebellion too far. Later on, when Mrs. Pankhurst resorted to attacks on property, two of her staunchest allies, Mr. and Mrs. Pethick-Lawrence, withdrew from the movement, but not even their defection could shake Emmeline's inflexible purpose. Her uncompromising comment reveals the fanaticism that possessed her: "The W.S.P.U. is simply a suffrage army in the field. It is purely a volunteer army, and no one is obliged to remain in it. We declared that we would wage war not only on all anti-suffrage forces, but on all neutral and non-active forces. Every man with a vote was considered to be a foe to women's suffrage unless prepared actively to be a friend."

Mrs. Pankhurst's militancy may not have been responsible for the drift away from Liberalism, but the vigour and persistence with which she conducted her campaign unquestionably brought suffrage into the political limelight. The subject was debated at length in the House and prominent M.P.s of all parties were drawn into the argument. The fundamental importance of the issue was generally recognized; the only danger was that the Cabinet, reacting to suffragette breaches of the peace, would lose patience and deliberately procrastinate.

Guerrilla warfare continued according to pattern, with Mrs. Pankhurst's shock troops hammering away on all fronts and the government gradually tightening their defences. That the situation was deteriorating emerges from

Mrs. Pankhurst's address to her forces on 16 February, 1912: "We don't want to use any weapons that are unnecessarily strong. If the argument of the stone, the time-honoured, official, political argument, is sufficient, then we will never use any stronger argument. And that is the weapon and the argument that we are going to use next time."

Within a fortnight bands of determined suffragettes, armed with hammers, went out on a window-smashing spree in Piccadilly Circus, Regent Street and Oxford Street. Mrs. Pankhurst herself and two of her lieutenants took a taxi to Downing Street and hurled stones at the windows of the Prime Minister's residence. A few days later more shop windows were smashed, this time in Kensington. Of the two hundred and odd women who were arrested and sent to prison, many started a hunger-strike and had to be forcibly fed, but for once the public had little sympathy with their sufferings.

Mrs. Pankhurst, however, was soon on the warpath again. Not only did she incite her followers to try their hands at arson; she also arranged for two bombs to go off in Lloyd George's new house near Walton Heath golf course. As a consequence she was tried at the Old Bailey and there, in a masterly speech from the dock, she traced the evolution of the women's suffrage movement and asserted that the evils ravaging civilization would never be removed until women were given the vote.

Thereafter, until the outbreak of war in 1914, the acknowledged Queen of the Suffragettes was in and out of prison with monotonous regularity, but nothing could quell her insuppressive spirit. She saw to it that buildings were fired, windows smashed, bombs planted, valuable pictures slashed in art galleries. She infuriated politicians and antagonized public opinion, but she achieved her aim. Everybody was so interested in her exploits that no one was allowed to forget the cause for which she was fighting.

Nobody was surprised when Emmeline Pankhurst ordered a "Cease Fire" shortly after the war started. As loyal Englishwomen, she and her army of militants were eager to operate on the national front. Emmeline's abundant energy was channelled into patriotic activities and her slogan was changed almost overnight from the Right to

Vote to the Right to Serve. With the menfolk fully occupied in their country's defence, women at last had an opportunity to prove that they could keep the wheels of commerce and industry turning. They told themselves they could always resume their crusade after victory was won.

Before the war ended, however, the Electoral Reform Bill became law and all women were given the right to vote at the age of thirty and upwards, a circumstance that reduced Mrs. Pankhurst to the status of a rebel without a cause. She could not even fight for women's entitlement to become M.P.s, for in November 1918 another Bill enabling women to stand as election candidates was approved by both Houses. Then, in 1928, the year of her death, came the greatest success of all – votes for women at twenty-one.

By that time the woman who had "discovered, stimulated, and through her personal initiative, harnessed for action, the Spirit of Revolt" was a frail old lady of seventy, but as she sat in the Ladies' Gallery on the day the Bill had its Second Reading in the House of Commons, she must have known a deep and abiding satisfaction. Although she had worn herself out in pursuit of an ideal, her rebel spark had quickened into such effective action during her lifetime that Mrs. Pankhurst's final victory had been inevitable.

Chapter 16
Lenin
1870 – 1924

Vladimir Ilyich Ulyanov, later to be known as Lenin, was born in the town of Simbirsk on the Volga at a time when Russia was seething with discontent and a revolution was inevitable. Already for about fourteen years the vast backward state had been copying such capitalist countries as Britain, Germany and France. The Tsar Alexander II had belatedly abolished serfdom in 1860. An educated but politically inexperienced middle class, inspired by what they had read about socialism, working-class movements, trade unions and co-operative societies, were becoming more and more critical of the Tsar and his government. Outbreaks of terrorism and violence bred repressive measures, very often directed against the Liberal reformers who were trying to eliminate the conditions in which revolution thrived.

It was in this atmosphere of conflict that little Vladimir spent his formative years. His father was employed in the educational service of the Province of Simbirsk; his mother came from land-owning stock, although her father was a professional man, a doctor named Berg. Altogether they had six children, three boys and three girls, all of whom were at one time or another caught up in the tangled web of revolutionary thought and activity. In fact, one of the determining factors in Vladimir's life was the execution of his eldest brother for the part he played in the unsuccessful attempt on the life of Alexander III.

The boy was still attending the Simbirsk High School when his brother was marched to the scaffold. The execution was something he never forgot, but it did not prevent him from continuing to study the Marxist, Socialist and revolutionary literature in which he was already reasonably well versed. He put in another year at school, coming first in his final examinations and winning the gold medal. When he left he had picked up more than a sound knowledge of academic subjects. He had also learned two valuable lessons: that isolated terrorist acts were not likely to achieve very much, and that the workers' only satisfactory method of seizing power was by first gaining control of the nation's economy. Then again, he had made a point of talking to the inhabitants of Simbirsk whenever the opportunity presented itself and had acquired some insight into the thoughts and emotions of peasants and workers.

In 1887 he was enrolled as a student at Kazan University with the intention of studying law. He realized immediately that many of his fellow students were the very stuff of rebellion. They came from poor homes where they had suffered all manner of privations. A judicious word here and there, cryptic references to governmental abuses, a few revealing facts and figures, and they were soon convinced that they were little better than slaves, hounded and ground down by a select group of moneyed idlers who jealously guarded their own rights and privileges. With such a firebrand on the premises, it is not surprising that the peace of Kazan University was shattered by protesters and demonstrators shortly after Vladimir's arrival. It is even less surprising that the young revolutionary was named as one of the ring-leaders and sent down. His university career had lasted exactly four weeks.

Banished to the country, he still pursued his law studies, but kept in touch with Marxism and those who professed it when he was allowed to return to Kazan in 1889. As an external student attached to St. Petersburg University, he read all the set books and followed the prescribed course and succeeded in passing the law examination that qualified him as a barrister. He practised in Samara, acting as defence counsel in a number of trials, but he was by no means enamoured of his chosen profession. He was far more interested in the teachings of Marx and in how to propagate them, first of all in Russia and subsequently throughout the world.

He decided to launch his Marxist campaign in St. Petersburg. Legal work claimed him in the beginning, but when his commitments as a barrister encroached upon the time he believed should be devoted to his political activities, he abandoned the law in order to concentrate exclusively on the coming struggle. He had already dashed off pamphlets and theses, and was rapidly building up a reputation as a socialist propagandist. He was also meeting prominent Marxians, including his future wife and collaborator, Nadezhda Konstantinova Krupskaya.

In 1894 Vladimir had become one of the leading controversialists among the Social Democrats. Wherever he went he stirred others to revolt by talking of his own personal rebellion against the Tsar's conservative policies, against the rich nobles and landowners, against those who wished to compromise, against misguided revolutionaries who were on the wrong tack, and even against the moderates in his own party. Because of police spies everything had to be done secretly, very often under cover of darkness. Vladimir's pamphlet *The Friends of the People,* for instance, in which he clearly set out in manuscript form the aims of his organization had to be circulated by hand. Care, too, had to be exercised in the distribution of his other broadsheets, such as *The Law of Fines, On Strikes* and *On Industrial Courts.*

The following year Vladimir was taken ill, so he persuaded the authorities to let him go abroad to recuperate. Once he had crossed the frontier, he forgot his ill health in the excitement of meeting the leaders of Russian Social Democracy in exile. He talked with Plekhanov, Axelrod and members of the *Deliverance of Labour* group. He chatted with Berlin factory workers, collected a trunk filled with illegal literature in Switzerland, and returned to

St. Petersburg bursting with new ideas and plans for the future.

Shortly afterwards he was responsible for building up a vitally important propaganda outfit called the *Union for the Liberation of the Working Class* and followed this up with extensive preparations for printing a clandestine newspaper which was to be called *The Workmen's Cause.* The first edition was scheduled to be ready for issue in December, but the police got wind of the project and rounded up the staff. Vladimir, who was picked up with the others, was sent to prison.

During his imprisonment, by an elaborate system of codes and invisible inks, he was able to correspond regularly with his supporters and friends. He also began work on his book *The Development of Capitalism in Russia.* For the best part of a year he was kept in solitary confinement, and then, in accordance with Russian legal procedure, his sentence was pronounced. Considering the serious nature of his "crime", his punishment was not excessively severe. He was banished for three years to Siberia.

He was sent to the village of Shushenskoya in the Yenisei province in eastern Siberia. By pretending to be his fiancée, Krupskaya who had shared so much of his revolutionary work in St. Petersburg managed to join him in his exile. They were married in 1898, entering on a husband-wife relationship that was to endure without friction for the next 26 years.

To help pass the time in Shushenskoya, Vladimir hunted, skated during the winter frosts, played chess and gardened. He read a great deal, especially philosophical works, completed his book on Russian capitalism, and in collaboration with his wife translated the Webbs' *History of Trade Unionism.* Not for one moment did he forget that he was a working-class leader. He preached rebellion to his fellow exiles and was never out of touch with the movement generally. If the authorities thought that exile was going to cool Lenin's revolutionary ardour, they were clearly in for a surprise when he returned to the main stream.

It was during his stay in Shushenskoya that, following the usual practice of revolutionaries, he assumed the name of Lenin.

When his exile ended in February 1900 Lenin was not

allowed to go back to St. Petersburg, so he made for Pskov. He had not been there long when his superiors in the party revived the idea of a clandestine newspaper, but this time they proceeded with caution. It was too dangerous to print it in Russia, so they arranged for Lenin and two of his comrades to get out of the country and establish contact with Plekhanov who was then in Switzerland. Between them they could devise a scheme whereby the party organ could be published abroad and then smuggled into Russia.

In the beginning everything went according to plan. Lenin and Plekhanov got together, pooled their resources and eventually agreed that the newspaper would be printed in Munich largely under Lenin's direction. It was to be called *Iskra* ("The Spark") and at the same time there would be a companion paper Zarya ("The Dawn"). The former would present the Marxian interpretation of the Revolution, while the latter would concentrate on the theoretical aspects of socialism. Lenin's wife was to act as editorial secretary.

Thanks to a spate of contributions from Lenin and Krupskaya's indefatigable efforts as circulation manager, the first number of *Iskra* came off the Munich presses towards the end of the year. From their little house in a Munich suburb, Lenin and his wife built up a secret communication network that enabled them to deliver copies of "The Spark" to various distributing points inside Russia. Lenin's revolutionary message was getting through to the people. More important still, although he was so far away from the scene of operations, Lenin himself had become a central figure in the Russian Socialist movement. When the day of rebellion dawned, the masses would undoubtedly turn to him as their natural leader.

It came as a cruel blow to Lenin when in 1902, just at a time when the underground organization behind the publication and distribution of *Iskra* had reached a peak of efficiency, the Munich branch had to be shut down. The printers regrettably decided that the enterprise was too dangerous. The Russian editorial board discussed the situation and by a majority vote London was chosen as a suitable alternative to Munich. Consequently, in the spring of 1902 Lenin and his wife moved to their new location in Holford Square, between the British Museum and Highgate cemetery. In the reading-room of the Museum was all the literature Lenin needed to further his revolutionary career; in the cemetery was the grave of his great hero, Karl Marx. He started to learn English (partly from books and partly by listening to the Hyde Park orators). He also found time to study the rich variety of London life and was particularly struck by the existence side by side of the "two nations", the "haves" and the "have-nots".

Although he was in poor health, Lenin could not afford to relax, for apart from all his other work he was expected to draw up the programme for the Party Congress. This important gathering was supposed to take place in a large flour warehouse in Brussels, but the Belgian police were showing more than an ordinary interest in the proceedings, so the fifty-odd delegates converged on London.

When the discussions began, it became evident that the main issue boiled down to a question of method. Some were in favour of a leisurely, orderly evolutionary development towards political and economic reforms. Others, led by Lenin, believed that changes could be effected only by a mass movement of the people guided by a small group of competent professional revolutionaries. As far as Lenin was concerned, it was no use mincing words. The terms "revolution" and "class war" meant precisely what they said. Any attempt to equate the policy of the proletariat with that of the liberal *bourgeoisie* would lead only to disaster. The natural allies of the proletariat were surely the peasants. "The cause alone was worthy" was Lenin's slogan, and those who thought otherwise would be well advised to leave the movement.

After the Congress of July and August 1903 had accepted the views of Lenin (and Plekhanov) by a very narrow majority, came the historic split of the party into Bolsheviks (Majority) and Mensheviks (Minority). The former supported Lenin's uncompromising revolutionary tactics; the latter wanted to collaborate with the liberals.

Then, in 1905 events in Russia combined to create the revolutionary atmosphere for which Lenin had been waiting. First of all the Tsar had foolishly plunged the nation into the Russo-Japanese War and had suffered a series of ignominious defeats. Secondly, frank expressions of dissatisfaction were finding their way into the Russian press.

Thirdly, the Tsar's troops had fired on a peaceful demonstration of petitioning citizens heading for the Winter Palace and had killed at least two hundred of them.

When news of local risings filtered through to Lenin from different areas of Russia, he knew exactly what he had to do. The people were in the right frame of mind and ripe for revolt, but not even a rebellion *en masse* could hope to succeed against armed and disciplined troops. The insurrectionists had to be supplied with weapons, leaders had to be trained, the Tsar's soldiers had to be diverted from their misplaced allegiance to an oppressive régime.

Lenin who was always thorough pored over volumes dealing with military techniques and strategy. He also had a visit from Father Gapon, the man who had led the petitioners to the Winter Palace, and from him he obtained detailed information about the massacre. Furthermore, the belligerent Father was able to help Lenin in connection with supplying the Fighting Committee of Bolsheviks with arms and ammunition.

In November 1905, just after a successful general strike, Lenin made up his mind to return to his native land. Travelling by way of Stockholm, the generally accepted leader of the Social Democrats arrived in St. Petersburg. He started off by living with his friends, but when he discovered that the police were keeping him under constant surveillance, he moved into less conspicuous quarters. His twin aims remained unchanged: to persuade more and more industrial workers to join the movement, and to establish a firm link between proletariat and peasantry.

It was about this time that the Soviet of Workers' Deputies was inaugurated. This new organization soon became the symbol of working-class power and Lenin was not slow to recognize its value to the cause. After attending some of its meetings in disguise, he was better able to assess its capabilities. He was, in fact, so impressed that he advised many of his supporters to take an interest in its activities.

Lenin now felt that it was the moment to take up his position at the very centre of the growing rebellion – Moscow. He could see at once that the citizens were spoiling for a fight. Among all the popular discontent and disturbances, the government was watching events with mounting apprehension. The rulers of Russia knew only too well that they could rely neither on the army nor the navy. After the calamitous war with Japan, the national debt had become an intolerable burden. A loan from France had helped to bolster up the tottering economy temporarily, but the Tsar and his ministers were uncomfortably aware that they could not afford to pay for all the emergency measures that would be necessary to crush the rebellion when it came.

The opening gambit was a declaration by the Soviet of Moscow workers in favour of a general strike. The strike leaders expected that the army would be called in to deal with the crisis, but they were confident that most of the soldiers were on their side. When the anticipated counter-moves were made, their next step was an armed rebellion. There was a certain amount of sporadic shooting and a number of home-made bombs were thrown, but the rising lacked proper direction and cohesion. When the Tsar's artillery began to fire shells into the crowd, the workers faltered, broke ranks and all was confusion. Nevertheless they managed to maintain a sort of disorderly resistance for the space of five days before they were forced to admit defeat. They had made no material gains, but their brief battle had left them richer in experience. They would not make the same mistakes next time.

When at last order was restored, the Tsar and his minister Stolypin embarked on a punitive campaign that the Russians never forgot or forgave. A thousand workers were executed without trial and 70,000 were thrown into prison. Another 14,000 had been killed in the scattered risings. It was a heavy price to pay, but Lenin was far from discouraged. For one glorious moment the people had been within an ace of snatching political liberty, and they had known the thrill of hitting back at their oppressors. All that was necessary now was a short period of recuperation before they made their second bid for freedom.

So the incorrigible rebel went back to St. Petersburg to continue with his underground work and to make preparations for a full-scale revolution. He kept up the pressure until the police net began closing in on him and it was becoming increasingly difficult to find a safe refuge in the Russian capital. Compelled to flee at last, he made his way to Finland. He was far enough away from the Russian scene to feel reasonably secure, but he was near enough to maintain regular contact with his supporters and to travel to St. Petersburg or Moscow on matters of extreme urgency. He was also able to preside over the fourth congress of the Bolshevik party in Stockholm in April 1906 when two major decisions were made: that a new paper, the *Volna,* should be started as soon as possible, and that party members should in future take part in the elections to the *Duma,* the first representative parliament granted by the Tsar. Lenin at first was against the second proposition, urging his followers to boycott the institution, but subsequently he changed his tactics and advised them to co-operate.

The police were now on Lenin's trail in Finland, so he was again driven to take evasive action. On 20 January, 1908, he arrived in Geneva where he became embroiled in a philosophic dispute with those party members who wanted to revise the Marxist theories on which his whole revolutionary policy was based. Lenin's ruthless analysis of the reformers' false position appeared in his book, *Materialism and Empirio-Criticism.*

In 1912, at a special Congress in Prague, the Bolsheviks finally disowned the Mensheviks who had advocated the liquidation of the "underground" party. During that same year several events occurred in Russia that suggested to Lenin a new wave of rebellion was sweeping across the country. In the Lena goldfields the police had shot about two hundred strikers in cold blood; workers everywhere were beginning to lay down tools; social and industrial unrest was spreading. Lenin had little doubt that the Tsar's day of reckoning was not very far away. The better to keep his finger on the political pulse, he transferred his headquarters to Poronin near Cracow and within walking distance of the Russo-Polish border.

Lenin's revolutionary interests inside the country were well taken care of when half a dozen Bolshevik Deputies were elected to the *Duma.* Together the six delegates formed a small but useful independent group that could operate under Lenin's direction. Quite apart from this close link with the *Duma,* the communication network reached out to every nerve centre in Russia, and the underground information service was keeping Lenin up-to-date with all branch activities. Conversely he was able to transmit to the workers and peasants his constantly reiterated message that the only answer to their problems lay in the elimination of the Tsar.

On the outbreak of the 1914-18 war, Lenin was rudely jerked out of his Socialist dreams. According to his theories, the Socialists of Europe should have protested against the war and refused to fight, brother against brother. Instead, industrial and agricultural workers everywhere were lining up behind their respective rulers. The powerful Socialist movement in Germany supported the government's war aims one hundred per cent. But the bitterest pill Lenin had to swallow was the fact that the Russian proletariat responded immediately to the Tsar's appeal to their patriotism. To a man they put the needs of Holy Mother Russia before the high-sounding resolutions of the Second International.

Recovering quickly from the initial shock, Lenin set out to prove to the European Socialists that their patriotic fervour was quite misplaced. He withdrew to Switzerland and issued a flood of pamphlets in which he carefully and concisely analysed the causes of the war, showing that the capitalist imperialists were responsible and that the ones who would suffer most, whether they were on the winning or the losing side, would be the working classes. It was the solemn duty of all men, irrespective of nationalities, to rise up in their thousands and insist on a cessation of hostilities.

Lenin's propaganda certainly had its effect on the Russian people. They blamed the Tsar for joining the Allies; they blamed his wife for being *against* the Allies; they blamed the malign influence of Rasputin. As the war dragged on, they were affected by stories of what was happening to Russian soldiers at the front. They resented the extra efforts they were called upon to make in order to step up arms production. The Soviet of Workers' Deputies enjoyed a new lease of life, whipping up local feeling and encouraging strikes, first in the munitions factories and then generally. And behind these manifestations and demonstrations, skilfully manipulating events to suit his own ends, lurked the arch-rebel Lenin. He had even used a European war to his advantage.

The murder of Rasputin came too late to help the Tsar,

just as the Tsar's abdication in favour of his brother, the Grand Duke Michael, came too late to save the situation. Within twenty-four hours Michael had also abdicated and authority lay in the hands of the *Duma*.

Lenin did not hesitate. Travelling across Germany, he reached St. Petersburg on 16 April, 1917. Plekhanov had already arrived and Trotsky was on his way. But it was their great commander the people wanted to see. He left the station and climbed on to an armoured car to address the huge crowd before moving on in triumph to the Bolshevik party headquarters, the Khesinkaya palace.

Some of his more tolerant comrades were not too enthusiastic about Lenin's immediate programme. Russia's participation in the war was to be considered as an imperialist blunder and the provisional government had to bring the soldiers home without delay. Lenin urged the "confiscation of all private lands; immediate merger of all the banks in the country into one general national bank; immediate placing of the Soviet of Workers' Deputies in control of social production and distribution of goods". He also insisted that the name of the party should be changed from Socialist to Communist. When a coalition government was formed on 18 May, Lenin promptly denounced it as useless on the grounds that it would neither get Russia out of the war nor further the revolutionary cause. What he envisaged was a republic of Soviets and "the abolition of the police, the army, and the bureaucracy". In short, he wanted the whole revolutionary process to be accelerated.

Meanwhile discontent was spreading among Russian soldiers and sailors. A number of front-line regiments were disbanded, because they refused to take the offensive; mutinous sailors at Sebastopol put their own officers under arrest; sailors elsewhere were demanding the resignation of Admiral Koltchak. And not satisfied with provoking the army and navy to mutiny, Lenin was also busy stirring up the peasants. He was making sure that his rebellious message was reaching military and civilians alike. Every day he would stride on to the balcony of the Khesinkaya palace to thunder out his impassioned exhortation: "Seize power and use it!"

Kerensky managed to boost the morale of the fighting services, but after the soldiers had made a notable advance they were exhausted and had no further desire to fight. In Petrograd (formerly St. Petersburg) there were riots and disturbances. The government had to find a scapegoat, so they picked on Lenin who had criticized them so harshly, and issued a warrant for his arrest on a charge of treachery. Before they could act, however, their quarry had escaped to Finland.

With the government divided and unstable, Lenin felt confident that this time nothing could go wrong. The Party was stronger than ever; the borough and city elections indicated that it enjoyed the support of the people; the peasants were on his side. He had once written: "When a revolutionary party has not the support of a majority either among the vanguard of the revolutionary class, or among the rural population, there can be no question of a rising." Both conditions, he could now claim, had been fulfilled. Why, in less than three months Party membership had almost trebled. Besides, the government as it was then constituted was totally ineffective. It had lost control of the military forces; it was unable to safeguard the nation's industries. Now, while the opposition was thoroughly demoralized, was the moment to strike.

Lenin assured his comrades that an armed insurrection was imperative. It was essential to fix the date and plan the details. Bolshevik propagandists were instructed to go out and talk to the workers and peasants. Trotsky, in his capacity of President of the Petrograd Soviet, was expected to countermand all orders emanating from the Provisional Government.

The date selected for the uprising was 7 November, the opening day of the all-Russian congress of Soviets. As the final touches were being given to the preparations, Lenin moved to the outskirts of the capital.

In the early hours of the morning, government troops were sent to suppress all Bolshevik newspapers. The Soviet reacted sharply by despatching *their* soldiers to sabotage the government press and to reopen their own. More soldiers marched into government buildings, meeting only the feeblest resistance. A printed proclamation informed the people that the Soviets had taken over from the Provisional Government. The new President was Lenin, with Trotsky as his Foreign Minister.

By the evening of the following day Lenin had already appointed his government and was in a position to outline his peace policy to the Congress of Soviets. Some historians have accused him of acting with immoderate haste, but he knew that if he was to carry out his vast programme of reforms, he needed peace quickly. The negotiations were left in the capable hands of Trotsky who under the circumstances was obliged to accept the terms put forward at Brest-Litovsk. The Germans had naturally demanded their pound of flesh, but Lenin had known all along that they would take full advantage of the situation. He had declared: "By prolonging the war . . . we unusually strengthen German imperialism, and the peace will have to be concluded anyway, but then the peace will be worse because it will be concluded by some one other than ourselves. No doubt that the peace which we are now being forced to conclude is an indecent peace, but if war commences, our government will be swept away and the peace will be concluded by another government."

The Brest-Litovsk peace treaty was certainly a humiliating document for the Russians to sign, but as one of their delegates said, surely in a flash of prophecy: "We do not doubt for a moment that this triumph of imperialism and militarism over the international proletariat will prove only temporary and transitory."

Although Lenin was opposed to excessive and unnecessary violence, the Tsar and his family were duly executed. It must also be remembered that many of the killings that followed the social upheaval were the work of anti-Bolsheviks who were using the Revolution as an excuse for all manner of crimes including looting and murder and private revenge. Not that the Bolsheviks were by any means against the use of force, but they believed with their leader that strong-arm methods were permissible only if they contributed to the creation of the new Russia. To quote Lenin's own opinion: "There has been no revolution, no epoch of civil war, in which there were no executions." On the other hand, for many of the wanton liquidations that followed the 1917 Revolution, he could find no justification. He had hoped for a period of peaceful reconstruction during which Russian miners, factory workers, builders and peasants would have pooled all their efforts and produced the ideal state. Unfortunately his hopes were never realized.

For the next two years Lenin and his supporters had their hands full dealing with attacks by counter-revolutionaries. Lenin himself was shot at in August 1918 by a female Social Revolutionary, but he recovered with his prestige enhanced and by the spring of 1921 his government was at last getting down to putting some of his economic and agricultural reforms into operation. Gradually, however, his physical health deteriorated and after a severe stroke (his third) in March 1923, he died at the beginning of the following year at the age of fifty-four.

Perhaps one of the strangest tributes to the rebel who had died forty years previously appeared in *Pravda* on 31 October, 1963. It said: "The radiant genius of the great teacher of the toilers of the world, V. I. Lenin, lights the path of mankind to Communism. In the preparation of the Programme, our party and its Central Committee constantly took counsel with Lenin and made their point of departure his brilliant ideas regarding the construction of socialism and communism. Therefore the Programme of the Soviet Communist Party is, with complete justification, called Leninist."

Chapter 17
Bertrand Russell
1872–

Philosopher, mathematician, writer and champion of humanity, Bertrand Russell was born on 18 May, 1872 into one of the oldest families in England. If heredity counts for anything, then any account of Bertrand Russell's rebellious nature must take into consideration the fact that his grandfather, Lord John Russell, fought a life-long battle for free trade, for free education and for Jewish emancipation, and that his father, Lord Amberley, also had a free-thinking outlook. It is furthermore relevant to add that after his parents and his grandfather died, as a small boy Bertrand became the responsibility of his grandmother with whose opinions he generally disagreed but who nevertheless wielded a tremendous influence over him.

Bertrand and his elder brother Frank were brought up in the aristocratic environment of Pembroke Lodge at Richmond. Their education had been entrusted to their puritanical grandmother, a lady who had very pronounced views on a variety of subjects including religion, politics, Home Rule for Ireland, and the British Empire. Abstemious and sparing in her diet, she was a strict disciplinarian. She provided governesses for her grandsons' formal instruction, but as far as Bertrand was concerned much of his knowledge was derived from the numerous history books in his grandfather's library. In addition to being a voracious reader the younger brother was fascinated by mathematics, but he was obliged to indulge his passion for figures clandestinely, for the eccentric old lady would not allow the governesses to teach either mathematics or philosophy to their young charges.

It is significant that in his wide reading Bertrand preferred the revolutionary Shelley to the more down-to-earth Gibbon or the bitterly satiric Swift. As he grew older he developed a genuine interest in religion, growing increasingly sceptical, until in the end he believed only in that which could be proved by experience. It is also worth noting that in those far-off days it was Frank who was the rebel. Bertrand was quiet, retiring and usually wrapped up in his own thoughts.

Because his grandmother was firmly opposed to boarding-school life, Bertrand had to rely on a private tutor to coach him in Greek and Latin with a view to getting him into Cambridge. Fortunately, when he sat for the entrance examination, he made a good impression on the eminent mathematician Alfred Whitehead who was able to introduce the young undergraduate to students of the same intellectual calibre and to ensure that he did not lack friends.

In the stimulating atmosphere of Cambridge, Russell soon came out of his shell. Although his principal subject was mathematics, he also yielded to the lure of philosophy. He loved to express his own ideas, to listen to the ideas of others and to exchange ideas with original thinkers. It was this passion for discussion that prompted him to become a member of an exclusive undergraduate society called "The Apostles". The group usually met at weekends when they were free to talk over their problems without interruption, sometimes pursuing elusive solutions until the small hours of the morning. It was a period of question and answer leading to knowledge, not only of the subjects under discussion but also of himself.

During Russell's Cambridge years his fundamentally rebellious nature was beginning to emerge. Once he had started to inquire beyond mathematics into the philosophy of mathematics, the orthodox approach of many of his tutors failed to satisfy him. After three years of mathematical studies, attracted no doubt by the colourful personalities – Keynes, Rutherford and Whitehead among them – who were transforming his university career into a perpetual voyage of discovery, he began to take interest in wider intellectual questions. When he went down in 1894 his inquiring mind was bent on a particular course – philosophy, with the emphasis on the philosophy of mathematics.

Cambridge had also given Russell the confidence and assurance he needed after being subjected to his grandmother's autocratic treatment. He was, however, still not sure of himself in the presence of young women. He overcame his shyness to a certain extent when he met Alys Pearsall Smith and promptly fell in love with her. He was no dashing Lothario, but his suit was meeting with a measure of success until his grandmother intervened. With her aristocratic outlook, she had obviously expected her grandson would have chosen his future wife from her own social *milieu.* She voiced her disapproval and was somewhat taken aback when Bertrand expressed his determination to marry the girl. It was probably the first time he had rebelled against the old lady's authority.

Eventually she was forced to compromise. She promised to review the situation after a short probationary period. Hoping that Bertrand would find other distractions and forget Alys, she arranged for him to go to Paris as an attaché to the British Ambassador.

She was chagrined to learn that for once she had miscalculated. Bertrand went to Paris, but it did not take him long to discover that he was not cut out for a career in the diplomatic service. His duties did not even remotely tax his intelligence and the social functions he had to attend seemed trivial and boring. So at twenty-two he handed in his resignation, shook the dust of Paris off his feet and returned to London and his beloved Alys whom he married in 1894.

His grandmother chose to regard Bertrand's behaviour as an act of rebellion. In her eyes he had broken faith with a long line of illustrious ancestors. Over the years she might have reconciled herself to the fact that he had "married beneath him", but she could never bring herself to accept his deliberate abandonment of a career that was eminently suitable for the grandson of Lord John Russell, third son of the Duke of Bedford and twice Prime Minister of England. On reflection it was far worse than rebellion. It was a betrayal.

After this painful family break, although philosophy still had first claim on his attention, Russell was attracted for a time towards politics. The only choice that existed lay between Conservatism and Liberalism and Russell's natural inclination was towards the latter, but like many educated people of those days he had given a good deal of thought to the political doctrines held by members of the Fabian Society. Founded in 1884, the Society already numbered among its supporters such distinguished intellectuals as George Bernard Shaw, H. G. Wells and the Webbs, all of whom subscribed to the Fabian principle of reforming mankind strictly "in accordance with the highest moral possibilities". The fundamental difference between Marxism and Fabianism, then, was one of method. Both systems wanted to change existing institutions, but whereas the Marxist believed in wiping the slate clean and starting afresh, the Fabian preferred to build a new world on the foundations of the old.

Russell, who appreciated these broad distinctions and who was looking for a system of political reconstruction that lay somewhere between the harsh radicalism of the one and the leisurely constitutionalism of the other, found the answer in Socialism. The Independent Labour Party, founded by Keir Hardie in 1893, undoubtedly had plenty to offer to one who could see that Marxism ultimately meant violence while Fabianism meant interminable delays.

Shortly after their marriage, then, the Russells went to Germany, and in Berlin Bertrand took the opportunity of examining the German Socialist movement at first hand. Thanks to his sound knowledge of German, he was able to follow the proceedings at meetings of the Social Democrats. Quickly realizing that there was nothing to be learned at those stormy gatherings, he turned to Marx's *Das Kapital* and the *Manifesto of the Communist Party*. In them, especially in the latter document, he found much food for thought. The rebel in him sympathized with the Manifesto's rejection of all conventional values. He, too, had no room for a religion and a morality based mainly on worn-out traditions. Instead of scrambling after pie in the sky, man should strip himself of his illusions and try to fashion a world where Reason was supreme.

When he got back to London, Russell delivered a series of lectures at the London School of Economics, expounding his views on German Socialism to students and to members of the Fabian Society. Later, in 1896, he published a book on the subject entitled *German Social Democracy*. Scorning sensationalism and wishful thinking, he presented objectively an exact picture of what was happening in Germany at that moment and he took a dispassionate look at what lay ahead. His arguments, invariably logical extensions of the known facts, were wholly convincing. His literary style could not be faulted. Language for Bertrand Russell had to reflect reality.

Despite his aristocratic background, Russell understood all the implications of poverty and was always ready to support those who advocated a more even distribution of wealth and property. It was the Socialists' concern for justice, for equality of opportunity and for social welfare that aroused his enthusiasm. On the other hand, as a Liberal by conviction, he was not prepared to go all the way with Marxism. He could see the inevitability of nationalization, but his logical mind objected to a political system that was in favour of nationalizing everything at one go. Nationalization, if it was to be successful, had to be introduced gradually over a period of years.

By and large Russell's experiences in Germany had taught him many valuable lessons. If socialism was to be the universal panacea for political ills, then before applying it as a practical programme, it was a case of "physician heal thyself". To begin with, there was too much banging of the big drum and far too much aggressive propaganda. Most of the Socialists he had come across in Germany were loud-mouthed, doctrinaire, intolerant fanatics, so enamoured of their own dogmas that they were blind to everything that was good in other political systems. Their arrogant assumption that because they were right everybody else must be wrong cut them off completely from progressive organizations elsewhere. In Russell's view it was the isolation they had brought upon themselves that would prove their undoing. He was right when he maintained that in the long run the German people would rather endure economic difficulties and submit to a military dictatorship then accept a political programme that had such little regard for religion, for the family, and for national feeling. Perhaps the Socialists in England would be warned in time and introduce their reforms in a manner that would not alienate possible sympathizers.

After spending an interesting three months in America on a lecture tour, Bertrand Russell settled in Sussex with the intention of concentrating on his philosophical studies. He also took a critical look at the writings of Hegel, Bradley and Leibniz, was present at the sittings of the international philosophical congress in Paris, and was busy putting the finishing touches to the first draft of his *The Principles of Mathematics.*

His mathematical research brought him into contact with his old friend Whitehead and they decided to write *Principia Mathematica,* a work that obviously would benefit if it was treated as a joint effort. Consequently they collaborated on the project from 1900 until 1910, Whitehead taking care of the mathematical aspect while Russell was the philosophical expert. Throughout the three volumes that eventually appeared, Russell's philosophical approach to mathematics is entirely revolutionary. His reverential attitude towards the subject was already apparent; an attitude he described later in *Mysticism and Logic* in the following terms: "Mathematics, rightly viewed, possesses not only truth but supreme beauty – a beauty cold and austere, like that of sculpture, without appeal to any part of our weaker nature, without the gorgeous trappings of painting or music, yet sublimely pure, and capable of a stern perfection such as only the greatest art can show."

Although his main concern was with *Principia Mathematica,* Russell occasionally interrupted his tremendous labours to dash off articles and reviews for scientific and philosophical journals, to dabble with politics once again, and to figure on public platforms as an advocate of Free Trade. He even had two shots at entering Parliament as a Liberal candidate, but he was defeated on both occasions. He would almost certainly have pulled it off in 1910, if the electorate had not been influenced by his revolutionary comments on religion.

Until the outbreak of the First World War, he lectured at Cambridge, wrote, visited friends and travelled abroad, both on the Continent and in America. During his stay in America he met T. S. Eliot with whom he was particularly impressed. Later in England Russell helped to get him started as a reviewer for philosophical journals. Then, in 1911 he separated from his wife. It took ten years before he could get a divorce. Meanwhile he had become friendly with the half-sister to the Duke of Portland, Ottoline Morrell, at whose home near Oxford he was often to be seen exchanging ideas with his witty hostess and her entertaining guests.

Before the 1914-18 war, Russell had always been of the opinion that his fellow men were reasonable human beings who could distinguish between good and evil. When he saw them massing in their millions for the sole purpose of exterminating each other, his whole being rose in instinctive revolt against such lunacy. In those highly emotional days, when peace was an ugly word, Bertrand Russell dared to stand up and openly denounce the war and the people who were waging it. So powerful were his anti-war feelings that he even urged patriotic Englishmen to put an end to the madness by voluntarily submitting to Germany.

Impervious to the danger that threatened all pacifist demonstrators, Russell appeared on public platforms up and down the country and fearlessly addressed hostile crowds on the folly and futility of war, stripping it of its false glamour and exposing it in all its brutality and savagery. He pointed out prophetically that neither side would gain a decisive victory. Crippled and exhausted, Germany and the Allies would call off hostilities, but as soon as they had recovered their strength they would again be at each other's throat. Russell wrote to the same effect in *The Labour Leader* and shocked everybody by joining the No-Conscription Fellowship. At a time when soldiers were heroes and conscientious objectors were cowards, Russell was looked upon as a traitor and a social outcast. One of the few places where he could rub shoulders with his own kind was the home of Ottoline Morrell whose kindness and hospitality in those troubled years were warmly appreciated by many intellectual pacifists.

Even at Cambridge, where a degree of toleration might have been expected, Russell was made to feel *persona non grata.* The authorities there were soon given an opportunity to deal with the rebel.

A youthful pacifist named Everett who refused to fight for his country was prosecuted and given two years' hard labour. Several members of the No-Conscription Fellowship were also arrested for distributing a leaflet condemning the vicious sentence. Russell promptly sent a letter to *The Times* in which he not only registered a strong protest, but also announced that he had written the leaflet. The result was that he, too, was charged and put in the dock. The proceedings were hushed up, but he was convicted and had to pay a fine of a hundred pounds. His appearance in court gave the Cambridge authorities the excuse they had been waiting for. They dismissed the "criminal" from his post at Trinity College.

The rebel in Russell was now thoroughly roused. From anti-war propaganda he turned to other matters that in his opinion needed reforming. In a series of trenchant articles he attacked marriage, government, religion and education. Encouraged by the publisher Stanley Unwin, Russell collected the articles together and had them published in 1916 in book form under the title *Principles of Social Reconstruction.* The surprisingly good sales of the volume led the author to pursue the literary career that was to bring him fame and fortune.

But after his dismissal from Cambridge and before his royalties started to come in, Russell was left without an income, so he arranged to tour the country as a lecturer. Although his subject, the philosophical basis of politics, seemed hardly likely to spread alarm and despondency, he was not allowed by the War Office to give lectures inside the specially protected coastal zones. He was still considered to be a dangerous character.

As the war was drawing to a close, Russell began to dissociate himself from the pacifist movement's activities. It was, however, typical of the man to choose such a moment for sending a startlingly outspoken contribution on post-war conditions to the *Tribunal.* In the article he forecast a European famine that would lead to renewed bloodshed. He also predicted that in the event of an Allied victory, Britain and France would be occupied by American troops whose job would be to break the numerous strikes that were inevitable when peace came. For good measure the author wound up with a scathing attack on the British government.

Nobody who read the article was surprised when Russell made another brief appearance in court. This time he was sentenced to six months' imprisonment without the right to appeal.

In the spring of 1918, a few months before the armistice, the rebel was at last caged. Conditions in Brixton were not as unpleasant as they might have been. The prisoner had a comfortable cell, was provided with a carpet and a desk, had permission to read and write, and could receive visitors once a week. He employed the time usefully, writing his *Introduction to Mathematical Philosophy* and dividing his reading equally between philosophical and recreational literature. Nevertheless, for a man of Russell's temperament it was a frustrating experience. He was deprived of a stimulating conversation, and his freedom-loving nature cried out against such a circumscribed existence.

After his release from Brixton, Russell lectured for three years, continued with his literary work, and in 1920, when a Labour Party delegation visited Soviet Russia, he went along in the capacity of unofficial observer. He met Lenin and Trotsky, was not taken in by the specially laid on receptions and banquets, but noted for future reference the appalling conditions in which ordinary Russian people lived. He left Russia convinced that on balance the Revolution had failed to achieve its aims and recorded his unfavourable impressions later that year in *The Practice and Theory of Bolshevism.* On one point he had no reservations. Any system of Communist government in Great Britain would be a calamity.

Shortly after his Russian venture, he was off on another long trip, this time to Peking to lecture at the university. The Chinese fascinated the philosopher by virtue of their traditional imperturbability and exquisite courtesy. It saddened him, however, to see that the days of the bland, leisurely, ritualistic China were already numbered. Too many smilingly corrupt government officials were feathering their nests while the nation's economy was slowly grinding to a standstill. There was no transport worthy of the name, and such road and rail systems as existed could never cope with the needs of so vast a country. Russell was painfully aware that China's salvation would have to come in the form of a rebellion. With expansionist Japan on one side and Bolshevik Russia on the other, the Chinese people could not afford to rely on the old regime to protect them. Russell's forecast was that a military and socialist rising was inevitable. Subsequently he was to sum up his findings in *The Problem of China.*

Unfortunately Russell's Chinese visit had an almost tragic conclusion. As a result of over-work and nervous exhaustion he had little resistance to offer to a severe attack of pneumonia contracted in Peking. For days he hovered between life and death, but at last he took a turn for the better and miraculously struggled back towards health. When he got back to England in the autumn of 1921, he learned that he was free to marry again. Soon he was setting up a new household in Chelsea with his second wife; Dora Black had already accompanied him to China.

At the next General Election, Russell stood as a Labour candidate, but he was defeated by Samuel Hoare. He then settled down to write popular books and articles, managed to fit in another lecture tour in America, studied the new atomic theories, and in 1927 he and his wife were running their own "freedom" school for young children. It was one of those establishments where corporal punishment was taboo, sex was discussed freely, and the only discipline came from the pupils themselves. It took Russell a few years to discover that his revolutionary methods did not work, so he abandoned the project. The termination of this educational experiment coincided with the end of his second marriage.

Within a year Russell had another young wife, Patricia Helen Spence, a student who had worked for some time as his assistant. Although his unorthodox views on sex and marriage shocked many of his contemporaries, he nevertheless believed in marriage as an institution, if only for the sake of the children. His *Marriage and Morals* makes it clear that he rebelled against those popular conceptions that condemned pre-marital sex, unmarried mothers, and sexual relations between unmarried couples. His revolutionary attitude in this field can be traced back to his youthful reactions towards the warped sexual morality of the hypocritical Victorians.

During the 1930s he continued to disseminate his rebellious notions in a number of books that were calculated to appeal to the masses. He dealt with such diverse subjects as man's eternal search for happiness, life as an accidental occurrence, the proper use of money, the enjoyment of leisure, the dangers of power, and most important of all, the preservation of peace. He had no illusions about what was happening in Nazi Germany and was confident that a Second World War could not be avoided. Misunderstanding Hitler completely, Russell at first preached neutrality, advocating that Great Britain should leave Nazi Germany and Soviet Russia to fight over Poland, but as soon as hostilities started he changed his tune. He realized at last that Hitlerism meant the end of civilization.

Russell went to America in 1939 to lecture at the University of California. He had expected to move on to a teaching appointment in New York, but at the last minute he found that the offer had been withdrawn on account of his anti-religious and unconventional views. An inimical press treated him as a moral leper, dragging up and distorting incidents from his private life. He moved to Pennsylvania and for a while enjoyed comparative tranquillity in a farmhouse near Philadelphia, but the persecution started again so in 1944 he decided to return to England.

The Labour Party's election victory the following year seemed to promise a period of peaceful reconstruction, but the dropping of the atom bomb on Hiroshima convinced Russell that the world was no more ready for Socialism than for pacifism and drove him to the reluctant conclusion that the only sure shield against the forces of evil was Western capitalism. It was as an envoy preaching Western Unity, sponsored by the Foreign Office, that he departed on an overseas lecture tour. By that time, of course, he had an international reputation both as an original speaker and as a rebel, so it is not surprising that wherever he appeared thousands flocked to listen to him.

His old allegiances emerged, however, when in 1948 he

was asked to deliver the Reith Lectures. The subject could not have been more appropriate – Authority and the Individual. Russell's main argument was that every man, no matter to what social class he belonged, should enjoy every possible liberty that was consistent with the efficient organization of the community as a whole, but at the same time, taking his cue from the Socialist Party programme, he recommended that all heavy industries in Britain should be nationalized. Deep down he must have been aware that the two propositions were not altogether consistent.

In the summer of 1950, the year when he was awarded the Nobel Prize for literature, he took advantage of an invitation to tour Australia, lecturing and broadcasting. Two years later his third marriage ended on the rocks and at the age of eighty he embarked on yet another marital venture.

Despite his advanced years, Russell was as mentally alert as ever before, writing newspaper articles, appearing on television, invading the short-story market, rebelliously refusing to cut down either his heavy smoking or his moderate drinking. Thanks to his tough constitution, he survived a critical operation in 1953 when he was prostrated by a severe attack of pneumonia.

At eighty-odd he was still an incorrigible rebel, launching a world-wide appeal against the manufacture of the hydrogen bomb. He was actually within seven months of his ninetieth birthday when, as a member of the Committee of One Hundred, he was sentenced to a week's imprisonment for the part he had played in a public demonstration against nuclear weapons.

As these words are being written, Bertrand Russell is still a force to be reckoned with.

Chapter 18
Epstein
1880–1959

In his monumental autobiography Jacob Epstein tells us that his earliest memories were of the densely populated East Side district of New York, for he was born in 1880 in Hester Street with its crowded open-air market where people of a dozen nationalities rubbed shoulders daily. His own parents were of Russian-Polish origin and from them he inherited the patience, tolerance and imperturbability that sustained him in later life. In Hester Street one learned to accept the vicissitudes of life with equanimity. Brought up in such an environment, a boy like Jacob Epstein soon appreciated that "sufferance is the badge of all our tribe".

Young Epstein learned something else during those formative years in Hester Street. He learned about humanity in all its rich variety. He was able to study shapes and sizes, angles and curves, textures and colours, and the dignity of the miraculous creation that was man. Furthermore, he was already recording his impressions in the form of forceful sketches, for in spite of his mother's conviction that he was born to be a pianist, little Jacob preferred to set down what he saw in terms of light and shade and significant line. Even as a very small child he was passionately devoted to drawing. His favourite subjects at school were art, literature and history, but art always came first.

Soon he was attending the Art Students' League, drawing from models, painting, and learning about the rules that govern the different forms of art. When he went up town to art school, he was intensely aware of the contrast between the huge stores and apartment blocks and the tiny people scurrying like ants along the straight smooth-sided canyons of the streets. Although mankind seemed to be dwarfed by the mammoth buildings, Epstein obstinately told himself that the real giants were the human beings whose imaginations had first seen the possibility of creating those walls of offices with their thousands of unseeing eyes. It was undoubtedly this concept of man's limitless vision that subsequently influenced his approach to sculpture. His colossal stone figures were in a sense the protests of a man who had looked up at so many uninspiring slabs of concrete in his youth that he wanted to look up later at something of real value.

Although his sessions at the art school taught him something, it was on the world centred round Hester Street that he depended for his education. As the tide of humanity moved sluggishly past the street traders, Epstein would single out a Jewish rabbi, or a Polish carpenter, or an Italian ice-cream vendor and try to capture his particular features on his drawing-pad. He was so fascinated by the Hester Street characters that when his parents set up home in a better-class neighbourhood, he stayed on there in a rented room so that he could continue with his true-to-life drawings. It was indeed a sad day for Epstein when the building caught fire in his absence and he returned to find the room gutted and all his East Side studies reduced to ashes. He wasted no time bemoaning his losses, however. He simply found other accommodation in the same area and started a new series of sketches.

When he was not busy drawing or reading in Hester Street, he liked to roam round the New York docks, admiring the tall ships and the agile sailors furling or unfurling the rigging, the mountainous stevedores handling cargoes, eager immigrants with their pathetic bundles, and the hauntingly expressive faces of the coloured workers. He also explored the Jewish and Irish quarters, the Bowery, Chinatown, Harlem, Coney Island, Central Park, and as his interest in art developed he began to visit the galleries and study sculpture. The first time he felt clay under his fingers he was sure he had found the artistic outlet he had been groping towards. Thereafter the longing to create in plastic form never left him.

He knew what his next move had to be. Somehow or other he had to get to the city which seemed to attract all artists. Like hundreds of painters, musicians, poets and sculptors, he resolved to go to Paris.

Fortunately, Epstein soon found an opportunity to earn sufficient money for his fare. The writer Hutchins Hapgood had just finished a book about New York's East Side and was looking for someone to supply the illustrations. Epstein was commissioned to do the job. His past experience made him eminently suitable for such a task and his drawings of various East Side types were immediately accepted. He was twenty-two years old, unknown and a comparative beginner in a highly specialized field. But he was quietly confident of his own ability.

Paris lived up to his expectations. The *Ecole des Beaux Arts* offered the type of training that suited him. Although he was a born sculptor, naturally endowed with a capacity for giving shape, significance and life to otherwise meaningless material, there were certain techniques that only experts could teach him. There were also written and unwritten rules that sculptors had evolved throughout the centuries, a system of "do's" and "don'ts" that served as a useful guide to those who chose to practise the art. Epstein, for all his originality, realized the importance and validity of those rules and never regretted the time spent in learning them. That he rebelled against so many of them later in no way rendered them obsolete. In his great wisdom Epstein knew that any form of art is greater than the rules that govern it.

At the *Beaux Arts* school, too, he was gradually formulating those principles of conduct that were to sustain him in his life-long battle with the forces of ignorance and prejudice. He was always prepared to consider both sides of an argument, but once he had made up his mind, no power on earth could budge him. Even in minor matters, if he thought he was right, Epstein would never yield to external pressure. The *Beaux Arts,* for instance, subscribed to the English public school system of fagging. During his few weeks there, Epstein flatly refused to be at the beck and call of the older students. It was an infringement of personal liberty that his freedom-loving nature rejected as iniquitous. Rather than subject himself to such degradation, he left the *Beaux Arts* and joined the Julian Academy where he was treated more reasonably.

To Epstein Paris almost meant the Louvre and all its dazzling abundance. He was strongly influenced by the primitive Egyptian sculpture, although it was the work of the French sculptor Auguste Rodin (1840-1917) that made the deepest impression because of its incredible vigour. He worshipped at the shrines of the early Greek sculptors, but he had to wait until destiny took him to London before he found what he had been searching for without knowing it – the Polynesian and African carvings that set his feet on the path which finally led him to fame and fortune.

Meanwhile Epstein continued to profit from his sojourn among the artists of Paris, for at that time the cultural centre of Europe was also the cultural centre of the world, an inexhaustible treasure-house of beauty and inspiration. His material gains were considerable, but there were also the spiritual and mental advantages of living in a city whose very stones were reminders of the great social upheaval that had liberated a whole nation. Paradoxically, too, it was in Paris whose battle-cry was liberty that Epstein began to appreciate that the sculptor, perhaps more than any other artist, had to cultivate discipline. It was his business to express his inner vision in whatever material he was working on, yet it was vital to exercise self-control. A man hacking away frenziedly with a chisel might be the popular conception of a sculptor at work; it was certainly not Epstein's. Energy was an essential attribute, especially when the medium was intractable stone, but uncontrolled violence was only a dissipation of the sculptor's power. Epstein believed that the urge for expression had to be satisfied, but not at the expense of order and cogency.

When he was twenty-five Epstein wondered whether he should go back to America or pursue his chosen career in another country. He decided to settle in London. It was a curious choice, for sculpture in England had reached an abysmally low level. Such work as was emerging during that period was conventional, representational and totally lacking in imagination. The art had flourished between the end of the thirteenth century and 1450, when it had been inspired by religious motives, but then a decline had set in when the Italian baroque with all its complicated florid excesses spread to England. Thereafter English sculptors had tended to reflect the whims of their wealthy patrons.

The only worthwhile attempt to restore the old simplicity and restraint had been made by a Frenchman, Jules Dalou, who had fled to England after the French Revolution and had established modelling classes in South Kensington. Progress, however, had been slow. When Epstein moved into his studio in the Camden Town district, sculpture was still virtually in the doldrums. It was not surprising therefore that he was soon discouraged by so bleak an outlook and began to wonder if he had made the wrong decision.

Acting on a sudden impulse, he returned to New York, travelling steerage and rather enjoying the experience. His stay in his native city was short-lived, for a letter from a friend convinced him that he ought to give England another try. Within a fortnight he was back in London, this time taking a dingy studio in Fulham where he proposed to concentrate on modelling, drawing and carving.

For the next two years Epstein dedicated himself to perfecting his techniques, working indefatigably and spending his few leisure hours in the British Museum. Although he saw little evidence to indicate that the people in England had any interest in sculptors, especially foreign ones, he never lost faith in himself. He was encouraged, too, by a Scotswoman named Margaret Dunlop who devoted herself to furthering his career. He married her in 1907.

Epstein's great opportunity came in the spring of 1907 when he was commissioned to decorate the façade of the new British Medical Association building in the Strand. It took him fourteen months to complete eighteen nude figures of both sexes, illustrating the human life cycle from birth to old age. These "Strand Statues" marked the beginning of a Press war against Epstein that was to continue almost to the end of his life. There were newspaper articles condemning them as improper, vituperative letters to *The Times,* even questions in the House. Everybody from bishops down to dustmen became an art critic overnight.

The opening shots were fired by the *Evening Standard.* The 23 June edition contained an impassioned plea that the "indecent and inartistic" statues should not be exposed to public view. The virulent attacks increased, leaving the ordinary man in the street with the impression that Jacob Epstein was deliberately pandering to mankind's basest instincts, that his work was obscene and pornographic.

The more intelligent *Times* promptly took up the cudgels on the sculptor's behalf, declaring that the figures were inoffensive and that there was no justification whatsoever for the adverse criticism. He found another worthy supporter in the author of the leading article in the 27 June issue of the *British Medical Journal.* Under the headline OLD MAID WITH A SPY-GLASS the writer stated categorically that he saw nothing indecent in the statues and that there was no intention of removing them. His views were endorsed the following week by a number of correspondents. But it was the voice of the *Evening Standard* (scandalized by the effect the figures would "produce on the minds of young people") that prevailed. Despite the able defence put up by the *Times,* by the Slade Professor of Fine Arts and others well qualified to judge, the superb statues were demolished. The Philistines had won the day.

For the next three or four years Epstein was busy with studies from models, busts and portraits, but in 1912 he was in the news again. This was the year in which he put the finishing touches to another piece of commissioned work, a tomb to go over the grave of Oscar Wilde in the Père Lachaise cemetery in Paris. The sculpture was the rebel's effective answer to his critics, for once more he refused to be restrained by classical and romantic formalism. Carved with the same imaginative vision as had been responsible for the Strand Statues, the Oscar Wilde tomb again stirred up controversy. According to the *Pall Mall Gazette* of 6 June, the design on the tomb was "unconventional and quite likely to shock people". Epstein was "a sculptor in revolt" who was in conflict "with the idea of current sculpture". On the other hand, the *Evening*

Standard and St. James's Gazette found it "a dignified piece of monumental sculpture".

Finding he could not settle down to work in Paris, Epstein returned to England, living for a time on the Sussex coast in a rented bungalow. With his usual zest he tackled new projects until, as a "foreigner", he ran foul of the authorities during the First World War and was obliged to move away from the coastal zone.

After serving without distinction in the armed forces from 1916 until the end of the war, he produced a bronze statue of Christ. When it was exhibited at the Leicester Galleries, it proved to be yet another subject of controversy. The revolutionary Epstein technique offended certain members of the press, the clergy, Royal Academicians and various social organizations. *Outlook* boldly asserted that "the figure is all wrong", that the statue was "an artistic mistake". More precise in its vilification was an article in *The Graphic* by Father Bernard Vaughan who wrote: "I felt ready to cry out with indignation that in this Christian England there should be exhibited the figure of a Christ which suggested to me some degraded Chaldean or African, which wore the appearance of an Asiatic-American or Hun-Jew, which reminded me of some emaciated Hindu, or a badly grown Egyptian swathed in the cerements of the grave. I call it positively wicked and insulting to perpetrate such a travesty of the Risen Christ, and to invite a Christian people, to whom the founder of Christianity is the Man-God, to come and admire it." After reading such a diatribe, Epstein must have turned with relief a week later to the more reasoned criticism by George Bernard Shaw in the same journal, or to the *Sunday Times* which said that he had done justice "to the power and mastery of the Saviour".

Although Epstein was no doubt astonished by the violent antipathies aroused by his work, his next major work, a piece of architectural sculpture for the Hudson Memorial in Hyde Park, bluntly warned his critics that his rebellion against conventional sculpture was only just beginning.

Precluded by the Office of Works from incorporating a figure of the famous naturalist William Henry Hudson himself in the design, Epstein decided to use as his centre-piece Rima, the heroine of Hudson's romance *Green Mansions.*

This nude shape surrounded by birds provoked the press into such spiteful comments as "obscene", "a horror", "ought to be removed from Hyde Park", "a piece of artistic anarchy". Vandals, no doubt responding to the newspaper campaign, daubed the memorial with green paint. Later on it was defiled with swastikas and the letters I.F.L. (Independent Fascist League). Police investigations, needless to add, led nowhere.

This desecration of a small and quite innocuous panel revolted Epstein, but as always he did not let ignorance and stupidity disturb his placid temperament. How could the ordinary run of mankind be expected to appreciate a conception that baffled men whose job it was to write knowledgeably about art? In any case, Epstein had more respect for the observations contained in a memorandum sent to the Office of Works on 29 November, 1925. There *Rima* was referred to as "a notable and dignified work", and Epstein was praised for attempting "to get back to real carving... and not the mere mechanical reproduction of clay originals".

Epstein's statues continued to puzzle the critics. For example, his two groups "Night" and "Day" produced in 1929, to go above the doors of the Underground Headquarters Buildings at St. James's Park, had a mixed response. But it was beginning to look as though the old hostility towards the rebel and his work was at last on the wane. Then Epstein dropped his biggest bombshell of all. From a block of Seravezza marble, bought in Paris and delivered to his Epping Forest "studio", he started to carve his conception of universal motherhood. He completed the task in his London work-shop at Hyde Park Gate and in 1931 was able to offer his most important work in marble to the Tate Gallery. He called it "Genesis".

The Tate turned it down as "sensational", but on 7 February it was given a private showing in the Leicester Galleries. As might have been expected, it occasioned a veritable storm of protest, for Epstein had obviously rebelled not only against the erotic nudes of his era, but against a whole generation of sculptors. The huge pregnant Mongolian type of woman, with one gigantic hand pressed protectively against the moving child within and the other resting with fingers outstretched against the broad thigh, is neither beautiful nor voluptuous, but it symbolizes the very beginning of life as we know it. It represents infinitely more than a woman in an advanced state of pregnancy. "Genesis" is Epstein's powerful vision of creation.

Most critics condemned the statue as "a bad joke in stone", as an anatomical absurdity, as "harsh and unsympathetic", as an "oddity of design and peculiarity of psychological conception". It was "coarse and repellent", "heavy and inartistic", "uncouth". One of the few reviewers who saw what Epstein was driving at stated in the *Observer* that the figure had "unusual merit", that "the divergencies of the forms, the contrasts of lightnesses and weight, and the downward-forward movement of the lines contribute to a significance which is undeniably primeval and profound".

It was the usual story. Epstein's creative intelligence dwarfed that of any other contemporary sculptor in England and his sculptural vision was far ahead of his time. He was expressing in stone deep spiritual truths that were not fully comprehensible to his generation. Because his work had a universality and elemental quality and because he expressed himself in a language that was altogether new and strange, he was understood only by a discerning minority. The rest, uncertain and bewildered in the presence of the unknown, sought relief in condemnation. How were they to know that Epstein's apparent distortions were all part of his artistic vision?

In any event the vehement newspaper attacks had no effect on the incorrigible rebel. In 1935 the largest figure he had so far attempted, "Ecce Homo", was damned by the ignorant as "ugly and vile", "an outrage", "an insult to religion", "grotesque". Epstein treated such irresponsible comments with the contempt they deserved, preferring to listen to the enlightened few who spoke of his "impressive energy", his "astonishing virtuosity", and recognized that he had given sculpture "a new lease of life".

There was the same strong division of opinion when his "Consummatum Est" was exhibited at the Leicester Galleries the following year. His "Adam" (1938-39) was also misunderstood by the press, although the work subsequently found a purchaser and was well reviewed in the *Birmingham Mail.*

By the time Epstein had reached his sixty-ninth year, although he had made no concessions to popular taste, he had moved into a position of unassailable superiority. He was never short of commissions for his exquisite portrait bronzes, while his studies from life and his water colours of Epping Forest always enjoyed a ready sale. Public bodies were beginning to appreciate his bigger carvings and the popular clamour had started to die down. He produced major works for the Festival of Britain, for the Convent of the Holy Child Jesus in Cavendish Square, for Llandaff Cathedral, for Westminster Abbey and for the new cathedral in Coventry. To crown his long run of successes, in 1958 the North Staffordshire University commissioned him to carve a bust of Princess Margaret, who sat for him until the work was interrupted by a temporary breakdown in the sculptor's health.

On 19 August, 1959, Epstein was busy on the Bowater House Group, a massive bronze that was scheduled to stand inside the new Duke of Edinburgh's Gate leading into Hyde Park. He had completed all the preliminaries and had arranged for his bronze moulder to do the casting. He added the finishing touches that same evening and then went to bed. He passed away peacefully during the night.

Finally, although it is right and fitting that Jacob Epstein should be included in a book about rebels, it is important to establish the special nature of his rebellion. As an innovator and visionary he was in revolt against convention, against smug respectability, against ignorance and prejudice, against the insincerity of sculpture in England. As one who shared the same artistic vision as the old masters, he was never in revolt against tradition. On the contrary his work, properly understood, combines the instinctive with the simplicity of the past. What he believed in all his life was the creative urge that has been the driving force behind every genuine artist since the beginning of time. He was original, inventive, intensely personal, and yet a traditionalist. In that paradox lies the key to his mystery.

Chapter 19
D. H. Lawrence
1885–1930

David Herbert Lawrence, the man whom E. M. Forster once described as "the greatest imaginative novelist of our time", was born on 11 September, 1885, in the Nottinghamshire mining village of Eastwood, up on the hills above the Erewash Valley. His father, who was employed in the nearby colliery at Brinsley, had all the virtues and vices of a typical miner. In short, he worked hard and he played hard. It must have been his industrious side that had appealed to Mrs. Lawrence, for she was a pious self-righteous woman, a censorious evangelist who viewed most of her husband's little pleasures with strong disapproval. They had five children altogether, David Herbert being the youngest of three sons. His parents' constant bickering and sometimes violent quarrels contributed to the depressing home background of David's formative years.

Eastwood had little to offer in the way of entertainment for a growing boy. The fair introduced a little colour and variety every September and November; strolling players gave dramatic performances ranging from Shakespeare to

"Sweeney Todd"; the Literary Society held weekly discussions. Then there was the Congregational chapel in Albert Street. From David's point of view the most rewarding spare-time occupation was wandering about the surrounding countryside, and there is no doubt that his solitary rambles made a deep and lasting impression on him. His novels and short stories are full of references to such places as Greasley with its fourteenth-century castle, the ruins of Beauvale Priory, High Park Wood and Moor Green Reservoir. Years later, when he was in Italy, he summed up his feelings for the area in one sincere sentence: "That's the country of my heart." The woods, hills and fields around Eastwood became known as "the Lawrence country" and Lawrence himself is as much a regional novelist as Hardy or Phillpotts or Trollope. A recurring theme in his books is the sharp contrast between the pit-head gears and slag-heaps of Eastwood and the green world beyond.

Not very robust, a typical mother's boy, David spent five miserable years at the Beauvale Board School. His unequivocal attitude towards organized games kept him in constant conflict with the authorities, while the other boys taunted him for his effeminacy. He had plenty of courage, however, and in spite of his poor physique, he was not slow to defend himself with his tongue when attacked.

Encouraged by his mother to break loose from his working-class environment, David won a scholarship at twelve and so became a pupil at the Nottingham High School. With eight miles each way to be covered in all weathers, he had a long hard day, usually leaving home at seven in the morning and returning at seven in the evening. His winter journeys must have aggravated the hacking cough that was to trouble him until the end of his life.

Lawrence was not yet sixteen when he met Jessie Chambers at her parents' farm. Their curiously complicated relationship (one of the central themes of *Sons and Lovers*) had a profoundly emotional effect on the sensitive youth and was destined to continue for the next twelve years. Their serious attitude towards life, together with their love of books, formed a powerful link between them and the hours Lawrence spent with Jessie, reading and studying, played an important part in his artistic development.

That same year Lawrence left school and took up a

clerical appointment in Nottingham. His employers who made surgical appliances and sold pharmaceutical products paid him the princely wage of thirteen shillings for a six-day week. His experiences as a city clerk later served as a basis for certain episodes in *Sons and Lovers.*

A severe attack of pneumonia from which he almost died brought his clerical activities to an end and he never went back to his ledgers. After a happy period of recuperation at Skegness, Lawrence taught for four years as a pupil-teacher at the British School in Eastwood. Then he and Jessie attended the Pupil-Teacher Centre at Ilkeston. Although he detested his tutor (the headmaster), he distinguished himself in the King's Scholarship examination, taking first place in England and Wales. Fussed over by his mother to the point of embarrassment, he was over-anxious in the Matriculation examination and the result was less creditable.

He now had all the proper qualifications for a place at University College, Nottingham, but he needed the sum of twenty pounds to put down as advance fees, so he had to teach for an additional year. In his leisure hours he embarked on his first novel, *The White Peacock,* using his own village and local scenery (especially Felley Mill) as a setting. He also tried his hand at writing poetry. During this first spell of literary activity he was influenced largely by the books he had read, usually in Jessie's company, but for his Nottinghamshire lore he was indebted to his friends, William Hopkin and his wife.

Since adolescence sex had been a disturbing problem for him, particularly in connection with his relationship with Jessie. In 1906, whilst on holiday in Mablethorpe, he decided he had to free himself from a partnership that seemed mutually destructive, so he frankly admitted to Jessie that although he was very fond of her, he could never marry her. It was a painful confrontation, but Lawrence was convinced it was for the best. As for poor Jessie, she had no alternative but to agree that henceforth they would see less of each other.

At twenty-one, then, Lawrence began his two-year training course at Nottingham University College. It did not take him long to discover that college life did not come up to his expectations. Apart from Professor Ernest Weekley, for whom he conceived an instant admiration, the lecturers were dull and uninspiring. The budding novelist did not take very kindly to the fact that his written exercises were being corrected by quibbling pedants who could not boast half his literary ability. When one of his poems was turned down by the editorial board of the college magazine, he was on the verge of rebellion.

With nothing to show for his two years' stint save a Teachers' Certificate and a profound contempt for the pseudo-education he had received, Lawrence left college in June 1908, and four months later he set out for London to tackle his first teaching appointment at the Davidson Road School, a recently built and comparatively well-equipped establishment in Croydon. His starting salary was ninety-five pounds a year.

Lawrence was a remarkably good teacher, especially if he was dealing with a subject that interested him, and throughout his three years at the school he was extremely popular both with staff and pupils. He had his own strict views on discipline and made sure that any rules he laid down were observed to the letter. For his own part, he reacted sharply to any attempts by the authorities to pin him down with regulations. If the headmaster or any senior teacher tried to change his methods, he immediately rebelled. Personal liberty to Lawrence was sacred.

It was while he was employed at the Davidson Road School that he became friendly with Helen Corke who taught at a neighbouring school. They both enjoyed the open air and often set out on walking expeditions on Wimbledon Common or in Richmond Park or across the Downs. They sometimes sat in Hyde Park listening to band concerts, and if they were feeling extravagant, they went to see a play in the West End. Like Jessie Chambers, Helen was essential to Lawrence at a vital stage of his life. She was physically desirable, bubbling over with vitality, and she genuinely appreciated Lawrence's quick brain and rare sensitivity. She was intelligent enough to give his rebellious nature free rein and to avoid any suggestion of cramping domesticity. In any case, as long as his mother was still alive, Lawrence would never have allowed himself to form a permanent attachment to another woman.

Meanwhile he had kept in touch with Jessie Chambers

who had sent some of his work, under a pseudonym, to Ford Madox Hueffer (later Ford), the editor of the *English Review*. Her faith in Lawrence was soon justified, for some of his poems and short stories were accepted for publication. Moreover, there were other interesting repercussions. The editor naturally wanted to meet his new "discovery", and at the literary parties that followed, Lawrence was introduced to several eminent writers of the period including Ezra Pound and W. B. Yeats. The young elementary school teacher's extra-mural activities were certainly leading him into an alien world.

Back in his Croydon lodgings, Lawrence completed his first novel, *The White Peacock,* the book he had started four years previously. In spite of all its shortcomings – stilted dialogue, too much literary chatter, immaturity – it was full of promise and Heinemann went ahead with publication. It should have been a great moment for the obscure schoolmaster, but his success had come at a time when any form of celebration was out of the question. His mother was dying slowly of cancer and Lawrence was inconsolable. Although Heinemann had accelerated publication so that the author was able to give her a copy, Mrs. Lawrence was too ill to read it. When the end came, Lawrence was racked with grief. His mother had meant everything to him. His health steadily declined and for the next twelve months he was unable to concentrate on his writing. There was even a possibility of consumption, so he put in a request for sick leave and went away to convalesce.

Before his mother had fallen ill, Lawrence had written the first draft of a second novel, *The Trespasser.* As his strength returned, he sought relief from his anguish in literary work, tackling the rewrite of *The Trespasser* and then plunging into his third book, *Sons and Lovers.* The former, which many critics believe to be his worst novel, was published in May 1912. Lawrence himself did not care for it, but the story occasionally catches something of his genius, and there are intermittent passages of authentic Lawrence. The latter, a moving presentation of an impressionable working-class boy's adolescence, was to mark a notable advance in characterization, scene-painting and story-telling.

But while he was still working on *Sons and Lovers,* he

met somebody who was going to be responsible for a dramatic change in his domestic circumstances and in his whole attitude towards life and art. In the April of 1912 he was introduced to Mrs. Frieda Weekley, wife of his favourite professor at University College. The encounter soon led to Lawrence's first open rebellion against conventional behaviour.

At the time Lawrence was thinking of applying for a lectureship in a German university, so he went to Nottingham to enlist the aid of Professor Weekley. He immediately fell under the spell of Frieda Weekley, blonde, beautiful and aristocratic, the Baroness von Richthofen before her marriage. Her continental charm, her attractive accent and her eager vivacity were altogether outside Lawrence's previous experience. He was flattered by her obvious interest in his literary aspirations and he could see that she treated her elderly husband with undisguised indifference.

Completely infatuated, Lawrence began calling regularly on the Weekleys, and one week-end, when the Professor was not at home, Frieda invited him to spend the night with her. But he refused to settle for a casual love affair. He wanted her to run away with him so that they could start a new life together.

Frieda was no longer in love with her husband, but she had to consider her three children and inevitable social ostracism. Nevertheless she allowed herself to be persuaded and on 3 May she and Lawrence left England. At one stroke Lawrence had cut himself off from his teaching career, from his family and friends, from his own country. He had rebelled against middle-class morality, against the social code and against every principle instilled into him by his God-fearing mother. In a word, he had rebelled against the past.

The lovers first stayed at Metz where Lawrence was nearly arrested as a spy. Then they went on to Trier and later to Icking, not far from Munich, where they settled happily in a house overlooking the Isar. While they were there, *The Trespasser* was published by Duckworth, and Lawrence wrote poetry and worked on *Sons and Lovers*. He was gay, at peace with the world and confident that he had made the right move. His feelings for Frieda are expressed in his poetry:

"You are the call and I am the answer,
You are the wish and I the fulfilment,
You are the night, and I the day."

In August Lawrence and Frieda moved to Gargnano on Lake Garda and soon he had put the finishing touches to *Sons and Lovers,* a novel that was to establish him as one of the significant authors of his day. He was also turning over in his mind ideas that were eventually to emerge as his two masterpieces, *The Rainbow* and *Women in Love.*

The following summer they went back to England on a visit, in time to read the encouraging reviews of *Sons and Lovers.* During their stay they became firm friends with Middleton Murry and Katherine Mansfield, "the only spontaneous and jolly friendship that we had", as Frieda put it years later in her memoir, *Not I, But the Wind.* Other interesting people they met were Professor Raleigh, Edward Marsh and the Asquiths. Herbert Asquith, the son of the Prime Minister, made a most significant comment about Lawrence. He said that the writer was "a poet living on a plane far removed from the dust of politics, but *more deeply in revolt against the values of the day* than any political leader". (The italics are the author's.)

After enjoying the experience of being a notability in England, Lawrence took Frieda back to the Continent where they travelled for a while before settling in a rented house in Fiascherino near Lerici. From a literary angle it was not a particularly productive period, but Lawrence was by no means idle. He had already decided that contemporary writers such as Bennett and Galsworthy had little to offer that was likely to endure. He now concentrated on the Futurists and asked himself if they were heading in the right direction. He came to the conclusion that they were justified in moving away from worn-out traditional forms, but he questioned the way they were going about their revolution. In Lawrence's view their work was often built on inadequate knowledge of the human psyche. Man's actions, beliefs, desires and motives had to be explained in terms of the unconscious mind. In other words, Lawrence had discovered Freud.

In the spring of 1914 Frieda's decree *nisi* was finalized and she was free to marry Lawrence. The ceremony was performed at the Registry Office in Kensington on 13 July. Within a month England was at war with Germany, a circumstance that shocked and disgusted Lawrence. He was soon corresponding with another pacifist, Bertrand Russell, and agreeing with him that war was a monstrosity. In his letters to Russell, Lawrence stressed the necessity for a revolution that would "smash the frame" of the present way of living. After he had met and talked with the philosopher, he was not so sure that his new friend would make a good ally. He was convinced that Russell "sustained simultaneously a pair of opinions ludicrously incompatible. He held that in fact human affairs were carried on after a most irrational fashion, but that the remedy was quite simple and easy, since all we had to do was to carry them on rationally." Russell for his part discovered "that we differed from each other more than we differed from the Kaiser". It is not altogether surprising that in rather less than twelve months their hectic friendship came to an end.

Lawrence soon had another reason for rebelling against the established order of things. When Methuen published *The Rainbow* in September, a police-court magistrate ruled that the book was obscene and all available copies had to be destroyed. The *New Statesman* reported on the prosecution in the following terms: "Last Saturday, at Bow Street, Mr. D. H. Lawrence's new novel *The Rainbow* was brought before the bench and sentenced to death. Who lodged an information against the book I don't know. It is conceivable, at a time when the patriotism of our criminals must leave our policemen plenty of leisure, that some cultured constable may have got hold of the work and rushed to his superiors with it. But it is likelier that the prosecution was the work of some society or individual set upon Mr. Lawrence's track by one of the violent attacks upon the book which appeared in the Press."

Accused of obscenity and pro-Germanism at the same time, Lawrence decided to press on with a venture he had already planned – a trip to America. The furore over *The Rainbow,* however, put so many difficulties in his path that he abandoned the notion, and instead he took Frieda to Zennor in Cornwall where he devoted much of his time to the completion of *Women in Love,* his fifth, and in the opinion of many critics, his best novel. Like *The Rainbow,* its sequel was also written in that new and revolutionary idiom that had upset so many traditionalists. The author, still in revolt against ancient methods, techniques and form, had set out to present a comprehensive picture of twentieth century England that was as far removed from similar offerings by contemporary novelists as is the music of Stravinsky from that of Ketelby. He had succeeded gloriously.

Neither Lawrence nor Frieda was left in peace in Cornwall. The local inhabitants viewed them both with suspicion and were positive that the Lawrence cottage was a nest of spies. They even broke in one day while the occupants were away and turned everything upside-down in a frantic search for evidence. The final straw was an order from the military giving the Lawrences three days to get out of the county. Their future movements were severely restricted and wherever they were they had to report their whereabouts to the police. This unwarranted persecution deeply wounded Lawrence and it rankled for a long time.

The unfortunate couple went first to London, then to a mountain cottage in Derbyshire where they remained until the war was over. This was another barren period as far as novel-writing was concerned, although Lawrence was not exactly idle. Among the shorter pieces he wrote were several essays on American authors. He also expressed his revolutionary views in a series of articles for *The Times* under the title *Education of the People.*

In 1919, when Frieda set off to visit her mother in Germany, Lawrence headed for Florence where Frieda subsequently joined him. Thereafter they travelled extensively in Italy, not staying long in any one spot until they had crossed over into Sicily and had fallen in love with Taormina. There they lingered for two years at the Villa Fontana Vecchia, "a nice big house, with fine rooms and a handy kitchen, set in a big garden, mostly vegetables, green with almond trees, on a steep slope at some distance above the sea".

As usual Italy had acted as a stimulus to Lawrence's creative imagination. At Taormina, amid the olive groves and lemon trees, he finished two novels, *The Lost Girl* and *Aaron's Rod,* wrote a magnificent travel book entitled *Sea and Sardinia,* and also found time for poetry, essays and short stories. Moreover, the vivid colours, the perpetual sunshine and the sense of freedom stirred the rebel in him, for he again felt the urge to join the revolutionary socialists and march with them when they rose up against their oppressors to fight for their rights and for liberty.

But there was no revolution and at the end of their two years in Paradise, the Lawrences were on the move once more. They spent six weeks in Ceylon, where Lawrence found the intense heat too much for him, and then toured Western Australia, a trip that inspired Lawrence to write *Kangaroo,* the theme of which was man's single-handed battle against conformity.

From Australia Lawrence and Frieda sailed to America, disembarking at San Francisco and taking the train to Lamy. Friends met them there and they were driven across the desert to Santa Fé. The scenery of New Mexico fascinated Lawrence. He wrote later that it was "the greatest experience from the outside world that I have ever had. It certainly changed me for ever." He and Frieda visited Taos, the Del Monte valley, Mexico City, and lived for a time in an adobe house in the village of Chappala. It was in Chappala that the novelist started the book that he at first believed was his masterpiece, *The Plumed Serpent.*

From Chappala the Lawrences went by way of New Orleans and Washington to New York. Frieda sailed for England, while Lawrence spent a lonely, restless and unhappy month in Los Angeles. He then had a look at Mexico, travelling down the west coast with a friend, and at last was on his way to England to rejoin Frieda.

After three depressing months in Europe, the Lawrences returned to America and were soon installed in a small ranch up in the Sangre de Cristo mountains. That same ranch served as the setting for Lawrence's "dramatic poem", *St. Mawr.* Seven months later they were living in the small Mexican town of Oaxaca (the place where Lawrence met Somerset Maugham and found him "a bit rancid"). There, in February 1925, he finished the ambitious *Plumed Serpent* with its superb prose, its brilliant landscape pictures, and unfortunately far from satisfactory finishing chapters. There can be no doubt that the inferiority of the last third of the book was due to Lawrence's first serious attack of tuberculosis.

Lawrence gradually recuperated and in September he

and Frieda said farewell to America and by the end of the month they were back in England. In the spring of the following year they moved to the most famous of the many habitations they had known – the Villa Mirenda at Spotorno just outside Florence. It was there that Lawrence wrote his most controversial novel of all, *Lady Chatterley's Lover,* a book which he had to rewrite three times. Privately printed and circulated, it was banned in England and in the United States on the grounds of obscenity, for on this occasion the author had shown the sanctimonious objectors to *The Rainbow* what he could do when he was really trying. With its four-letter words and frank descriptions of the sex act, the book was assuredly a deliberate challenge to the conformists, but it was more than that. It was a warning that overintellectualization and industrialization were slowly destroying mankind by throwing all physical and spiritual processes out of balance. The only chance of salvation for future generations lay in restoring a harmonious relationship between body and soul.

In the Villa Mirenda, too, Lawrence turned seriously to painting, a relaxation which he kept up later in Switzerland. He liked to do landscapes and portraits and preferred rich eye-catching colours. Even here he contrived to express himself in a revolutionary fashion, freely mixing religion and eroticism and sometimes choosing subjects that were deliberately provocative. In *Throwing Back the Apple,* for instance, Adam and Eve are seen hurling apples at their Maker and driving Him out of Eden.

After a walking tour of the Etruscan tombs and ruined cities along central Italy's western coast, Lawrence used his experiences in a series of essays that appeared in book form after his death under the title *Etruscan Places.* Chronic bronchial congestion was attacking him more frequently, so he went to Les Diablerets in Switzerland for the altitude, the snow and the sun. With renewed strength he returned to the Villa Mirenda, but five months later, in June 1928, the Lawrences were back in Switzerland, living in a chalet at Gsteig bei Gstaad.

They spent the winter in Bandol, travelled around Europe for a time, but by then Lawrence was well aware that he was near death. On 6 February 1930, on the recommendation of his doctor, he went as a patient to the *Ad Astra* sanatorium at Vence. There he had many distinguished visitors, including H. G. Wells, the Huxleys and the Aga Khan. His illness was now burning him away, but he could still appreciate the beautiful view from his balcony of blossoming mimosas and almond, "the coast-line and Cannes five miles off".

Lawrence preserved his dignity right up to the end, and when he felt that his time had almost come, he insisted on leaving the sanatorium so that he could die in less clinical surroundings. He was taken to the Villa Robermond in the village of Vence, but on the following day, 2 March, at ten o'clock in the evening, the tired, emaciated, Christ-like visionary died.

In his last prose piece, *Apocalypse,* Lawrence has a close look at Christianity and presents his own revolutionary panacea for setting the world to rights: "What we want to destroy is our false, inorganic connections, especially those related to money, and re-establish the living organic connections, with the cosmos, the sun and earth, with mankind and nation and family. Start with the sun, and the rest will slowly, slowly happen."

Chapter 20
Michael Collins
1890–1922

The popular young Republican leader and politician Michael Collins was born in 1890 in the hamlet of Sam's Cross, not far from Clonakilty in County Cork. His father was a carpenter and builder, but he had found time to read widely and intelligently and he had a detailed knowledge of his country's checkered history. His tales of the exploits of the famous Irish patriots, such as Wolfe Tone and Robert Emmet, contributed a great deal to his son's fervent patriotism, for the boy Michael admired and respected his father almost to the point of hero-worship.

Michael was born into a troubled Ireland, for in 1890 the reputation of the country's greatest patriot had been irretrievably damaged by the scandalous O'Shea divorce proceedings, and large areas along the west coast were threatened by famine during that black period. By the time he was four, however, the situation had improved a little. In a splendid upsurge of Irish nationalism, the Gaelic League and Sinn Fein ("Ourselves alone") had come into being and the Home Rulers' pressure on the British Government was beginning to prove embarrassing.

As a pupil at the Clonakilty School, Michael followed the example set by his father and became an avid reader. His favourite authors included Dickens, Scott and Thackeray, but he also developed an interest in books dealing with political themes. Like most Irish lads of his age, he would not hear a word said against Arthur Griffith or Charles Parnell. He was proud of his Irish blood and was eager to do something for Ireland. His schoolmaster at Clonakilty School, a patriot and a member of the Irish Republican Brotherhood, is credited with the remark that Michael Collins had "a certain restlessness in temperament".

At his school many of the pupils were keen to get into the British postal service, so the headmaster had initiated special civil service classes for the older boys. Michael eventually enrolled in these classes, and when he was fifteen, was entered for the Post Office examination. He was successful and in 1906 he set out for London to be a junior postal clerk at the Post Office Savings Bank in West Kensington. Away from his friends and the familiar neighbourhood of Sam's Cross, the boy was lonely and miserable at first, but after a few weeks he had formed new ties of affection with other Irish youths who banded together to form their own little community in an alien land, meeting regularly, discussing Irish problems and indulging in sporting activities. Michael who was finding his job rather tedious and uninspiring had also started to attend evening classes at King's College with a view to improving his prospects.

At eighteen he was beginning to devote most of his spare time to political matters. He joined the Irish Republican Brotherhood and soon demonstrated his extraordinary talent for organization. His tireless energy and capacity for hard work were quickly rewarded. First of all he became a Section Master and later on was appointed Treasurer for the London and South England district.

Thanks to his studies at King's College, he was able to hand in his notice at the P.O. Savings Bank and take up a more lucrative clerical post at the Board of Trade. Always eager to try something new, in 1915 he took a job with a firm of stockbrokers. In the same year he made another move, this time to the London office of the Guaranty Trust Company of New York.

Although he really hankered after an engineering career in America, he could not help noticing that one by one his friends and acquaintances were going back to Ireland. At last he too could no longer resist the *nostalgie du pays* that was tugging at his heart-strings, so off he went to Dublin.

Collins's premonitions were correct. The Irish leaders had decided to take advantage of the situation in Europe. They reasoned that Britain would be too occupied fighting Germany to cope with an insurrection in Ireland. Now was the moment to strike.

Meanwhile Collins had found employment with a firm of accountants in Dublin, but he had joined the Irish volunteers so that he would be ready for the battle when it came.

The rank and file were in good heart, but what about their leaders? They were Cathal Brugha, President of the Gaelic League, Padraic Pearse, barrister and poet, and James Connolly, a man of action who hated oppression and injustice. Their right-hand men were Tom Clarke who ran a newspaper and tobacco business; Sean MacDiarmada, a brilliant party organizer; Thomas MacDruagh, whose main interests were education and poetry; Eamonn Ceanut, clerk in the City Treasurer's department; Joseph Plunkett, a literary man. Such was the group of practical men and dreamers who were responsible for planning the coup. Their theory was that a popular rising in the capital would be the signal for similar outbreaks in the provinces. Zero hour was fixed for noon precisely on Easter Monday, 24 April, 1916.

The ill-fated venture was doomed from the outset. To begin with, the supply of weapons and ammunition from Germany, promised by Sir Roger Casement, failed to materialize. Then again, although the men at the top had decided to postpone the whole venture, the Easter Rising was launched at the time previously arranged. The Volunteers (and Michael Collins was one of them) took up their appointed places; general headquarters was established at the Post Office; all telegraph links with England and Scotland were sabotaged. Snipers moved into requisitioned buildings and other strategic positions were occupied. A swift surprise attack won the city block housing the *Daily Express* offices.

Although the British had been taken completely by surprise, they were swift to react to the situation. Reinforcements poured in from Dun Laoghaire, and in six days, after bloody fighting had caused heavy casualties on both sides, the insurrection had been suppressed. Brugha was severely wounded, buildings lay in ruins and fires blazed everywhere. Collins who had fought bravely under Pearse in the Post Office building, escaped the general round-up of prisoners but he was picked up later.

For Michael Collins detention at Frongoch, in Wales, was not altogether without purpose. His leadership qualities were readily recognized and the other prisoners came to rely on him when camp rules and regulations became too irksome. It was Collins who taught them foolproof methods of smuggling messages and information to the world beyond the wire. The clandestine system of communications he devised was useful preparation for his subsequent work as head of the I.R.A.'s intelligence department.

After a bleak depressing winter at Frongoch, the internees were suddenly released and sent back to Ireland.

On his return to Dublin, Collins realized that the British had committed a grave error in executing so many prominent Irishmen after the Easter Rising. The people were more determined than ever before to rid the land of their oppressors and many were not even prepared to co-operate with the Irish Parliamentary Party. The majority were turning towards the Sinn Fein as the most likely political party to control the affairs of Ireland.

On 25 October, 1917, the American-born politician de Valera was elected President of the Sinn Fein; Michael Collins stepped into prominence, first as a member of the Executive Committee, and later as the Director of Organization and a member of the Executive of Volunteers. In the spring of the following year, however, the Sinn Fein temporarily lost its President as a result of Lloyd George's modification of the Defence of the Realm Act. (Fearing a Sinn Fein rising at a time when the German armies were approaching the Marne, the crafty Welshman legalized the deportation of Irish troublemakers without a public trial.

De Valera walked deliberately into the trap with a view to winning sympathizers to the Irish cause.)

De Valera's sudden removal left Collins, together with Harry Boland, to keep the movement alive in the leader's absence. As Adjutant-General, Director of Intelligence, and Minister of Finance in the Dail Eireann government, he became a kingpin in the Party.

In the capacity of Director of Organization, Collins considered that his main concern was the efficiency of the Volunteers. In the belief that no army could function without strict discipline, from his Dublin H.Q. he made it his business to visit the various brigades to ensure that officers and men were carrying out the training programmes to the best of their ability. Although the British were hot on his trail, he somehow managed to be everywhere at once and yet steer clear of trouble. His physical strength coupled with his tremendous zeal kept him going for anything up to twenty hours a day. He seemed indefatigable.

Shortly after the armistice, the Sinn Feiners had their reward. In the December elections they captured almost three-quarters of the seats – seventy-three out of a hundred and five. Collins's own political victories were gained in West Cork and Armagh.

Collins's next move was one of supreme effrontery. He crossed over to England and personally arranged de Valera's escape from Lincoln Gaol. It was Collins himself who opened the outside gate and escorted the escapee to his first hideout in Manchester. His services to the Cause were recognized shortly after de Valera's American visit when Collins joined the cabinet as Minister for Home Affairs and became one of the four most important men in the Dail Eireann (The other three were de Valera, Griffith and Brugha.) The British certainly appreciated his growing value to Ireland, for on 25 January, 1920, they offered a substantial reward for the body of Michael Collins, dead or alive.

Driven to desperation by Collins' widespread activities, the British decided to try a new approach to the problem. So far they had relied on their two terror groups, "G" Division and the Auxiliaries, to keep order in Dublin and even beyond the city limits, and above all to capture Collins. They now brought back sixteen British officers from the Middle East and turned them into a special task force. They were given intensive training in intelligence work and sent out on their secret mission, the object of which was to deal once and for all with Collins and his organization. They had been supplied with up-to-date descriptions of their quarry, but they had never actually seen him. Collins was at an even greater disadvantage at first, because the officers had been smuggled quietly into Dublin and he had no idea what they looked like.

After a period of preliminary sparring, a British spy gave the whole game away, so Collins was able to have his adversaries' correspondence intercepted and to arrange for regular reports on their movements. Then on Sunday, 21 November, (referred to subsequently as "Bloody Sunday"), the Dublin Brigade rounded up fourteen of the British spies and put them to death. The Auxiliaries' reply was to fire into the crowd at a football match in Croke Park, causing many deaths and casualties. Collins again showed his contempt for the Occupying Power by putting in a personal appearance at the funeral services held over the bodies of the dead Irishmen.

With Collins still at large and their terror gangs being worsted on all fronts, the British completely reversed their policy with regard to Ireland and tried to effect a settlement by peaceful means. De Valera was not easily wooed, but as the weeks passed, the Irish freedom fighters were forced to acknowledge that without reinforcements and supplies they could not resist much longer. Consequently, on 11 July, 1921, the Irish leaders called off hostilities and agreed to send a delegation to London to discuss peace terms. The outcome, as far as Collins was concerned, proved disastrous.

The tragedy was that Collins, who had clearly demonstrated that he was a soldier rather than a politician, allowed himself to be persuaded into accompanying the delegation as one of its members. He arrived in London on 8 October, was accommodated at 22 Hans Place and was soon involved in the tricky negotiations. His immediate impressions of the British delegates were unfavourable. The only one he felt he could trust was Lord Birkenhead. The rest struck him as being smooth, double-tongued and lacking in moral scruples. After the preliminary discussions,

Collins was far from satisfied with the way things were going. His own solution was that Ireland should have full Dominion status, but he foresaw that certain Irish politicians would object to some of the conditions on which the British were insisting. He was also unhappy about the great weight of responsibility that had fallen on his own shoulders, for Griffith had been taken ill, leaving Collins as the unofficial leader of the Irish delegation.

The Treaty that the delegates took back to Ireland for de Valera's approval offered Ireland Dominion status, committed the British to withdraw their troops and police from Irish soil, acknowledged the independence of the Irish Parliament and the creation of the Irish Free State. Britain was granted certain concessions with regard to harbour facilities, and the Six Counties were free to choose whether they wanted to be incorporated with the rest of Ireland or remain part of the United Kingdom. The Irish press for the most part found the terms acceptable, but to Collins' dismay de Valera and thousands of Irishmen rejected them out of hand. To Collins the split was highly significant and a warning that Ireland was on the brink of civil war.

When the Dail met to ratify the Treaty under de Valera's presidency, Collins spoke fervently in favour of the agreement as the best bargain obtainable under the circumstances, while de Valera and others voiced their objections. When the matter went to the vote, the Treaty was carried by a handsome majority, whereupon de Valera promptly resigned. Griffith, although a tired and disillusioned man, was elected in his stead and Collins remained as Minister for Finance. It was in one sense a political triumph for Michael Collins, but in another sense it was a personal tragedy. All the bitterness and anger of the anti-Treaty group were now focused on the man who had been largely instrumental in dividing Ireland into two camps. How could Ireland consider herself independent, they asked, when Irishmen still had to take the Oath of Allegiance to the British Crown and when part of her territory continued to be part of the United Kingdom?

Nevertheless the Treaty was ratified on 14 January and a Provisional Government, under the chairmanship of Michael Collins, was given the task of drawing up a new constitution. The country was now at sixes and sevens, with no fewer than four authoritative bodies controlling its destinies – Collins' Provisional Government, the Dail Eireann, the Republican Party and the Independent Republican Army, the notorious I.R.A.

The British Government was watching developments in Ireland with considerable alarm. First of all, the Irish elections which should have been held quickly, if only to get the voters' reactions to the Treaty, were postponed for three months. Then, on 13 April, 1922, the I.R.A. showed its teeth by occupying the Four Courts in Dublin City. The immediate British reply was to stop the evacuation of their troops and demand an explanation from Collins and Griffith. The two Irish leaders went to London and managed to smooth things over, promising an early election and effective measures to control the I.R.A.

The General Election was at last held on 16 June and the result was by no means reassuring. Out of the 128 seats, the pro-Treaty candidates won fifty-eight; the Labour, Farmers and Independents (who were also in favour of the Treaty) captured thirty-five; the remaining thirty-five fell to the anti-Treaty party. Clearly most Irishmen were willing to accept the provisions of the Treaty, but a considerable body of public opinion had no love of the contract. As Collins had feared, the situation was bristling with ugly possibilities.

Events certainly took an ironic turn when Collins gave orders that the I.R.A. garrison had to pull out of the Four Courts. Their refusal to move meant that one of Ireland's greatest rebels was now expected to crush a rebellion set in motion by his fellow countrymen. It was probably the hardest decision he had ever been called upon to make, for he was well aware that the use of force at that stage could precipitate the civil war he had always dreaded. He was, however, a soldier and a disciplinarian. His orders had been disobeyed and appropriate action had to be taken.

Collins instructed the National Guard to clear the Four Courts.

The first shot fired in anger was the signal for the civil war to begin and a sorry tale of bloodshed and murder it turned out to be. Brugha was killed, Boland was riddled with National Army bullets, Griffith fell dead on 12 August.

Collins, inevitably, assumed chief command. There are various versions of the events that led up to his tragic death in the fields between Skibbereen and Cork, but the ascertainable facts are these: Collins visited Curragh and Limerick on a tour of inspection. Confident that he would be reasonably safe in his own county, he ordered the convoy to proceed towards Mallow in County Cork. *En route* they were ambushed and found that trees had been laid across the road leading to Clonakilty. Thinking of the return journey, Collins left instructions with the local commander that the obstacle was to be removed. The convoy then went another way round and reached Mallow without further mishap. Collins ran a professional eye over the garrison and then moved on to Cork where he spent the night at the Imperial Hotel. It was Sunday, 20 August, 1922.

Early on Tuesday morning the convoy moved off towards Skibbereen, with Collins travelling in the open touring car. The party passed through Skibbereen and Bandon without incident, then after a detour to his birth-place, Sam's Cross, where he chatted for a time with members of his family, they went back to Skibbereen and Collins inspected the garrison there. Soon they were on the road again and nothing untoward happened until they discovered that for some reason or other the roadblock near Clonakilty had not been removed. Consequently the convoy had to take the alternative route through the valley of Beal na mBlath.

At the head of the convoy Collins was sitting in the tourer grasping his rifle. He had every reason to be on the alert, for after negotiating a blind corner, he saw that a brewer's cart had been dragged across the narrow road. There was a sudden burst of machine-gun fire, whereupon Collins' men dashed for cover and began firing back. Collins was standing in the middle of the road reloading his rifle when a single shot rang out. He slumped to the ground and lay still. When his soldiers got to him, they found that the sniper's bullet had entered his head a few inches from his left ear.

The great rebel leader was dead.

Chapter 21
Aneurin Bevan
1897–1960

The seeds of Aneurin Bevan's rebelliousness were undoubtedly sown in his childhood. Brought up as he was in the South Wales coal-area, in daily contact with penury, unemployment, appalling housing conditions, ill health, and all the humiliations that go hand in hand with abject poverty, it is hardly surprising that he grew up with bitter resentment in his heart and a burning desire to put things right. Like Michael Collins, he was a rebel from birth.

Aneurin was born on 15 November, 1897, at 32 Charles Street, Tredegar, a typical miners' town where most of the population were connected with the pits either above or below ground. His father was a miner, a good-looking man, a dreamer, a lover of books, and like nearly all Welshmen, very fond of music. His mother, a hard-working housewife who never allowed her large family to go hungry, had only one ambition in life. She wanted her children to be respectable, God-fearing, and to get on in the world. She sent each of them in turn to the elementary school in Sirhowy, a place of purgatory for Aneurin who was constantly at loggerheads with the bullying headmaster. In those early years there was nothing to indicate that little Aneurin Bevan had any particularly outstanding qualities. He rebelled against the headmaster's harsh discipline, but no more than most lively boys of his age.

Aneurin left school at thirteen to go and work in the pits. As he grew older he began to take more than a passing interest in union activities and it was not long before the members of the Miners Federation realized that they had in their midst an energetic and popular leader. The only snag was that to be effective a union leader had to be a fluent speaker. Young Bevan had all the other qualities they were looking for, but unfortunately he also had a bad stammer. His contributions to the Federation's discussions often proved embarrassing.

In those days speech therapy was still in its infancy, so Bevan had to rid himself of his impediment entirely by his own efforts. The chairman of the South Wales Medical Society set him on the right track by diagnosing his malady. He attributed most of Bevan's verbal hesitancies to the fact that the young man was not sufficiently well acquainted with the topics discussed at the union meetings. Bevan then decided that the remedy lay in perfecting his knowledge of such relevant subjects as industrial history, sociology and philosophy. Whenever it was possible he would retire to the workmen's library and spend hours poring over books, memorizing facts and figures, so that next time he spoke in public they would roll effortlessly off his tongue. At the same time he set out to educate himself in geography and art. As his intellectual and cultural horizons widened, his self-confidence increased; as he became surer of himself, he began to stutter less frequently. Then one day, when leading a miners' delegation to discuss a new contract with the owner's representative, he conducted the whole business without a single stammer.

Recognizing Bevan's potentialities, the Miners Union decided it would be worthwhile to send the young man to the Central Labour College in London. There he worked hard, developed his interest in political matters and eventually, influenced by the works of Karl Marx and by the political ideas of Marx's American admirers, he became a Socialist. When he returned to South Wales as the miners' agent, the mine owners blacklisted him, so he took a job as a day labourer on a building site. As he looked round him and saw poverty and misery everywhere, he became more than ever convinced that social reforms were long overdue. His smouldering dislike of capitalists blazed up into fierce flames of uncompromising hatred. He firmly believed that the wealthy classes were insatiable taskmasters, ruthlessly squeezing the last ounce of energy out of the poor, grudgingly giving them a starvation wage, and throwing them on the scrap-heap when they were too old or too weak to work. He resolved there and then to fight abuses wherever he found them.

Bevan jumped into the attack during the General Strike in 1926, urging the miners not to compromise or surrender, but the end of it was that the coal owners emerged victoriously from the struggle. The miners returned to work at the same wage but with longer hours, a result which bitterly disappointed their most ardent champion, Aneurin Bevan. In his determination to improve industrial relations, he became so involved in union activities that he found himself unemployed for years afterwards. He felt helpless, frustrated and humiliated, but his rhetorical outbursts on behalf of the miners had not been entirely wasted. His reputation as a fearless and fiery supporter of the underdog was growing steadily. All who listened to his bold denunciations of the moneyed classes felt certain that his wild talk would inevitably lead to an insurrection.

In the General Election of 1929 Aneurin Bevan, the 32-year-old Socialist candidate for Ebbw Vale, triumphed handsomely over his opponents in a three-cornered contest. He had a majority of rather more than eleven thousand over the combined total of his Tory and Liberal rivals for the seat. His stammer had almost disappeared and he had demonstrated throughout his election campaign that he was a brilliant orator. When Labour won the election, it seemed that Bevan, although then only an obscure backbencher, was destined to figure prominently in the political arena.

The second Labour Government in British history set out to do great things, but it was doomed from the start. Only a strong competent government could have survived the economic depression that shattered world trade between

1929 and 1932. Ramsay MacDonald's government, dependent for its very existence on a shaky alliance with Lloyd George's Liberals, had no way of damming the rising tide of unemployment. By July 1931 at least one-third of the nation's income was being spent in rates and taxes, and in the same month, when the gold standard was threatened, the Bank of England lost 45 million pounds in gold in the space of one month. MacDonald and his Chancellor of the Exchequer, Snowden, were determined to balance the Budget, but neither the Trades Union Congress nor the Labour Party would co-operate. Even if they could have come up with a solution, they would have needed the support of Lloyd George who was exploiting the balance of power for himself.

Watching all this dithering and inefficiency, Aneurin Bevan was gradually losing his patience. Up to a point he had confined his verbal onslaughts in the House to the Tories whom he hated and the Liberals whom he despised. As Ramsay MacDonald's attempts to shore up the tottering economy proved more and more futile, Bevan's fury steadily mounted until he could no longer prevent himself from castigating members of his own party. After MacDonald finally sold the pass, the fiery Welshman did not mince his words when he expressed his disillusionment with the Labour leader and his vacillating policies. At least Bevan's own political beliefs had a solid basis. His views in 1931 were entirely consistent with those he had held seven years previously when he had said: "Although we believe in loyalty, a disastrous blow would be struck at the heart of the movement if the Government remains in office longer than is necessary for immediate requirements. We all realize the Labour Government is being prevented by a series of hindering influences from bringing any emancipation of any value to the country. If the Government cannot put a policy into effect for dealing with the nation's economic problems, the sooner it gives up, the better. The Government must not cling to office for the sake of office; if it does so the reaction on the ideals of the miners is bound to be serious."

In 1931, of course, Bevan was painfully aware that MacDonald had done more than resign. In so far as he had agreed to form a coalition government, in Bevan's eyes his leader had defected.

As might have been expected, the Labour Party, which had "brought the country to the brink of disaster", suffered a crushing defeat in the October General Election. Panicked by the threat of inflation, the voters returned 471 Conservatives to Parliament and only 52 Labour members. Bevan, strongly entrenched in his Ebbw Vale constituency, was one of the few who weathered the storm.

For the next five years Aneurin Bevan continued to plead for improved conditions for the working classes and for an all-out attack on the unemployment problem. After Mussolini invaded Abyssinia in 1935, however, the member for Ebbw Vale began to show a genuine concern for what was happening abroad. He was alarmed by the aggressiveness of Mussolini and Hitler. He and his supporters roundly condemned the conciliatory policies of George Lansbury and his pacifist group. In fact, it was Bevan's relentless pressure that brought about Lansbury's resignation at the Party's 35th Annual Conference in Brighton.

The international situation was rapidly deteriorating and Bevan, following Sir Stafford Cripps's lead, believed that the only answer lay in a United Front. Hitler had marched into the Rhineland, and Republican Spain needed protection from the Nationalists. Cripps wanted the Labour Party to throw in its lot with the Independent Labour Party and the British Communist Party, thus producing a solid body of working-class voters who would return a Socialist government at the next election. In Cripps's opinion, war was inevitable if the Socialists did not get back into power. The Independent Labour Party and the Communists endorsed his plan, but when the Labour Party voted on the issue, only Bevan and George Strauss backed Cripps.

Looking ahead to the 1939 General Election, Attlee, Bevin and Morrison naturally rejected the United Front proposition. The very idea of an alliance with the Communists would alienate the middle classes up and down the country, and they knew that they had to capture a large section of the middle-class vote if they were to win the election. At the same time Transport House was committed to fighting the British Fascists as represented by Sir Oswald Mosley's supporters. The Labour leaders could not logically attack the Mosleyites and join hands with the Communists at one and the same time.

Party rebels Bevan and Cripps continued to advocate a United Front, and to make matters worse they started making public appearances on the same platforms as the Communist leaders, Harry Pollitt and William Gallacher. Not only did they repudiate the Labour Party's policy with regard to the United Front; they also made it abundantly clear that they were dissatisfied with the Party leadership. Moreover, in 1937, in association with two or three others of the Left, Bevan and Cripps founded a new Socialist weekly called *The Tribune* in which they could express their objections to the Party line.

At last Aneurin Bevan was able to record his views without fear of interruption. "What is our common purpose in the immediate issue before us?" he demanded in the issue of 25 November, 1938: "It is to make the Parliamentary Labour Party an efficient instrument of opposition to the National Government and an effective expression of the rank and file of the Party outside the House. It cannot honestly be claimed that it is so at present. There is something wrong with it that cannot easily be defined, and as we have just started a new Parliamentary Session it is just as well that we should try to understand what is wrong. The Parliamentary Labour Party is not getting across to the country as it should.... It presents the appearance of a second-class exponent of a first-class case."

Hoping to silence the rebel, the Labour Party executive sent out an appeal asking for party loyalty from all its members. The immediate response of the United Front was to issue a manifesto urging the workers to band together against "Fascism, Reaction and War". These exchanges were followed by a declaration by the Labour Party leaders to the effect that members appearing on platforms with Communists would be automatically expelled. Bevan and Cripps henceforth respected the Party's wishes on that particular issue, but Bevan's scathing comments on the ban blistered the pages of the *Daily Herald* where he pointed out that the rule had often been broken by the Party's own leaders, and mentioned Attlee, Greenwood and Bevin by name. "I trust," he wrote, "that all these distinguished persons will not cause you to falter in the pursuit of virtue. Please don't be deterred in the fanatical application of your sterile logic. Let a Labour Conference be called and declare its own expulsion!"

Then, early in 1939, Cripps was expelled from the Party for publishing a memorandum setting out his arguments in favour of a Popular Front and for refusing to withdraw it when ordered to do so. The expulsion of Bevan and Strauss who made it known that they supported Cripps followed shortly afterwards. Cripps was to remain in the political wilderness for six years; the cautious rebel Bevan, after informing the Executive he would in future observe the Party's disciplinary measures, was welcomed back into the Party only six months later.

When the war-time Coalition Government was formed under Churchill's leadership, Bevan was simply one of the rank and file, but the fact that he was only a backbencher did not prevent him from raising his rebellious voice whenever the occasion presented itself. He lashed out in all directions with munificent impartiality and was always prepared to run down Labour members as well as Tories. For instance, when Morrison, who was the Home Secretary, suppressed the *Daily Worker* at the beginning of 1941, Bevan moved a resolution in the House deprecating Morrison's high-handed behaviour. In the subsequent debate he had this to say: "The Prime Minister uses unexampled eloquence over the radio and talks about freedom and democracy. What does freedom mean if not that men may not be yanked off to prison by policemen without having a chance of defending themselves, and that a newspaper will not be suppressed without having a chance of being heard in its own defence? These are not idle forms; they are the citadels of our democratic institutions." The motion was heavily defeated, but Bevan had enjoyed the satisfaction of standing up for a principle. No doubt he had also enjoyed tilting at Herbert Morrison whom he strongly disliked.

As soon as Germany attacked Russia Bevan was again on the warpath. He began to clamour for Anglo-Russian co-operation and for a Second Front. The need for a Second Front became such an obsession with him that he toured the country and addressed large crowds on the subject. He also used the *Tribune* as a platform for his views, writing in these terms: "There is only one question for us in these swift days: what can we do to help ourselves by coming to the aid of the Soviet armies? . . . It seems to me that a decision to engage in no land venture of any kind at this moment is to admit the impossibility of victory in the event of Russia being beaten. . . . . The people of Great Britain are not content to play a passive role. . . ."

As the war neared its end, Bevan urged the Labour Party to disassociate itself from the Coalition Government and start thinking about the forthcoming General Election. He was confident that the people were ready for a change of government. Although he continued to berate the Coalition in general terms and the Conservative leaders as individuals, he no longer trounced members of his own Party. On the contrary, the *Tribune* began to find nothing but good in Attlee, Bevin, and even Morrison. He was already thinking in terms of his political future as the leader of the Left in the next government.

There was nothing of the rebel in the Bevan who endorsed the Labour Party's manifesto in 1945. Its authors, after urging the electorate to Face the Future, demanded nationalization of the Bank of England and of practically everything else, the expansion of public services, a moderate foreign policy, and that everybody should work for peace. A safe middle-of-the-road programme calculated to appeal to the average citizen.

Exactly as Bevan had predicted, the Labour Party swept into power on the backs of the middle-class voters. To retain this middle-class support, the Party leaders had no intention of rushing ahead with a programme of Socialist reforms. They were in for an unpleasant surprise from Bevan and Cripps (now back in the Party), both of whom were resolved to press for an early implementation of the Party's election promises.

Bevan, who had so suddenly given his full political allegiance to the Party, was rewarded with the Ministry of Health and Housing. He had been hoping for the Foreign Office or the Exchequer, but he had no complaints and settled down to do something he had long dreamed of doing – to improve the lot of the working man and his family. Thanks to Bevan's skilful negotiations, the National Health Service became law in 1948. He also did a remarkably good job in Housing and was largely responsible for pushing the Town and Country Planning Act through Parliament.

In 1948, as a reward for good behaviour during the Crossman-Bevin clash on foreign affairs, Bevan was offered a seat on the National Executive Committee. His popularity was steadily rising. At the Labour Party Annual Conference of 1950 he was actually praised by the Party leaders. If only the Labour Party could get back into power, there was no knowing to what heights he might soar. . . .

Labour *did* get back into power in the 1950 General Election, but with such a reduced majority that it was fairly obvious that its days were numbered. The delicate situation was not helped when Bevan who had been comparatively quiet for so long suddenly erupted. For some time he had been unhappy about the Party's foreign policy. As distinct from Attlee, Bevin and Morrison, Bevan was pro-Russia, anti-America and anti-armaments. It seemed to him that fundamental issues were at stake and he had to make a stand.

On 21 April, 1951, Aneurin Bevan resigned from the Government.

In that momentous year Attlee dissolved Parliament and in the election that followed, the Conservatives had a clear majority. Bevan's immediate goal was the Opposition Front Bench as a member of the Shadow Cabinet. As soon as he had achieved that ambition, he hankered after a more influential position, in finance or foreign affairs. His anti-American attitude remained unchanged, but in order to demonstrate that there were no cracks in the Labour Party, he did his best to avoid friction with his colleagues. His policy seemed to be one of compromise and conciliation.

He knew he had no chance of ousting Morrison, but in 1952 and again in 1953 he was a candidate for the Deputy Leader's post in the Shadow Cabinet. He was defeated on each occasion, but the two attempts amounted to Bevan's declaration of intent. He would never rest until he had won the highest honour of all – the Party leadership.

Towards the end of 1953 the rebel cut loose again, this time making a move that shocked both Press and Parliament and caused even his own Party to repudiate him. At a moment when Great Britain was involved in tricky negotiations with Egypt, Bevan sent an article to an Egyptian newspaper in which he said categorically that the presence of British troops in Egypt was an infringement of that country's territorial rights. Attlee was quick to point out that neither he nor the Labour Party had any sympathy with Bevan's irresponsible statement. Politicians' reactions everywhere indicated that the reckless Welshman had badly blundered. Just after the incident Bevan visited Egypt and Israel, accompanied by Jennie Lee, the M.P. for North Lanark, whom he had married in 1934. In both places his hosts treated him with a frigid courtesy which left him in no doubt that he had overshot the mark.

After his Middle East tour, Bevan felt the need to break away from the restraints imposed by his position in the Shadow Cabinet and as a member of the Executive Committee. If he was to challenge the Party leadership effectively, he had to have the freedom of the back bench. All he wanted was a reasonable excuse to hand in his resignation.

His chance came on 13 April, 1954, the day on which Attlee spoke in the House approving Eden's decision to join the American-sponsored South-east Asia defence alliance; S.E.A.T.O. In a flagrant breach of Party discipline Bevan addressed a startled House, expressing his out-and-out opposition to his leader's views. After dropping this bombshell he resigned from the Shadow Cabinet and set out on his new course – to stir up a national campaign against the way in which his Party's leaders were mishandling foreign policy.

Gradually Bevan built up his position among his many supporters (now known as Bevanites), until in 1955 he decided to have another crack at the Labour triumvirate: Attlee, Morrison and Gaitskell. On 2 March, during the debate on the Government's White Paper on Defence, Bevan attacked the Labour Party leadership as ineffective and inefficient, especially with regard to its views on the use of thermo-nuclear weapons against possible aggression by Russia.

At first it appeared as if Bevan's appreciation of the situation had been off the mark, for at the end of his "trial" in the New Palace of Westminster, the anti-Bevanites triumphed and Bevan faced expulsion after all. However, after he had apologized to the disciplinary committee, it was decided to take no further action against him. Bevan emerged from the struggle in a stronger position than ever before as a fancied contender for the Party leadership.

After the Conservatives' election victory, Bevan opposed Gaitskell, first of all in a fight for the treasuryship of Labour's Shadow Cabinet, and then, when Attlee resigned, in a contest for the Party leadership. He was beaten on both occasions, precisely as he had expected to be, so he harboured no feelings of resentment. What *did* hurt him was his defeat by Griffith in the election of the Party's Deputy Leader. He had no quarrel with the inoffensive Griffith. He knew that his path to power was being deliberately blocked by his arch enemy Deakin, leader of the influential T.U.C. All the same, in a speech he gave at Manchester, he did not miss the opportunity to say exactly what he thought of Hugh Gaitskell and the Labour bureaucracy.

Gaitskell, anxious to avoid a Party split and hoping to win Left Wing support, overlooked Bevan's Manchester speech and offered "Nye" the post of Colonial Secretary in the Shadow Cabinet. Bevan accepted the olive branch and thereafter was a changed man. The ageing rebel suddenly became a good-tempered, co-operative, imperturbable "elder statesman", backing his leader and supporting his Party's policies. It was difficult to reconcile Gaitskell's well-behaved amiable second lieutenant with the explosive and unpredictable rebel of the old days.

In 1956 Bevan had a brief spell as Party Treasurer before stepping into the post he had long coveted, that of Foreign Secretary in the Shadow Cabinet. He travelled a good deal, visiting India, Russia, Poland and Germany, clearly preparing himself for the great day when Labour would be returning to power. In support of the new image he was creating, he modified his views on nationalization, on the manufacture and testing of nuclear weapons, even on Bevanism itself.

Three years later the "New Nye" had graduated to the deputy leadership, working hand in hand with Gaitskell, a loyal and trusted colleague with a firm stake in the Party. He had assuredly mellowed with the years, but it is interesting to speculate on what might have happened if Aneurin Bevan had not died in 1960. Those who knew him best are inclined to think that the volcano was sleeping but by no means extinct.

Bibliography

Buddha:
Hilliard, F. H., *Buddha, the Prophet and the Christ*, (Allen & Unwin, 1956).
Morgan, K. (ed.), *The Path of the Buddha*, (Luzac, 1956).
Percheron, M., *Buddha and Buddhism*, (Longmans, Green, 1957).

Socrates:
Chroust, A-H., *Socrates, Man and Myth*, (Routledge, 1957).
Jowett, B. (tran.), *Four Socratic Dialogues*, (O.U.P.)
Plato, *Last Days of Socrates*, (Penguin).

Julian the Apostate:
Bidez, J., *La Vie de l'empereur Julien*, (1930).
Gibbon, E., *Decline and Fall of the Roman Empire*, (Dent).

Wat Tyler:
Clayton, J., *Leaders of the People*, (Martin Secker, 1910).
Lindsay & Groves, *The Peasants' Revolt*, (Hutchinson, 1955).
Maurice, C. E., *Lives of English Popular Leaders, Volume II*, (London, 1872).
Oman, Sir Charles, *The Great Revolt*, (O.U.P., 1906).

Martin Luther:
Bainton, R., *Here I Stand*, (Hodder & Stoughton, 1951).
Davey, C. J., *Martin Luther: the Monk Who Shook the World*, (Lutterworth, 1960).
Osborne, J., *Luther*, (Faber, 1961).

Galileo:
Fahie, J. H., *Galileo, His Life and Work*, (Murray, 1903).
Santillana, G. de, *The Crime of Galileo*, (Heinemann, 1958).

John Hampden:
Lindsay, P., *For King or Parliament*, (Evans, 1949).
Wedgwood, C. V., *The King's Peace*, (Collins, 1955).
Williamson, H. R., *John Hampden, a Life*, (Hodder, 1933).

Toussaint L'Ouverture:
Alexis, S., *Black Liberator: the Life of Toussaint L'Ouverture*, (Benn, 1949).

Alexander Hamilton
Miller, J. C., *Alexander Hamilton: Portrait in Paradox*, (Harper, 1959).
Mitchell, B., *Alexander Hamilton, Youth to Maturity*, (New York, 1957).
Schachner, N., *Alexander Hamilton*, (Yoseloff, 1946).

Danton:
Madelin, L., *Danton*, (1914).
Mathiez, A., *Danton et la Paix*, (1919).
Robinet, J. F. E., *Danton, homme d'état*, (1889).

Mary Wollstonecraft:
Wollstonecraft, Mary, *The Rights of Woman*, (Everyman's Library).
Wardle, R. M., *Mary Wollstonecraft*, (Richards Press, 1951).
Brailsford, H. N., *Shelley, Godwin and Their Circle*, (Oxford).

Shelley:
Brailsford, H. N., *Shelley, Godwin, and their Circle*, (Home University Library, 1913)
Dowden, E., *Life of Shelley*, (Kegan Paul, 1926).
Elton, E., *Shelley*, (Arnold, 1924).
Hogg, T. J., *Shelley at Oxford*, (Methuen, 1904).
Maurois, A., *Ariel*, (Lane, 1927).

John Brown:
Furnas, J. C., *The Road to Harper's Ferry*, (Faber, 1961).
Karsner, D., *John Brown, Terrible Saint*, (New York, 1934).
Villard, O. G., *John Brown, 1800–59. A Biography Fifty Years After*, (Alfred A. Knopf, New York, 1943).

Wagner:
Lidgey, C. A., *Wagner*, (Dent, 1904).
Newman, E., *The Life of Richard Wagner, in 4 volumes*, (Cassell, 1933–47).
Wagner, R., *My Life*, (Librairie Plon, Paris).

Emmeline Pankhurst:
Emmeline Pankhurst, *My Own Story*, (Nash, 1914).
E. S. Pankhurst, *The Life of Emmeline Pankhurst*, (Laurie, 1935).
Fulford, R., *Votes for Women*, (Faber, 1957).
Mitchell, D., *The Fighting Pankhursts*, (Cape, 1967).

Lenin:
Gorky, M., *Lenin*, (Centrizdat, 1931).
Krupskaya, N. K., *Memories of Lenin*, (Martin Lawrence, 1930).
Mirsky, D. S., *Lenin*, (The Holme Press, 1931).
Trotsky, L., *Lenin*, (Harrap, 1925).

Bertrand Russell:
Gottschalk, H., *Bertrand Russell: a Life*, (John Baker, 1965).
Schilpp, P. A., *Philosophy of Bertrand Russell*, (Evanston: Illinois, 1944).
Wood, A., *Bertrand Russell*, (Allen & Unwin, 1957).

Epstein:
Epstein, J., *Autobiography*, (Studio Vista, 1945).
Powell, L. B., *Jacob Epstein*, (Chapman & Hall, 1932).
Wellington, H., *Jacob Epstein*, (1925).

D. H. Lawrence:
Aldington, R., *Portrait of a Genius, But . . .*, (Duell, Sloan & Pearce, 1950).
Lawrence, F., *Not I But the Wind*, (New York, 1934).
Leavis, F. R., *D. H. Lawrence, Novelist*, (Chatto & Windus, 1955).
Murry, M., *Son of Woman*, (Cape & Smith, 1939).
Seligmann, H. J., *D. H. Lawrence: an Appreciation*, (New York, 1924).

Michael Collins
O'Connor, F., *The Big Fellow*, (Nelson, 1937).
Taylor, R., *Michael Collins*, (Hutchinson, 1958).

Aneurin Bevan:
Bevan, A., *In Place of Fear*, (Heinemann, 1952).
Foot, M., *Aneurin Bevan*, (4-Square Books, 1966).
Krug, M. M., *Aneurin Bevan: Cautious Rebel*, (Yoseloff, 1961).

Index

Index